EXPLORATIONS IN SOCIOLOGY
British Sociological Association conference volume series

* *also published by Macmillan and St. Martin's*

† *also published by Macmillan*

Gender Relations in Public and Private

New Research Perspectives

Edited by

Lydia Morris
Professor of Sociology
University of Essex
Colchester

and

E. Stina Lyon
Principal Lecturer and Head of the Sociology Division
South Bank University
London

First published in Great Britain 1996 by
MACMILLAN PRESS LTD
Houndmills, Basingstoke, Hampshire RG21 6XS
and London
Companies and representatives
throughout the world

A catalogue record for this book is available
from the British Library.

ISBN 0–333–63087–4 (hardcover)
ISBN 0–333–63088–2 (paperback)

First published in the United States of America 1996 by
ST. MARTIN'S PRESS, INC.,
Scholarly and Reference Division,
175 Fifth Avenue,
New York, N.Y. 10010

ISBN 0–312–12869–X

Library of Congress Cataloging-in-Publication Data
Gender relations in public and private: new research perspectives /
edited by Lydia Morris, E. Stina Lyon.
p.   cm.
Includes bibliographical references and index.
ISBN 0–312–12869–X (cloth)
1. Sex role—Great Britain.   2. Sex role in the work environment–
–Great Britain.   3. Man–woman relationships—Great Britain.
I. Morris, Lydia, 1949–   .   II. Lyon, E. Stina.
HQ1075.5.G7G48   1996
305.3'0941—dc20   95–19104
                                                            CIP

10   9   8   7   6   5   4   3   2   1
05   04   03   02   01   00   99   98   97   96

Printed Great Britain by
Ipswich Book Co. Ltd, Ipswich, Suffolk

Contents

List of Figures

List of Tables

Notes on the Contributors

Lee Chalmers is from the Canadian prairies and has just completed her PhD in sociology at the University of Essex. She received her BA and MA degrees in psychology from the University of Regina, Canada, and has worked on a number of research projects ranging in focus from domestic violence to traffic accidents. She has been a sessional lecturer in sociology at the University of Regina, teaching courses on social problems. Her current research interests centre on gendering processes in organisations.

Angela Dale is Director of the Census Microdata Unit and Professor of Quantitative Social Research at the University of Manchester.

Andrea Doucet is a Canadian post-doctoral research fellow and affiliated lecturer in the Faculty of Social and Political Sciences, Cambridge University. Her post-doctoral research, funded by the Social Sciences and Humanities Research Council of Canada, is on issues of gender equality and gender differences in Swedish family life.

Jean Duncombe is a PhD student at the University of Essex and worked as a Senior Research Officer on an ESRC-fund project (with Dennis Marsden) on 'The Role of Ideologies of Love in the Social Construction of Coupledom'. She studied sociology at Cardiff, where her undergraduate project was on extra-marital sexual relationships. Subsequently her MA at Essex University was on 'Alexandra Kollontai and the crisis of heterosexual feminism'. She has published work on attitudes to women's work and on youth training schemes.

Janet Finch is Professor of Social Relations at Lancaster University. She is the author or co-author of various works on family responsibilities and family relationships including *Family Obligations and Social Change* (1989), *Negotiating Family Responsibilities* (1993) and *Wills, Inheritance and Families* (1995).

Pauline Fuller is a Lecturer in Sociology and Social Policy in the Faculty of Health Studies at the Buckinghamshire College of Brunel University. She is currently working on a book based on her research in the area of child sexual abuse and critical studies of men. Her research interests include gender studies, the sociology of childhood and the sociology of emotion.

Lynn Hayes is a Research Associate at Lancaster University working on the Inheritance Project and subsequently on the Migration and Household Change Project, both funded by the ESRC. She has also worked as an Administrator at the Central European University in Prague. She is co-author with Janet Finch of *Wills, Inheritance and Families* (1995).

Arlie Russell Hochschild is the author of *The Managed Heart: Commercialization of Human Feeling,* and *The Second Shift: Working Parents and the Revolution at Home.* She is currently working on gender and the sociology of time, and is a Professor of Sociology at the University of California, Berkeley.

Heather Joshi is an economic demographer who became the Deputy Director of the Social Statistics Research Unit at City University in 1994. This job entails responsibility for academic liaison with the OPCS Longitudinal Study and a number of research projects involving that Study and the National Child Development Study. Her research has been mainly concerned with the family and the labour market. Previous appointments have been at the London School of Hygiene and Tropical Medicine, Birkbeck College and with the Government Economic Service.

Elisabeth Lawrence is Senior Lecturer in Sociology at Sheffield Hallam University. She is the author of *Gender and Trade Unions* (1994) and teaches in the area of Industrial Sociology, Equal Opportunities and Women's Studies. She is an active member of NATFHE (National Association of Teachers in Further and Higher Education) and has held a variety of union offices over the years, including Regional Secretary for Yorkshire and Humberside and NEC member.

E. Stina Lyon is Principal Lecturer and Head of the Sociology Division at South Bank University. Her research and teaching expertise are in the areas of education and sociological research methodology. Her most recent research was on the relationship between higher education and the labour market, published as *Students, Courses and Jobs,* with J. Brennan, P. McGeaver and K. Murphy (1993).

Dennis Marsden is Professor of Sociology at the University of Essex. He has worked for the Institute of Community Studies where (with Brian Jackson) he wrote *Education and the Working Class*. After research at Salford Royal CAT, he moved to the University of Essex to work with Peter Townsend on *Poverty in the United Kingdom*, which led to the publication of *Mothers Alone*. He has researched and written on the impact of unemployment on family life, published as *Workless*, on family violence, the emotional costs of married daughters caring for elderly mothers, and comprehensive schools and youth training schemes.

Joan McKiernan is currently Investigation Officer with the Equal Opportunities Commission for Northern Ireland. Previously she was Research Officer in the Centre for Research on Women in the University of Ulster where she worked on projects on women's employment and child care and co-authored the study on domestic violence with Monica McWilliams. She has also lectured in sociology and women's studies.

Monica McWilliams is a Senior Lecturer in Social Policy and a member of the Centre for Research on Women at the University of Ulster. She has been responsible for both the postgraduate and outreach Women's Studies programmes at the University. She has published articles on the changing role of women and has co-authored a book, with Joan McKiernan, on domestic violence in Northern Ireland.

Albert J. Mills is Associate Dean, Faculty of Commerce, Saint Mary's University in Nova Scotia, Canada. His research activities centre on the impact of the organisation upon people, focusing on organisational change and human liberation. He is the co-author of two books: *Organisational Rules* (with S. Murgatroyd, 1991) and *Reading Organisation Theory: A Critical Approach* (with T. Simmons, 1994), and he has co-edited (with Peta Tancred, 1992) *Gendering Organisational Analysis*. A fourth book (co-edited with Prasad, Elemes and Prasad) on the *Management of Diversity* is forthcoming.

Jayne Mooney is Research Fellow and Lecturer, School of Sociology and Social Policy, Middlesex University. Her research interests include violence against women, methodology, deprivation and crime, and her past publications include: *The Miranda Crime and Community Survey* (1993); *The Hidden Figure: Domestic Violence in North London* (1993). She is at present completing a PhD on domestic violence.

Lydia Morris is Professor of Sociology at the University of Essex. Her research interests cover unemployment, the underclass, gender relations, and labour market changes as well as the social policy issues relevant to all of these. She is author of *The Workings of the Household, Dangerous Classes* and *Social Divisions*.

Kate Purcell has been Reader in the School of Hotel and Catering Management at Oxford Brookes University since 1989. She has taught, researched and published widely on employment-related issues, with particular interests in gender and divisions of labour. Her current research focuses on the hospitality industry, including studies of the transition from vocational education to employment, the impact of equal opportunities legislation on women's employment in four European countries, and management training needs in the Bulgarian tourism industry.

Clare Ward is the Information Manager in the Housing Service at Reading Borough Council. Before that she was a research fellow at the Social Statistics Research Unit, City University.

1 Introduction

LYDIA MORRIS and E. STINA LYON

The gendered nature of the public and private spheres, economy and polity versus home and family, has long operated as given in traditional sociology. The sociological task has been to document the emergence of these spheres, to understand their interrelations, and to reveal the ideological dimension of their operation. In the course of this task, the artificial nature of the division itself has become apparent, manifest for example in arguments about the productive nature of domestic work, the gendered assumptions and controls embedded in aspects of social policy, gender segregation in the labour market, etc. There is still, however, a need for research which records the way in which aspects of the public sphere can be shaped around assumptions carried over from the private, and the way in which the private sphere is shaped by influences generated in the public. Thus, in the spirit of C. Wright Mills (1973) and his concern to link private troubles to public issues, we offer here some documentation of the inter-connections of the public and private spheres.

The papers collected in this volume have in common an attempt to lay bare some of these interconnections, often bringing together substantive areas commonly treated separately. They differ radically both in substance and approach, and some focus principally on methodological problems, rather than on research 'findings'. Whilst they by no means provide a full overview of the potential field, and readers will no doubt identify a number of omissions, they all represent some aspect of changing research perspectives on public and private gender relations. This is not, however, a collection of papers built around a research problem, but a research focus which emerges from a selection of the papers offered at the 1993 British Sociological Association conference on Research Imaginations.

Many of the papers in the collection reflect recent theoretical and methodological developments in feminist sociological research, but they also, as outlined above, collectively go beyond the traditional concerns of a 'women's sociology'. Much of the impact on sociology of feminist research is found in the study of the inter-linkage between the public and the private spheres of social relations and in the reconceptualisation of central sociological categories such as 'work', 'sexualities, 'class' in relation to the all-pervasive nature of structured gender relationships of unequal power. The overarching aim of bringing women 'out of the margins' has meant

1

changing research perspectives characterised first by a strong wish to locate in the public sociological domain the individual and personal experiences of women within the domestic sphere; experience which until relatively recently had remained largely invisible to the sociological eye (see, for example, Smith, 1987; Aaron and Walby, 1991). Much of this research has looked at the subordinate position of women in the economic and occupational structure relative to the hidden and devalued domestic roles of child bearing and house keeping. Secondly, feminist research perspectives have focused on the largely invisible nature of 'gendered' relations within organisations and institutions in the public sphere and their effect on women's progress and status within them, and on the ways in which occupational roles reflect the gendered characterisations of their majority practitioners

Explorations of the domestic, the personal, the private and the hidden in social relations, and the extent to which socially constructed gender characterisations infuse and determine the nature of day-to-day activities in ways not immediately discernible have led to a strong focus on qualitative research in the exploration of feelings and emotions. Such research has facilitated the study of aspects of social life hitherto seen as inaccessible, especially to quantitative survey research techniques; the role of sexualities or emotions in the work place, the role of violence in the domestic sphere, the importance of publicly defined gender characteristics in the construction of identities and the legitimation of selves. This achievement should not, however, stand as a denial of the validity and utility of quantitative techniques, which have contributed to a number of the papers presented here.

Though feminist research strategies have primarily aimed to validate and legitimate the experiences of women, the extent to which all social relations have become seen to be 'gendered' unto their innermost parts, has also brought to the fore the ways in which men's public and private roles are gender-defined, albeit from a different position of power in the social and economic spheres. It is in the relationship *between* women and men that gender differences need to be understood, however, and in the exploration of the ever-receding private areas of all our selves. The necessity for integrating into the analysis of gender relations the concepts of 'power' and 'inequality', in order to avoid merely cataloguing differences between the social roles of men and women, is brought to the fore by several of the papers in this selection.

A final key tenet of feminist research strategies has been that of presenting knowledge and research in such a way as to empower its subjects, to point to spheres of activity where change is possible and action designed to alleviate subjugation can be realistically envisaged. There is a shared focus in the papers, which work together to illuminate the close nature of the relationship between 'structure' and 'agency'. Emphasis is on the perceptions and aspirations of the actors themselves and their varied responses to gender-defined structures within households, organisations, and the economy at large. As C. Wright Mills so keenly saw, it is in the critical and imaginative conjuncture between the public and the private in sociological research that informed social and political change towards a more equitable society becomes possible.

There has been increasing dissatisfaction with an over-simplified view of the public/private divide and its incapacity to explain the entrenched nature of gendered social structures. This concern may in part be related to aspects of social change which have anyway undermined the gendered nature of the opposition. Women are increasingly present in the public sphere of paid work, and men — albeit reluctantly — are increasingly present in the home. We know from a vast body of research in both Britain and America (see Morris, 1990 for a review), that this does not simply mean that men and women are exchanging places. Yet the change itself invites a reconsideration of the nature and sources of male and female divisions and identities. Significantly, four of our papers are concerned with the 'public' issues of employment, and two with the related area of material resources.

In the opening paper Hochschild discusses changes in the 'emotional culture' of family and workplace, with family life becoming more like work, and work more like home. She explores the impact of changing, and intensifying, working practices alongside growth in the female workforce and the emergence of a dual-earner norm. This is not, however, a study of the renegotiation of gender roles, but of a changing emotional geography in the link between work and home. With time-management advice increasingly invading the homes of working mothers, and 'family friendly strategies' appearing in the workplace, Hochschild asks why there is so little take-up for the latter. Her answer is that the removal of peripheral aspects of family activity in the drive for efficiency privatises the family and displaces the reciprocity of community and neighbourhood into the workplace, making this the new location for easy sociability and feelings of personal worth. Thus, the traditional 'emotional geography' of the public/private divide is being reversed, and many corporations have been quick to foster and capitalise on this possibility.

The paper by Lawrence considers the way in which gender difference can invade the experience of paid work by examining women's under-representation in trade union leadership. In doing so, however, she problematises the nature and source of gender difference by turning the focus away from barriers to participation, to ask under what conditions women do become active trade unionists. This move reveals constraints which include a management culture defining activism as unfeminine, women's frequently part-time presence in the workplace, and the nature of women's employment, in which flexibility and absences are harder to accommodate. The result of the last point is that union work has more probably to be accommodated in non-work time, and here of course the demands of family are significant. There are shades of Hochschild's argument from the female shop steward who feels lucky to live alone. Thus gender difference invades the workforce not simply through the conflict of work and family for women, but more subtly, through workplace structures and assumptions.

Papers by Chalmers and by Mills show in different ways how specific areas of employment can be build around (assumed) gender differences, and again notions from the private sphere invade the public sphere. The focus for Chalmers is marketing, its relatively low prestige in the management hierarchy, and the way that gender is deployed in the claim for status through a struggle to assert 'masculinity'. Thus gender operates in work relationships not only between men and women but among men. Chalmers reports on a study of computer marketing, and much of the text of her interviews incorporates vivid gender metaphors. Good marketing, we learn, needs 'killers instinct', a readiness to get 'kicked in the teeth', and ability to 'hammer things down', despite its unmanly public image. There is, however, a lurking fear that, seen as an essentially supportive activity, marketing may also be seen as essentially feminine.

Mills' focus starts from gender differentiation in British Airways recruitment strategy, but looks specifically at the appropriation of a variety of versions of female sexuality in the marketing of air travel. Thus we learn of the initial recruitment of a male-only piloting and maintenance crew, despite the availability of qualified women, and of the biological justification for women's exclusion from commercial piloting. In the early days of the industry it was assumed that the reassurance of the male presence also made men more appropriate for the cabin crew, but we are taken through a history of competitive marketing which eventually harnesses female sexuality as a selling point. We see a gradual process of feminisation, eroticisation, and professionalisation; not necessarily mutually exclusive. Again there is a juxtaposition of the features classically associated with 'separate spheres'; caring and/or sexuality, with marketing and professional status.

The next two papers consider what would conventionally be construed as issues of the private sphere, but serve to demonstrate how slippery the distinction can be. Their authors draw our attention to aspects of domestic finance and material resources which are, in some sense, public issues.

Ward *et al.* address the issue of women's dependency in marriage, which persists despite popular assumptions that an increased presence in the labour force has overturned this stereotype. The paper reveals a surprisingly high degree of marital dependence, a particular concern given rising rates of divorce, and considers the barriers to women achieving economic independence. The root cause of dependence is argued to be a weak position in the labour market, partly explained by domestic and child-care responsibility, which lends even greater salience to concerns about the impact of marital instability. Again the interweaving of public and private influences defies an easy separation.

Finch and Hayes consider the transmission of property and assets following a death. Echoing the issue of marital dependency, we find that women in a married or cohabiting couple show a pattern of property disposal which is similar to men, but differs from that of widows. The opportunity for married women to be testators is only slightly more than one hundred years old, and perhaps it is not surprising that their actions in this are constrained by their husbands. The data from the study reveal sharp gender differences in the perception of 'bequeathing', which appear as a difference of marital status; for men the central issue is control of assets, but for women it is the management of relationships. It is only in the status of widow that this becomes clear. Thus private practice may lag some way behind public legislation, though the authors also found a tendency for women to bypass formalised mechanisms by passing on property within their own lifetime, thus establishing a distribution of goods quite different from that reflected by their will. These findings bring us close to one of the more truly 'private' aspects of domestic life, and the papers in the second half of the volume focus their attention more closely on investigations into the intimacies of social life in the private and personal domain, and on the methodological and ethical issues raised by such investigations.

Duncombe and Marsden draw on their shared research experiences in the study of marital relations with their discussion of a series of methodological issues emerging from a project on 'coupledom'. With sociological research traditionally placed in the public sphere of information collection, there has been increasing interest in the possibility, or indeed desirability, of gaining access into the personal domain of couples in a way capable of generating sociologically valid and meaningful material. Duncombe and Marsden give a detailed overview of previous research into the emotional relationships of couples, together and apart. This shows that flexible research strategies, characterised by an active and reciprocal involvement for researchers, can generate sociological information capable of differentiating between ideologically acceptable 'narratives' of family life, publicly and collectively constructed, and emotional life as very differently experienced by individual men and women. The 'emotion work' carried out by women in managing domestic relationships is at the forefront of their concerns.

They underline the importance of such research, given the increasing sociological as well as political focus on the changing nature of the family, and on newer forms of close and intimate relationships. But the ethical dilemmas posed by such researcher involvement in attempts to 'open up' emotional aspects of the private sphere to public scrutiny have serious implications. In their view, the private sphere needs to be conceptualised as a Chinese box, starting with a shared public image moving through different layers of 'exposure', with each layer interlinked. The more boxes are revealed, the more emotional conflicts are laid bare, with the researcher's role changing from that of recording observer to that of confidante, therapist and marriage guidance counsellor, with potentially disturbing outcomes for both researchers and researched.

The following two papers in this section by Doucet and Purcell share this methodological concern with ways in which relations and processes of decision-making within households can be explored. They join Duncombe and Marsden in examining the methodological problems in bridging the gap between the ideology of domestic harmony and actual domestic divisions and conflicts as experienced by individuals. These can be tapped only by the use of new and more innovative research techniques which each of their papers explores. Doucet and Purcell both point to the fact that, despite the transfer of women's labour from the private to the public sphere, women continue to bear the main burden of household responsibilities and a large proportion of women fulfill the same functions collectively in the labour market as they do at home. They both note the implications of this for the labour market experiences of both men and women.

Doucet highlights weaknesses in earlier research approaches, which she sees as characterised by a simplification of the nature of domestic tasks and an implicit devaluation of domestic responsibilities and household 'chores'. If we wish to understand this 'outstanding stability' of divisions in household labour, she argues, we need new creative research approaches capable of generating a more participatory sociological language for the work of everyday caring, and based on detailed task descriptions by household members themselves in interaction and discussion with each other. Her own contribution to the debate is the introduction of the 'household portrait' as a research tool: a collectively constructed biographical picture of who does what in caring and parenting, developed through the use of coloured slips of paper signifying whether different tasks are either 'his' or 'hers' or 'shared'. Her innovative research shows that, just as there are varied meanings attached to household tasks, there are also diverse notions of what it means to 'share.'

For Purcell, 'food management' is one of the dimensions of domestic decision-making that closely relates to changes in women's labour market participation. The closeness of the interrelationship between the private and the public sphere is well illustrated here, with evidence showing that households substitute and supplement domestic labour with pre-processed food and labour-saving technologies, thereby paradoxically contributing to the growth of those sectors of the economy which are the main employers of women. With time a declining resource in most households, strategic differences in the management of food between and within different types of households have a bearing both on the position of women as continuing 'providers', and on the changing nature of food production, marketing and consumption. Purcell suggests a triangulated approach to the study of food management, with a combination of various forms of time-budget studies, the use of diaries of daily activities combined with the study of retail check-out slips, for example. It is an obvious conclusion to be drawn from her paper, that when the internal management of the domestic sphere is conceptualised as 'work', then research techniques developed for the study of the labour process can fruitfully be applied also in the private domain (cf. Oakley, 1974).

The last papers in this selection are devoted to the study of domestic violence and its relationship to the wider ideological and political contexts within which it is perpetrated. A large amount of violence, much of it directed against women, occurs within the confines of the domestic sphere, in 'private'. This presents obvious problems for assessing its extent, exploring its cause and developing adequate political and policy responses. In her paper on researching domestic violence, Mooney reports on a large survey undertaken in North London with the aim of providing data on male and female experiences of, and attitudes to, domestic violence. The extent of domestic violence exposed by the project and the thorough and detailed way in which the information was assembled, brought it to national attention through the Press. The use of 'vignettes' detailing typical conflict situations and asking respondents whether they would see themselves as exercising physical violence in particular contexts, reinforced the overall picture of high levels of hidden domestic violence. If this picture is correct, as the thoroughness of the data-collection procedures would make us believe, then the public sphere is woefully inadequate in its resources to respond. Similarly, popular and positive images of the 'haven' of domestic life are far from universally applicable.

The papers by Fuller, and McKiernan and McWilliams bring the debate about domestic violence firmly into the public domain. Having noted the paucity of studies into the links between the social construction of 'hegemonic' masculinity as a cultural norm and child sexual abuse, Fuller presents a detailed analysis of interview material gained from men who have committed the offence. The cultural 'scenarios' identified from her evidence show the significance of physical strength, denial of emotion, and superiority in the notion of 'manliness'. Such scenarios, she argues, act as enabling conditions for abuse. She concludes by noting that, in particular cultural contexts, the child abuser is, at least in his own eyes, a 'normal' man.

In a political context where violence in the public sphere has become the norm, the general cultural context of masculine ideology assumes a sharper form. The investigation undertaken by Mckiernan and McWilliams into the relationship between violence against women in the home and the political violence occurring in the wider society of Northern Ireland (before the ceasefire), shows perhaps more forcefully than any other paper in this volume how close the connection is between the nature of social relations in the private and the public domains. They point to the different degrees of 'acceptability' of different kinds of violence and how religious traditionalism and political conflict create an environment where violence in the home remains invisible. Where guns are easily available, the police militarised and trained to focus on terrorism, and where local communities are under the control of paramilitaries, women's domestic lives are subject to considerable constraints, with little protection against physical intimidation and attack by partners who exploit the 'hidden' nature of the home as a forum for unchecked and clandestine violence.

The papers in this collection show, in their different ways, the manner in which beliefs and constraints deriving from, or confirmed within, the 'private sphere' can shape and constrain the organisation of the 'public sphere'. This happens, for example, through the changing 'emotional geography' of work and home, the gendering of work roles, and the appropriation of sexuality for commercial gain. Correspondingly, we see many and diverse ways in which the public sphere shapes the private, whether through the structure of the labour market, the power of ideology, the assumptions of policy makers, or, as in the case of Northern Ireland, an all-pervading atmosphere of violence. What we hope this collection shows is that the connection between 'private troubles' and 'public issues' is permeated by questions of gender.

References

Aaron, J. and S. Walby (eds), (1991) *Out of the Margins* (London: The Falmer Press).

Mills, C. W. (1973), *The Sociological Imagination* (Harmondsworth, Middx: Penguin; first published 1959).

Morris, L. (1990), *The Workings of the Household* (Oxford: Polity Press).

Oakley, A. (1974), *The Sociology of Housework* (London: Robertson).

Smith, D. (1987), *The Everyday World as Problematic: A Feminist Sociology* (Milton Keynes: Open University Press).

Part I
Employment and Assets

2 The Emotional Geography of Work and Family Life

ARLIE RUSSELL HOCHSCHILD

Over the last two decades, American workers have increasingly divided into a majority who work too many hours and a minority with no work at all. This split hurts families at both extremes, but I focus here on the growing scarcity of time among the long-hours majority. For many of them, a speed-up at the office and factory has marginalised life at home, so that the very term 'work–family balance' seems to them a bland slogan with little bearing on real life. In this chapter, I describe the speed-up and review a range of cultural responses to it, including 'family-friendly reforms' such as flextime, job sharing, part time work and parental leave. Why, I ask, do people not resist the speed-up more than they do? When offered these reforms, why don't more take advantage of them? Drawing upon my on-going research in an American Fortune 500 company, I argue that a company's 'family-friendly' policy goes only as deep as the 'emotional geography' of the workplace and home, the drawn and redrawn boundaries between the sacred and the profane. I show how ways of talking about time (for example, separating 'quality' from 'quantity' time) become code words to describe that emotional geography.

I suggest how, for some of the people some of the time, family life is becoming more like work and work more like home; the cultures are reversing. Drawing from writing on cultural and linguistic approaches to time (Hareven, 1982; Bailyn, 1993), research on company culture (Martin, 1992; Alvesson and Berg, 1992) and especially its emotional aspect (Fineman, 1993), I show how the latest advances in corporate engineering increase the magnetic draw of work, while strain and fracture reduce the draw of family. To be sure, there are exceptions to this cultural reversal, variations within, and counter-tendencies against it. But in the end, I argue, we need to understand the new emotional geography of home and work, so we can attune our social policies and political movements to unexpected problems emerging from it.

A WORK–FAMILY SPEED-UP

Three factors are creating the current speed-up in work and family life in the United States. (By the term 'family', I refer to committed unmarried couples, same-sex couples, single mothers, two-job couples and wage-earner–housewife couples. My focus is on all families who raise children.) First of all, increasing numbers of mothers now work outside the home. In 1950, 22 per cent of American mothers of children eighteen and under worked for pay; in 1991, 67 per cent did. Half of the mothers of children age one year and younger work for pay.

Second, they work in jobs which generally lack flexibility. The very model of 'a job' and 'career' has been based, for the most part, on the model of a traditional man whose wife cared for the children at home. Third, over the last 20 years, both women and men have increased their hours of work. In her book, *The Overworked American* the economist, Juliet Schor, argues that over the last two decades American workers have added an extra 164 hours to their year's work – an extra month of work a year (Schor, 1992, p. 26). Compared to 20 years ago, workers take fewer unpaid absences, and even fewer *paid* ones. Over the last decade, vacations have shortened by 14 per cent (Schor, 1992, pp. 12–13). The number of families eating evening meals together has dropped by 10 per cent (Blyton, 1985; Fuchs, 1991).[1] Counting overtime and commuting time, a 1992 national sample of men averaged 48.8 hours of work, and women, 41.7 (Galinsky *et al.*, 1993, p. 9). Among young parents, close to half now work more than 8 hours a day. Compared to the 1970s, mothers take less time off for the birth of a child and are more likely to work through the summer. They are more likely to work continuously until they retire at age 65. Thus, whether they have children or not, women increasingly fit the profile of year-round, life-long paid workers, a profile that has long characterised men. Meanwhile, male workers have not reduced their hours but, instead, expanded them.

Not all working parents with more free time will spend it at home tending children or elderly relatives. Nor, needless to say, if parents do spend time at home, will all their children find them kind, helpful and fun. But without a chance for more time at home, the issue of using it well does not arise at all.

COOL MODERN, TRADITIONAL, WARM MODERN STANCES TOWARD THE SPEED-UP

Do the speed-up people think the speed-up is a problem? Does anybody else? If so, what cultural stances toward gender equity, family life and capitalism underly the practical solutions they favour? If we explore recent writing on the hurried life of a working parent, we can discern three stances toward it.

One is a *cool modern* stance, according to which the speed-up has become 'normal', even fashionable. Decline in time at home does not 'marginalise' family life, proponents say, it makes it different, even better. Like many other popular self-help books addressed to the busy working mother, *The Superwoman Syndrome*, by Majorie Schaevitz offers busy mothers tips on how to fend off appeals for help from neighbours, relatives, friends, how to stop feeling guilty about their mothering. It instructs the mother how to frugally measure out minutes of 'quality time' for her children and abandons as hopeless the project of getting men more involved at home (Schaevitz, 1984). Such books call for no changes in the workplace, no changes in the culture and no change in men. **The solution to rationalisation at work is rationalisation at home.** Tacitly such books accept the corrosive effects of global capitalism on family life and on the very notion of what people need to be happy and fulfilled. (Hochschild, 1994).

A second stance toward the work–family speed-up is **traditional** in that it calls for women's return to the home, or **quasi-traditional** in that it acquiesces to a secondary role, a lower rank 'mommy track', for women at work (Schwartz, 1989). Those who take this sort of stance acknowledge the speed-up as a problem but deny the fact that most women now have to work, want to work, and embrace the concept of gender equity. They essentialise different male and female 'natures', and notions of time, for men and women – 'industrial' time for men, and 'family' time for women (Hareven, 1975).[2]

A third **warm modern** stance is both humane (the speed-up is a problem) and egalitarian (equity at home and work is a goal). Those who take this approach question the terms of employment – both through a nationwide programme of worksharing, (as in Germany), a shorter working week, and through company-based family friendly reforms.[3] What are these family-friendly reforms?

- flextime; a workday with flexible starting and quitting times, but usually 40 hours of work and the opportunity to 'bank' hours at one time and reclaim them later;
- flexplace; home-based work, such as telecommuting.
- regular or permanent part-time; less than full-time work with full- or pro-rated benefits and promotional opportunities in proportion to one's skill and contribution;
- job sharing; two people voluntarily sharing one job with benefits and salary pro-rated;

- compressed working week; four 10-hour days with 3 days off, or three 12-hour days with 4 days off;
- paid parental leave;
- family obligations as a consideration in the allocation of shift work and required overtime.[4]

Together, worksharing and this range of family-friendly reforms could spread work, increase worker control over hours, and create a 'warm modern' world for women to be equal within.[5] As political goals in America over the last 50 years, worksharing and a shorter working week have 'died and gone to heaven' where they live on as Utopian ideals. In the 1990s, family-friendly reforms are the lesser offering on the capitalist bargaining table. But are companies in fact offering these reforms? Are working parents pressing for them?

The news is good and bad. Recent nationwide studies suggest that more and more American companies offer their workers family-friendly alternative work schedules. According to one recent study, 88 per cent of 188 companies surveyed offer part-time work, 77 per cent offer flextime of some sort, 48 per cent offer job-sharing, 35 per cent offer some form of flexplace, and 20 per cent offer a compressed working week (Galinksy *et al.*, 1991).[6] (But in most companies, the interested worker must seek and receive the approval of a supervisor or department head. Moreover, most policies do not apply to lower-level workers whose conditions of work are covered by union contracts.)

But even if offered, regardless of need, few workers actually take advantage of the reforms. One study of 384 companies noted that only nine companies reported even one father who took an official unpaid leave at the birth of his child (Friedman, 1992, p. 50). Few are on temporary or permanent part-time. Still fewer share a job. Of workers with children ages 12 and under, only 4 per cent of men and 13 per cent of women worked less that 40 hours a week (Galinsky *et al.*, 1991, p. 123).

INSIDE A FORTUNE 500 COMPANY

Why, when the opportunity presents itself, do so few working parents take it? To find out, I set about interviewing managers, and clerical and factory workers in a large manufacturing company in the northeastern United States – which I shall call, simply, the Company. I chose to study this Company because of its reputation as an especially progressive company. Over the last 15 years, for example, the Company devoted millions of dollars to informing workers of its family-friendly policies, hiring staff to train managers to implement them, making showcase promotions of workers who take extended maternity leaves or who work part-time. If change is to occur anywhere, I reasoned, it was likely to be within this Company.

But the first thing I discovered was that even in this enlightened Company, few young parents or workers tending elderly relatives took advantage of the chance to work more flexible or shorter hours. Among the 26 000 employees, the average working week ranged from 45 to 55 hours. Managers and factory workers often worked 50 or 60 hours a week while clerical workers tended to work a more normal, 40-hour, week. Everyone agreed the Company was a 'pretty workaholic place'. Moreover, for the last 5 years, hours of work had increased.

EXPLANATIONS THAT DON'T WORK

Perhaps workers shy away from applying for leaves or shortening their hours because they can't afford to earn less. This certainly explains why many young parents continue to work long hours. But it doesn't explain why the wealthiest workers, the managers and professional, are among the **least** interested in additional time off. Even among the Company's factory workers, who in 1993 averaged between eleven and twelve dollars an hour, and who routinely competed for optional overtime, two 40-hour-a-week paychecks with no overtime work were quite enough to support the family. A substantial number said they could get by on one paycheck if they sold one of their cars, put in a vegetable garden and cut down on 'extras'. Yet, the overwhelming majority did not want to.

Perhaps, then, employees shied away from using flexible or shorter hour schedules because they were afraid of having their names higher on the list of workers who might be laid off in a period of economic downturn. Through the 1980s, a third of America's largest companies experienced some layoffs, though this did not happen to managers or clerical workers at this company.

By union contract, production workers were assured that layoffs, should they occur, would be made according to seniority and not according to any other criteria – such as how many hours an employee had worked. Yet, the workaholism went on. Employees in the most profitable sectors of the Company showed no greater tendency to ask for shorter or more flexible hours for family reasons than employees in the least profitable sectors.

Is it, then, that workers who could afford shorter hours didn't *know* about the Company's family-friendly policies? No. All of the 130 working parents I spoke with had heard about alternative schedules and knew where they could find out more.

Perhaps the explanation lies not with the workers but with their managers. Managers responsible for implementing family-friendly polices may be openly or covertly undermining them. Even though Company policy allowed flexibility, the head of a division could, for reasons of production, openly refuse a worker permission to go part-time or to job-share, which some did. For example when asked about his views on flextime, the head of the engineering division of the Company replied flatly, 'My policy on flextime is that there is no flextime.' Other apparently permissive division heads had supervisors who were tough on this issue 'for them'. Thus, there seemed to be some truth to this explanation for why so few workers stepped forward.[7]

But even managers known to be co-operative had few employees asking for alternative schedules. Perhaps, then, workers ask for time off, but do so 'off the books'. To some extent, this 'off the books' hypothesis did hold, especially for new fathers who may take a few days to a week of sick leave for the birth of a baby instead of filing for 'parental leave', which they feared would mark them as unserious workers.

Even counting informal leaves, most women managers returned to full-time 40- to 55-hour work schedules fairly soon after their 6 weeks of paid maternity leave. Across ranks, most women secretaries returned after 6 months; most women production workers returned after 6 weeks. Most new fathers took a few days off at most. Thus, even 'off the books', working parents used very little of the opportunity to spend more time at home.

Far more important than all these factors seemed to be a company 'speed-up' in response to global competition. In the early years of the 1990s, workers each year spoke of working longer hours than they had the year before, a trend seen nationwide. When asked why, they explained that the Company was trying to 'reduce costs', in part by asking employees to do more than they were doing before.

But the sheer existence of a company speed-up doesn't explain why employees weren't trying to actively resist it, why there wasn't much back-talk. Parents were eager to tell me how their families came first, how they were clear about that. (National polls show that next to a belief in God, Americans most strongly believe in 'the family'.) But, practices that might express this belief – such as sharing breakfast and dinner – were shifting in the opposite direction. In the minds of many parents of young children, warm modern intentions seemed curiously, casually, fused with cool modern ideas and practices. In some ways, those within the work–family speed up don't seem to want to slow down. What about their experience makes this true?

AN APPROACH TO THE MISSING CULTURE OF RESISTANCE

In order to catch the full answer, we need to draw on a variety of perspectives in and outside the 'work-family' field.

The mainstream literature in the work-family field in the US is both helpful and unhelpful. Rapidly expanding, mildly optimistic, policy-oriented, quantitative, the voluminous research by Ellen Galinsky and Dana Friedman of the Family and Work Institute provides some of the best survey data we have on workers' attitudes toward work and family life, and corporate thinking and action on family-friendly reforms (Friedman, 1991; Galinsky *et al.*, 1991). But this line of work doesn't question how people really feel about their families and jobs, or about reforms that would alter the balance between them.

A second literature keeps a vigil on the de-institutionalisation of the *family* from either a declinist (Lasch, 1977; Popenoe, 1989) or an adaptationist (Skolnick, 1991) viewpoint. But by focusing on the family, this line of work misses the symbiotic – even parasitic – relationship between work and family. That research which does focus on the relation of family to work (Kanter, 1977; Zedek, *et al.*, 1992) doesn't give sufficient primacy to the cultural aspect of each sphere.

A third literature is devoted to 'corporate culture' (Hofstede, 1980; Kanter, 1989; Alvesson and Berg, 1992; Martin, 1992; Trice and Beyer, 1993). Recent, growing, and relevant, this literature is wide-ranging and theoretically fruitful, but rarely do authors focus on work–family balance, emotional culture, or gender (For exceptions see Van Maanen and Kunda, 1989; Bowen and Orthner, 1991; Negrey, 1993).

Surrounding these literatures, so to speak, are works which help us to see the issue of work–family balance in its larger context. Highlighting as it does the small ways in which big 'structures' change, Anthony Giddens' concept of 'structuration' elucidates what we might call 'famil-isation', and 'work-isation' (Giddens, 1976).

In this same spirit of 'liquefying' concepts, turning nouns into verbs, we may speak of ritualising and de-ritualising, sacrilegising and de-sacrilegising, moments in family and work life. We can see the recent history of work and family life as a history of these underlying processes. At the moment, work is becoming a little more ritualised and sacred, for some people in some classes at some historical periods of capitalist development, while the family becomes less so. But, depending on the logic of capitalism, and on the strength of the resistance to it, rituals and a sense of the sacred can also flow the other way.

WORK AND FAMILY AS EMOTIONAL CULTURES

Through its family-friendly reforms, the Company had earned a national reputation as a desirable family-friendly employer. But at the same time, it wasn't inconvenienced by having to arrange alternate schedules for very many employees. One can understand how this might benefit a company. But how about the working parents?

For the answer, we may need a better grasp of the emotional cultures, and the relative 'draw' of work and family. Instead of thinking of the workplace or the family as unyielding thing-like structures, Giddens suggests that we see structures as fluid and changeable. 'Structuration', Anthony Giddens tells us, is the 'dynamic process whereby structures come into being' (Giddens, 1976, pp. 121, 157). For structures to change, there must be changes in what people do. But in doing what they do, people unconsciously draw on resources, and depend on larger conditions to develop the skills they use to change what they do (*ibid.*, p. 157).

With this starting point, then, let us note that structures come with – and also 'are' – emotional cultures. A change in structure requires a change in emotional culture. What we lack, so far, is a vocabulary for describing this culture, and what follows is a crude attempt to create one. An emotional culture is a set of rituals, beliefs about feelings and rules governing feeling which induce emotional focus, and even a sense of the 'sacred'.[8] This sense of the sacred selects and favours some social bonds over others. It selects and reselects relationships into a core or periphery of family life.

Thus, families have a more or less *sacred core* of private rituals and shared meanings. In some families what is most sacred is sexuality and marital communication (back rubs, pillow talk, sex), and in other families the 'sacred' is reserved for parental bonds (bedtime cuddles with children, bathtime, meals, parental talk about children). In addition, families have secondary zones of less important daily, weekly, seasonal rituals which back up the core rituals. They also have a profane outer layer, in which members might describe themselves as 'doing nothing in particular' – doing chores, watching television, sleeping. The character and boundaries of the sacred and profane aspects of family life are in the eye of the beholder. 'Strong families' with 'thick ties' can base their sense of the sacred on very different animating ideas and practices. Families also differ widely on how much one member's sense of the sacred matches another's and on how much it is the occasion for expressing harmony or conflict. Furthermore, families creatively adapt to new circumstances by ritualising new activities – for example, couples in commuter marriages may 'ritualise' the phone call or the daily e-mail exchange. Couples with 'too much time together' may de-ritualise meals, sex, or family events. Furthermore, families have different structures of sacredness. Some have thick actual cores and thin peripheries, others have a porous core and extensive peripheral time in which people just 'hang out'. But in each case, emotional culture shapes the experience of family life.

Emotional cultures stand back-to-back with ideas about time. In the context of the work–family speed-up, many people speak of actively 'managing time, finding time, making time, guarding time, or fighting for time'. Less do they speak of simply 'having' or 'not having' time. In their attempt to take a more active grip on their schedules, many working parents turn a telephone answering machine on at dinner, turn down work assignments and social engagements, and actively fight to defend 'family time'.

One's talk about time is itself a verbal practice that does or doesn't reaffirm the ritual core of family life. In the core of family life, we may speak more of living in the moment. Because a sacred activity is an end in itself, and not a means to an end, the topic of time is less likely to arise. If it does, one speaks of 'enjoying time', or 'devoting time'. With the work–family speed-up, the term 'quality time' has arisen, as in 'I need more quality time with my daughter', a term referring to freedom from distraction, time spent in an attitude of intense focus. In general, we try to 'make' time for core family life because we feel it matters more.

In the intermediate and peripheral zones of family life, we may speak of 'having time on our hands, wasting or killing time'. In the new lexicon, we speak of 'quantity time'.[9] In general, we feel we can give up peripheral time, because it matters less. More hotly contested is the time to participate in a child's school events, help at the school auction, buy a birthday gift for a babysitter, or call an elderly neighbour.

With a decline in this periphery, the threads of reciprocity in the community and neighbourhood grow weaker. By forcing families to cut out what is 'least important', the speed-up thins out and weakens ties that bind it to society. Thus, under the press of the 'speed-up', families are forced to give up their periphery ties with neighbours, distant relatives, bonds sustained by 'extra time'. **The speed-up privatises the family.** The 'neighbourhood goes to work', where it serves the emotional interests of the workplace. Where are one's friends? At work.

Although the family in modern society is separated from the workplace, its emotional culture is ecologically linked to and drawn from it. Both the family and workplace are also linked to supportive realms. For the family, this often includes the neighbourhood, the church, the school. For the workplace, this includes the pub, the golf club, the commuter-van friendship network. A loss of supportive structure around the family may result in a gain for the workplace, and vice versa. Insofar as the 'periphery' of family life protected its ritual core, to a certain degree for working parents these ties are not so peripheral at all.

A gender pattern is clear. Because most women now must and for the most part want to work outside the home, they are performing family rituals less. At the same time, men are not doing them very much more. Together, these two facts result in a net loss in ritual life at home.

At the same time, at some workplaces, an alternative cultural magnet is drawing on the human need for a centre, a ritual core. As family life becomes de-ritualised, in certain sectors of the economy, the engineers of corporate cultures are re-ritualising the workplace. Thus, the contraction of emotional culture at home is linked to a socially engineered expansion of emotional culture at work.

WORK LIKE A FAMILY, AND FAMILY, FOR SOME, LIKE WORK

At a certain point, change in enough personal stories can be described as a change in culture, and I believe many families at the Company are coming to this turning-point now. Pulled toward work by one set of forces and propelled from the family by another set of forces, a growing number of workers are unwittingly altering the twin cultures of work and family (Kanter, 1977; Lash, 1977). As the cultural shield surrounding work has grown stronger, the supportive cultural shield surrounding the family has weakened. Fewer neighbourhood 'consultants' talk to one when trouble arises at home, and for some, they are more to help out with problems at work.

These twin processes apply unevenly; the pull toward work is stronger at the top of the occupational ladder, and marginalisation of family life, more pronounced at the bottom. Indeed, the picture I shall draw is one in a *wide array* of work and family 'structurations' resulting from various combinations of social forces.

THE MODEL OF FAMILY AS A HAVEN IN A HEARTLESS WORLD

When I entered the field, I assumed that working parents would *want* more time at home. I imagined that they experienced home as a place where they could relax, feel emotionally sheltered and appreciated for who they 'really are'. I imagined home to feel to the weary worker like the place where he or she could take off a uniform, put on a bathrobe, have a beer, exhale – a picture summed up in the image of the worker coming in the door saying, 'Hi honey, I'm home!'. To be sure, home life has its emergencies and strains but I imagined that home was the place people thought about when they thought about rest, safety and appreciation. Given this, they would want to maximise time at home, especially time with their children. I also assumed that these working parents would not feel particularly relaxed, safe or appreciated at work, at least not more so than at home, and especially not factory workers.

When I interviewed workers at the Company, however, a picture emerged which partly belied this model of family life. For example, one 30-year-old factory shift supervisor, a remarried mother of two, described her return home after work in this way:

> I walk in the door and the minute I turn the key in the lock my oldest daughter is there. Granted she needs somebody to talk to about her day. The baby is still up ... she should have been in bed two hours ago and that upsets me. The oldest comes right up to the door and complains about anything her father said or did during the evening. She talks about her job. My husband is in the other room hollering to my daughter, 'Tracy, I don't ever get no time to talk to your mother because you're always monopolizing her time first before I even got a chance!' They all come at me at once.

The un-arbitrated quarrels, the dirty dishes, and the urgency of other people's demands she finds at home contrast with her account of going to work:

> I usually come to work early just to get away from the house. I go to be there at a quarter after the hour and people are there waiting. We sit. We

talk. We joke. I let them know what is going on, who has to be where, what changes I have made for the shift that day. We sit there and chit-chat for five or ten minutes. There is laughing. There is joking. There is fun. They aren't putting me down for any reason. Everything is done in humour and fun from beginning to end. It can get stressful, though, when a machine malfunctions and you can't get the production out.

Another 38-year-old working mother of two, also a factory worker, had this to say:

My husband is a great help (with caring for their son). But as far as doing housework, or even taking the baby when I'm at home, no. When I'm home, our son becomes my job. He figures he works five days a week, he's not going to come home and clean. But he doesn't stop to think that I work seven days a week ... Why should I have to come home and do the housework without help from anybody else? My husband and I have been through this over and over again. Even if he would pack up the kitchen table and stack the dishes for me when I'm at work, that would make a big difference. He does nothing. On his week-ends off, I have to provide a sitter for the baby so he can go fishing. When I have my day off, I have the baby all day long. He'll help out if I'm not here ... the minute I'm here he lets me do the work.

To this working mother, her family was not a haven, a zone of relief and relaxation. It was a workplace. More than that, she could only get relief from this domestic workplace by going to the factory. As she continued:

I take a lot of overtime. The more I get out of the house, the better I am. It's a terrible thing to say, but that's the way I feel!

I assumed that work would feel to workers like a place in which one could be fired at the whim of a profit-hungry employer, while in the family, for all its hassles, one was safe. Based as it is on the impersonal mechanism of supply and demand, profit and loss, work would feel insecure, like being in 'a jungle'. In fact, many workers I interviewed had worked for the Company for 20 years or more. But they were on their second or third marriages. To those employed, *work* was their rock, their major source of security, while they were receiving their 'pink slips' at home.

To be sure, most workers *wanted* to base their sense of stability at home, and many did. But I was also struck by the loyalty many felt toward the

Company and a loyalty *they felt* coming from it, despite what might seem like evidence to the contrary – the speed-up, the restructuring. When problems arose at work, many workers felt they could go to their supervisors or to a human resources worker and resolve it. If one division of the Company was doing poorly, the Company might 'de-hire' workers within that division and rehire in a more prosperous division. This happened to one female engineer, very much upsetting her, but her response to it was telling:

> I have done very well in the Company for twelve years, and I thought my boss thought very highly of me. He'd said as much. So when our division went down and several of us were de-hired, we were told to look for another position within the Company *or* outside. I though, 'Oh my God, *outside!*' I was stunned! Later, in the new division it was like a re-marriage ... I wondered if I could love again.

Work was not always 'there for you', but increasingly 'home', as they had known it, wasn't either. As one woman recounted, 'One day my husband came home and told me, "I've fallen in love with a woman at work ... .I want a divorce."'

Finally, the model of family-as-haven led me to assume that the individual would feel most known and appreciated at home and least so at work. Work might be where they felt unappreciated, 'a cog in the machine', – an image brought to mind by the Charlie Chaplin classic film on factory life, *Modern Times*. But the factory is no longer the archetypical workplace and, sadly, many workers felt more appreciated for what they were doing at work than for what they were doing at home. For example, when I asked one 40-year-old technician whether he felt more appreciated at home or at work, he said:

> I love my family. I put my family first ... but I'm not sure I feel more appreciated by them (laughs). My 14-year-old son doesn't talk too much to anyone when he gets home from school. He's a brooder. I don't know how good I've been as a father ... .we fix cars together on Saturday. My wife works opposite shifts to what I work, so we don't see each other except on weekends. We need more time together – need to get out to the lake more. I don't know ...

This worker seemed to feel better about his skill repairing machines in the factory than his way of relating to his son. This is not as unusual as it might seem. In a large-scale study, Arthur Emlen found that 59 per cent of employees rated their family performance 'good or unusually good' while

86 per cent gave a similar rating to their performance on the job (Friedman, 1988, p. 16).

This overall cultural shift may account for why many workers are going along with the work–family speed-up and not joining the resistance against it. A 1993 nationally representative study of 3400 workers conducted by The Families and Work Institute reflects two quite contradictory findings. On one hand, the study reports that 80 per cent of workers feel their jobs require 'working very hard' and 42 per cent 'often feel used up by the end of the work day'. On the other hand, when workers are asked to compare how much time and energy they *actually* devoted to their family, their job or career and themselves, with how much time they would *like* to devote to each, there was little difference (Galinsky *et al.* 1993, pp. 1, 98). Workers estimate that they actually spend 43 per cent of their time and energy on family and friends, 37 per cent on job or career, and 20 per cent on themselves. But they *want* to spend just about what they *are* spending – 47 per cent on family and friends, 30 per cent on the job, and 23 per cent on themselves (Galinsky *et al.* 1993, p. 98). Thus, the workers I spoke to who were 'giving' in to the work–family speed-up may be typical of a wider trend.

CAUSAL MECHANISMS

Three sets of factors may exacerbate this reversal of family and work cultures; trends in the family, trends at work, and a cultural consumerism which reinforces trends in the family and work.

First, half of marriages in America end in divorce – the highest divorce rate in the world. Because of the greater complexity of family life, the emotional skills of parenting, woefully underestimated to begin with, are more important than ever before. Many workers spoke with feeling about strained relationships with step-children and ex-wives or husbands (White and Riesmann, 1992). New in scope, too, are the numbers of working wives who work 'two shifts', one at home and one at work, and face their husband's resistance to helping fully with the load at home – a strain that often leaves both spouses feeling unappreciated (Hochschild, 1989).

Second, another set of factors apply at work. Many corporations have emotionally engineered for top and upper middle managers a world of friendly ritual and positive reinforcement. New corporate cultures call for 'valuing the individual' and honouring the 'internal customer' (so that requests made by employees within the Company are honoured as highly as those by customers outside the Company). Human relations employees give seminars on human problems at work. High-performance teams, based on co-operation between relative equals who 'manage themselves', tend to foster intense relations at work. The Company frequently gives out awards for outstanding work at award ceremonies. Compliments run freely. The halls are hung with new plaques praising one or another worker on recent accomplishments. Recognition luncheons, department gatherings and informal birthday remembrances are common. Career planning sessions with one's supervisor, team meetings to talk over 'modeling, work relations, and mentoring' with co-workers all verge on, even as they borrow from, psychotherapy. For all its aggravation and tensions, the workplace is where quite a few workers feel appreciated, honoured, and where they have real friends. By contrast, at home there are fewer 'award ceremonies' and little helpful feedback about mistakes.

In addition, courtship and mate selection, earlier more or less confined to the home-based community, may be moving into the sphere of work. The later age for marriage, the higher proportion of unmarried people, and the high divorce rate all create an ever-replenishing courtship pool at work. The gender desegregation of the workplace, and the lengthened working day also provide opportunity for people to meet and develop romantic or quasi-romantic ties. At the factory, romance may develop in the lunchroom, pub, or parking lot; and for upper management levels, at conferences, in 'fantasy settings' in hotels and dimly lit restaurants (Kanter, 1989, p. 281).

In a previous era, an undetermined number of men escaped the house for the pub, the fishing hole, and often the office. A common pattern, to quote from the title of an article by Jean Duncombe and Dennis Marsden, was that of 'workaholic men' and 'whining women' (Duncombe and Marsden, 1993). Now that women compose 45 per cent of the American labour force and come home to a 'second shift' of work at home, some women are escaping into work too – and as they do so, altering the cultures of work and home.

Forces pulling workers out of family life and into the workplace are set into perpetual motion by consumerism. Consumerism acts as a mechanism which maintains the emotional reversal of work and family (Schor, 1992). Exposed to advertisements, workers expand their material 'needs'. To buy what they now 'need', they need money. To earn money, they work longer hours. Being away from home so many hours, they make up for their absence at home with gifts which cost money. They 'materialise' love. And so the cycle continues.

Once work begins to become a more compelling arena of appreciation than home, a self-fulfilling prophecy takes hold. For, if workers flee into work from the tensions at home, tensions at home often grow worse. The worse the tensions at home, the firmer the grip of the workplace on the worker's human needs, and hence the escalation of the entire syndrome.

If more workers conceive of work as a haven, it is overwhelmingly in some sense *against their wishes*. Most workers in this and other studies say they value family life above all. Work is what they do. Family is why they live. So, I believe the logic I have described proceeds despite, not because of, the powerful intentions and deepest wishes of those in its grip.

MODELS OF FAMILY AND WORK IN THE FLIGHT PLAN OF CAPITALISM

To sum up, for some people work may be becoming more like family, and family life more like work. Instead of the model of the *family* as haven from work, more of us fit the model of *work* as haven from home. In this model, the tired parent leaves a world of unresolved quarrels, unwashed laundry and dirty dishes for the atmosphere of engineered cheer, appreciation and harmony at work. It is at work that one drops the job of *working* on relating to a brooding adolescent, an obstreperous toddler, rivaling siblings or a retreating spouse. At last, beyond the emotional shield of work, one says not, 'Hi honey, I'm home', but 'Hi fellas, I'm here!' For those who fit this model, the ritual core of family life is not simply smaller, it is less of a ritual core.

How extensive is this trend? I suspect it is a slight tendency in the lives of many working parents, and the basic reality for a small but growing minority. This trend holds for some people more than others and in some parts of society more than in others. Certain trends – such as the growth of the contingency labour force – may increase the importance of the family, and tend toward reinstalling the model of family as haven, and work as 'heartless world'. A growing rate of unemployment might be associated with yet a third 'double-negative' model according to which neither home nor work are emotional bases, but rather the gang at the pub, or on the street.

But the sense of sacred that we presume to be reliably attached to home may be more vulnerable than we might wish.

Most working parents more deeply want, or want to want, a fourth, 'double-positive' model of work–family balance. In the end, these four patterns are unevenly spread over the class structure – the 'haven in a heartless world' more at the top, the 'double-negative' more at the bottom, the 'reverse-haven' emerging in the middle.

Each pattern of work and family life is to be seen somewhere in the flight plan of late capitalism. For, capitalist competition is not simply a matter of market expansion around the globe, but of local geographies of emotion at home. The challenge, as I see it, is to understand the close links between economic trends, emotional geographies, and pockets of cultural resistance. For it is in those pockets that we can look for 'warm modern' answers.

Notes

1. Less time away from work means less time for children. Nationwide, half of children wish they could see their fathers more, and a third wish they could see their mothers more (Coolsen *et al.*, 1986; Hewlett 1991, p. 105). A growing number of commentators draw links, often carelessly, between this decline in family time and a host of problems, including school failure and alcohol and drug abuse (Hewlett, 1991).

2. In her book *When Giants Learn To Dance*, the sociologist Rosabeth Kanter suggests an alternative to mommy-tracking – company 'time outs'. A company requires workers to work ten weeks of 9- or 10-hour days preparing to ship a product, and then take a week-long 'time out' after the product is shipped. In contrast to 'mommy-tracking', these 'time outs' are available to men as well as women. Those who take advantage of them aren't placed on a lower track (Kanter, 1989). But by design, time-outs suit the needs of the *company* more than the worker. 'Time outs' presume the acceptance of an industrial notion of time for men and women, and pay the worker back for this acceptance, offering periodic rest-stops in it. It does not challenge the culture of capitalism but softens the worker up, the better to accept it (Kanter, 1989, p. 359).

3. On the political agenda for the 1950s, through the 1970s, bills proposing a shorter working week were vetoed by the United States Congress, strongly opposed by business, and have since disappeared from American public discourse. (McCarthy and McGaughey, 1981; Blyton, 1985; Owen, 1989).

4. Since factory workers are normally excluded in company consideration of these reforms, this option is normally excluded from 'family-friendly reforms'. In addition, seniority is the unquestioned principle applied in allocating shifts (see Engelstad, 1983). Unions often oppose it adamantly since it adds a principle that competes with the principle of seniority used to determine who gets to work which shift.

5. The option of shorter or more flexible schedules should not be confused with the growth of 'contingency jobs' which pair flexibility with a loss of job security and benefits. As activists in and outside companies conceive of family-friendly reforms, they make 'good' jobs better, and don't substitute bad jobs for good ones.

6. Many studies show that family-friendly reforms pay for themselves. Those who quit their jobs for family reasons are often the most, not the least, productive workers. In addition, each trained worker who quits, costs the company money in recruiting and training a replacement.

7. The CEO's pronouncement about family-friendly reforms and the managers' non-execution of them resemble an episode in Leo Tolstoy's *War*

and Peace. In the novel, the Russian Emperor Alexander dispatches an envoy, Balashev, to deliver a critical message to Napoleon, to halt this advance toward Moscow. Balashev is detained by a series of people and, when he meets Napoleon, forgets to deliver the message.

8. Taking inspiration from Emile Durkheim, Erving Goffman brilliantly applied a notion of the sacred to the individual, though Goffman does not apply this idea to the unit intermediate between society and the individual – the family.

9. The workplace speed-up has itself exacerbated a 'rationalization' of family life. In the nineteenth century, Tamara Hareven argues, events were measured in 'family time', according to a family timetable (births, marriages, deaths) and by family units (generations) and oriented to family needs (the need to tend newborns, the dying). Formerly resistant to rationalisation, in the last 30 years family life has become increasingly planned, and geared to the industrial clock. 'Quality time' is demarcated from 'quantity time', just as time at the office 'working' is designated as separate from time 'goofing off around the water cooler'. One shouldn't, one feels, be chatting aimlessly in a 'quantity' sort of way when one is having 'quality' time with a child. Even life-cycle events such as marriages and births are now sometimes planned according to the needs of the office (Martin, 1992).

References

Alvesson, Mats and Berg, Per Olof (1992), *Corporate Culture and Organizational Symbolism: An Overview Berlin* (New York: Walter de Gruyter).

Bailyn, Lotte (1993), *Breaking the Mold: Women, Men and Time in the New Corporate World* (New York: Free Press).

Blyton, Paul (1985), *Changes in Working Time: An International Review* (New York: St Martin's Press).

Bowen, Gary L. and Orthner, Dennis K. (1991), 'Effects of Organizational Culture on Fatherhood', in F. W. Bozett and S. M. H. Hanson (eds), *Fatherhood and Families in Cultural Context* (New York: Springer).

Coolsen, P., Seligson, M. and Garbino J. (1986), *When School's Out and Nobody's Home* (Chicago, IL: National Committee for the Prevention of Child Abuse).

Duncombe, Jean and Marsden, Dennis (1993), 'Workaholics and Whining Women, Theorizing Intimacy and Emotion Work: The Last Frontier of Gender Inequality?', unpublished paper, Department of Sociology, University of Essex, England.

Engelstad, Fredrik (1993), 'Family Structure and Institutional Interplay', in Leira, Annlang (ed.), *Family Sociology – Developing the Field* (Oslo: Institut fur Samfunnsforskning), pp. 72–90.

Fineman, Steven (ed.) (1993), *Emotion in Organizations* (London: Sage Publishers).

Friedman, D. (1991), *Linking Work–Family Issues to the Bottom Line* (New York: Conference Board). (Dana Friedman is co-president of the Families and Work Institute, New York).

Fuchs, V. (1991), 'Are Americans Under-investing in their Children?', *Society*, Sept/Oct, pp. 14–22.

Galinsky, Ellen, Friedman, Dana E. and Hernandez, Carol A. (1991), *The Corporate Reference Guide to Work Family Programs* (New York: Families and Work Institute).

Galinsky, Ellen, Bond, James and Friedman, Dana (1993), *The Changing Workforce: Highlights of the National Study* (New York: Family and Work Institute).

Giddens, Anthony (1976), *New Rules of Sociological Method* (New York: Basic Books).

Giddens, Anthony (1991), *Modernity and Self-Identity* (Stanford, CA: Stanford University Press).

Hareven, T. K. (1982), *Family Time and Industrial Time* (Cambridge: Cambridge University Press).

Hewlett, Sylvia Ann (1991), *When the Bough Breaks: The Cost of Neglecting Our Children* (New York: Basic Books).

Hochschild, Arlie (1983), *The Managed Heart: The Commercialization of Human Feeling* (Berkeley, CA: University of California Press).

Hochschild, Arlie (1994), 'The Commercial Spirit of Intimate Life and the Abduction of Feminism: Signs from Women's Advice Books', *Theory, Culture & Society*, vol. II (May), pp. 1–24.

Hochschild, Arlie with Anne Machung (1989), *The Second Shift: Working Parents and the Revolution at Home* (New York: Viking Press).

Hofstede, Geertz (1980), *Culture's Consequences, International Differences in Work-Related Values* (London: Sage Publishers).

Kanter, Rosabeth Moss (1977), *Work and Family in the United States: A Critical Review and Agenda for Research and Policy* (New York: Russell Sage Foundation).

Kanter, Rosabeth Moss (1983), *The Change Masters* (New York: Simon & Schuster).

Lasch, Christopher (1977), *Haven in a Heartless World* (New York: Basic Books).

Martin, Joanne (1992), *Cultures in Organizations: Three Perspectives* (New York: Oxford University Press).

McCarthy, Eugene and McGaughey, William (1981), *Nonfinancial Economics: The Case for Shorter Hours of Work* (New York: Praeger).

Negrey, Cynthia (1993), *Gender, Time and Reduced Work* (New York: SUNY Press).

Owen, John (1989), *Reduced Working Hours: Cure for Unemployment or Economic Burden?* (Baltimore, MD: Johns Hopkins Press).

Popenoe, David (1989), *Disturbing the Nest: Family Change and Decline in Modern Societies* (New York: Aldine De Gruyter).

Schaevitz, Marjorie Hansen (1984), *The Superwoman Syndrome* (New York: Warner Books).

Schor, Juliet B. (1992), *The Overworked American: The Unexpected Decline of Leisure* (New York: Basic Books).

Schwartz, Felice N. (1989), 'Management Women and the New Facts of Life', *Harvard Business Review*, 1, January–February, pp. 65–76.

Skolnick, Arlene (1991), *Embattled Paradise* (New York: Basic Books).

Tolstoy, Leo (1966), *War and Peace* (New York: W. W. Norton).

Trice, Harrison M. and Beyer, Janice M. (1993), *The Cultures of Work Organizations* (Englewood Cliffs, NJ: Prentice-Hall).

Van Maanen, John and Kunda, Gideon (1989), 'Real Feelings: Emotional Expression and Organizational Culture', *Research in Organizational Behavior*, vol. 11, pp. 43–103.

White, Lynn K. and Riesmann, Agnes (1992), 'When the Brady Bunch Grows Up: Step-, Half- and Full-Sibling Relationships in Adulthood', *Journal of Marriage and the Family*, vol. 54 (February), pp. 197–208.

Zedek, Sheldon, Maslach, Christina, Mosier, Kathleen, and Skitka, Linda (1992), 'Affective Response to Work and Quality of Family Life: Employee and Spouse Perspectives', in Goldsmith, Elizabeth (ed.), *Work and Family: Theory, Research and Applications* (London: Sage Publishers).

3 Gender and Office-holding in Trade Unions

ELISABETH LAWRENCE

INTRODUCTION

Discussion of women's union involvement in both academic and trade union circles has often contained an implicit assumption that women participate less then men, are less willing to join unions, and, once members, are less willing to be active and stand for union office (Purcell, 1979). Evidence of women's under-representation in union office-holding is often explained in terms of constraints on women's participation, rather than through an examination of reasons for participation or their absence. This belief in women's lower levels of union participation is held by many trade union members and officers, and often provides the starting point for researchers, seeking to explain why women participate less and are under-represented in unions. The validity of this starting point is, however, questionable. It should also be noted that participation and representation are not identical: a group can participate highly at some levels without being represented at other levels. Nor is it correct to assume that the reasons for women's under-representation in union leadership are necessarily a result of lower levels of participation at other levels of the union.

The work of Wertheimer and Nelson (1975), one of the first major studies of women's union involvement, has been interpreted by subsequent researchers in a manner which, I would argue, focused too much on barriers to participation, (which Wertheimer and Nelson classified into three groups: cultural–societal–personal, job-related and union-related), at the expense of looking at reasons for participation; the two are not always the same. For instance, while domestic responsibilities may present a barrier to union involvement, their absence does not necessarily mean that the extra time available will be spent on union work. As Wertheimer and Nelson note, among the union activists in their study, childcare was not a problem, because they were sufficiently committed to the union to find ways of arranging childcare or took their children along to the union meetings with them, while the inactive members, according to their informants, found time to work overtime or engage in leisure pursuits they were interested in, but not to attend the union meetings.

Lipset *et al.* in *Union Democracy* (1956) point out that much research on union participation contains an implicit assumption that members ought to participate. They write:

> Instead of asking why men do not attend union meetings (a question which follows on the assumption that they should) we might ask, 'Why do they go when they do, and what kinds of rewards are there for attendance?' (p. 262)

So it is important to ask about reasons for participating and to explore the factors which make union members willing to be active and to hold union office (Harrison, 1979). It can be argued that this is especially relevant in the case of women workers, given the poor historical record of many trade unions in representing adequately the interests of women members (Boston, 1987).

The research on which this chapter is based was a study of shop stewards in the Sheffield Local Government Branch of NALGO (National and Local Government Officers' Association), one of the predecessor unions of UNISON. UNISON is the largest trade union in the UK representing over 1.4 million members in public sector and related employment. The Sheffield branch was a large branch with over 7000 members at the time of the research (1986–90), covering a range of white-collar occupations, from filing clerk to senior executive, in nineteen departments of the City Council. Around 40 per cent of the members were male and 60 per cent female, whereas the shop stewards answering the questionnaire were 34.4 per cent female and 65.6 per cent male. The branch was selected for the research, because it offered a sufficiently large and varied sample to explore the influence of gender and occupation on union office-holding.

Some of the more recent research on women and unions (Cobble, 1990; Gordon, 1991; Briskin and McDermott, 1993;) has not started out with an assumption that women are less active in unions than men, but has identified work-related factors promoting female union activism and different forms that female activism and militancy have taken. Cobble's work argues that negotiating skills acquired by waitresses in dealing with customers assisted them in participating in formal union meetings. Gordon's work shows substantial evidence of militancy among female jute workers in Dundee, although it was not always expressed through formal union structures. The collection of articles edited by Briskin and McDermott, together with their own contributions, present an optimistic and affirmative view of the contributions that women workers and feminist ways of organising can make to revitalising trade unions.

Much of the general literature in industrial sociology on union participation has focused on work as a motivator for union activism (Spinrad, 1960, Perline and Lorenz, 1970, Dubin, 1973), although this approach has not always been applied in the case of women trade unionists. Studies of union participation have tended to focus on reasons for participation in the case of male workers and barriers to participation in the case of women workers. Thus, depending upon the gender of the workers being studied, researchers have adopted different starting points for investigation. This has also involved the relative neglect of the potential importance of women's work experiences for their union involvement. Women work at a variety of levels in local government, and there may be significant differences between women at different occupational levels, if work is a major factor affecting women's union involvement. For instance, a former Equal Opportunities Officer of the branch related in interview an attempt by the Equal Opportunities Committee to organise a women-only social. Only four women attended because many of the women in the branch saw a women-only social as a 'middle-class feminist' event and did not see the point of a women-only gathering. None the less, over fifty women had attended a meeting organised by the Equal Opportunities Committee of the branch on positive action in employment.

Feldberg and Glenn (1979) have argued that frequently in industrial sociology women's work experience has been studied through the perspective of a gender model, so that attitudes to work and to career progression were all explained in terms of family position and the feminine gender role. On the other hand, men's work experience was studied through the perspective of a work model, in which attitudes and behaviour at work were all explained in terms of the nature and experience of work, so neglecting the possible influence of family and the masculine gender role. They argued for the development of 'an integrated model which takes into account the interaction between job and gender factors' (p. 527). It can be argued that this principle should also be applied to the study of union involvement. It is important to take into account the effect of both work-related factors and external social factors, including gender roles and family situation, in studying the union involvement of women and men.

If the possible importance of work experience for women and gender role for men is acknowledged, for the study of areas such as attitudes to work and trade union involvement, then a more careful and precise study of gender differences becomes possible. It also allows for more recognition of similarities between women and men in various areas of work and union involvement. It is useful to ask the question whether differences in men's and women's union involvement are gender role differences or occupational differences, which arise from different experiences of employment.

The term 'gender difference' appears to be used in two ways in the social sciences. It can be used to refer to a difference which simply occurs along gender lines or to a difference which arises from gender roles in society. This is an important theoretical problem in women's studies and the sociology of gender. Because a difference occurs along gender lines, it does not automatically follow that it is the result of gender roles directly. For example, Fryer *et al.* (1978) in their work on facilities for shop stewards in NUPE (National Union of Public Employees, another of the predecessor unions of UNISON) showed that the main obstacle facing many women members of the union in becoming a shop steward was that they worked part-time, which made it difficult to be in full-time contact with members they would represent as a shop steward. Thus the factor directly inhibiting union office-holding was being a part-time worker (an occupational factor) although the reasons for working part-time were probably a mixture of occupational and gender role factors (occupational segregation by sex, part-time work being the only work available and family responsibilities restricting women's ability to take on full-time paid work).

Gender differences are often mediated via occupational and departmental differences. More 'room at the top', that is more higher graded posts, and hence more opportunity for promotion, is often to be found in male-dominated rather than female-dominated areas of employment, as shown in the report of the Positive Action Project, which investigated the employment provided by Sheffield City Council (Sheffield City Council Employment Department/Personnel Department; Store, 1984). This report divided council departments into 'male-dominated' (Cleansing, Environmental Health, Planning and Design, Recreation and Works), more or less evenly 'balanced' departments (Administration and Legal, Art Galleries, Employment, Estates, Housing, Museums and Treasury), and 'female-dominated' (Education, Family and Community Services and Libraries). These categories related to proportions of men and women in each department, not to their relative seniority.

There were also departmental variations perceived by the NALGO Branch Organiser (a local full-time union official) in levels of union awareness and involvement. His view was that in NALGO, as a general trend, departments of Housing and of Social Services (called in the Sheffield case Family and Community Services) tended to be the most active, and in Sheffield he added Education to the list of activist departments. He explained this tendency towards union activism in terms of the work content of the departments, which helped to make people aware of social issues, both because of the educational socialisation that professionals, such as social workers and housing administrators, in these fields received, and because they were dealing with social problems in their day-to-day work. Also in the case of Family and Community Services, the 1970 strike of field social workers had had a long-lasting radicalising effect (Joyce *et al.*, 1988). One of the male branch officers observed in interview that leading women union officers were most likely to come from Family and Community Services.

This chapter contains a short summary of the research process and then proceeds to discuss the research findings in three sections. The data are organised under the headings of (a) work-related factors affecting union office-holding, (b) family–societal–cultural factors affecting union office-holding and (c) union-related factors affecting union office-holding. These categories, taken from Wertheimer and Nelson (1975), are developed to explore factors which enable and support women's union participation, rather than focusing only on barriers to participation.

In the section on work situation there is material on jobs, pay (grade) levels, departmental distribution of shop stewards and the impact of work on the union role, particularly in relation to the operation of the union facilities agreement. This section indicates a number of significant gender differences, which suggests that work-related factors are important in the study of women's trade unionism. In the section on societal–cultural–personal factors, information is included on number and ages of children and responsibilities for care of children. These questions uncovered considerable gender differences. Particularly striking was the absence of mothers of young children among female shop stewards. The final section on union-related factors reports answers on how informants became shop stewards, and how union work affects performance of their job. There are also research findings reported on numbers of meetings attended and committee membership, which explore patterns of representation at different levels of the union branch. The conclusion then dicusses some of the implications of the research for understanding gender and occupational differences in relation to union involvement and for strategies to promote women's representation within trade unions.

THE RESEARCH PROCESS

Negotiations for research access were started in Summer 1985. A pilot questionnaire study was conducted in November 1986 and the main questionnaire survey carried out from Summer to Autumn 1987. Sixty-four questionnaires were returned in total. A computer analysis of these questionnaires, using SPSSX, was then conducted. From Autumn 1989 to Spring 1990, twenty-four interviews were conducted, using audiotape. Interviewees were selected by two methods: contacting informants who had returned the questionnaire indicating that they were prepared to be interviewed, and by approaching branch officers directly. An equal number of men and women were interviewed. In Summer 1990, a study of the branch records of shop stewards from 1983 to 1989 was carried out. The analysis of the branch records focused on rates of shop steward turnover, gender balance of shop stewards, and departmental variations in patterns of union organisation.

WORK-RELATED FACTORS AFFECTING UNION ACTIVISM

Seventeen (77.3 per cent) of the twenty-four female stewards worked in 'female-dominated' departments: Education, Family and Community Services, Libraries and Polytechnic. Four of them worked in the 'balanced departments' of Housing and Treasury. One female shop steward worked in the 'male-dominated' Environmental Health department. These figures tend to support the view that women find it easier to take on union representative posts when in a predominantly female environment (Wertheimer and Nelson, 1975; Cobble, 1990).

Gender differences among shop stewards answering the questionnaire survey were quite noticeable in regard to scale of posts and revealed a concentration of women on the lower pay grades. Of the forty-two male shop stewards, eighteen (42.9 per cent) were of high occupational status, twenty (47.6 per cent) were of middle status and three (7.1 per cent) were of low status. In the case of the twenty-two female shop stewards, two (9.1 per cent) were of high occupational status, nine (40.9 per cent) were of middle status and eleven (50 per cent) were of low occupational status. The categorisation of salary grades into high, middle and low status follows that used by Nicholson *et al.* (1981), in which grades 1 and 2 are defined as low, grades 3–6 as middle, and grades at senior officer and above are defined as high.

Thus when studying the shop steward population it was important to take into account the degree of overlap and of difference by grade and gender. While some of the shop stewards were also included in the interview stage of the research, other union officers were also included at this stage. There were twenty-four interviewees, including two NALGO employees. Among the remaining twenty-two interviewees, there were rather more women in higher status posts than in the case of the shop stewards surveyed in the questionnaire. Among the eleven male interviewees, seven were in high status posts and four in middle status posts. Among the eleven women interviewees, four were in high status posts, four in middle status posts and three in low status posts. Nicholson *et al.* (1981) noted the tendency for union activists to come disproportionately from higher status posts, and this seemed particularly so for senior female activists. It is also an important factor in explaining women's relative under-representation in union office-holding.

The importance of these status differences can be seen in answers to a number of questions about the relation between job and union work. In the questionnaire, informants were asked about the relation between job and union work to explore both how their job might help with union work and how it might conflict with it (see Table 3.1). The questions asked for yes/no responses to a number of statements about how the shop steward's job as a local government officer might support union work or present problems for its performance.

Table 3.1   *Job support for union work by gender**

	Male	Female
Informants agreeing their job helped them to be effective as a shop steward by:		
giving access to useful information	26 (61.9%)	13 (59.1%)
allowing easy access to your members	37 (88.1%)	13 (59.1%)
giving you flexibility in organising your time and work	36 (85.7%)	15 (68.2%)
helping you develop skills useful in union work (e.g. public speaking, organising meetings)	22 (52.4%)	11 (50.0%)
giving access to senior management	27 (64.3%)	9 (40.9%)
	(n = 64)	

*Percentages refer to total number of male and female shop stewards.

The questionnaire also revealed that 59.1 per cent of women and 61.9 per cent of men agreed that their job helped them to be effective as a shop steward, by giving access to useful information, showing minimal gender differences in this respect. But 59.1 per cent of women and 88.1 per cent of men thought their job allowed them easy access to their members: clearly, male shop stewards had some advantage here. And 68.2 per cent of women and 85.7 per cent of men agreed that they had flexibility in organising their time and their work, which assisted union office-holding. Half of the women and a slight majority of the men (52.4 per cent) agreed that their work helped them develop skills useful in union work, such as public speaking and organising meetings. A noticeable gender difference occurred when informants were asked whether their job helped by giving access to senior management: 64.3 per cent of the men, but only 40.9 per cent of the women, said yes.

To conclude on this point, men's jobs helped union office-holding more than women's in three respects: access to senior management, access to members and flexibility in management of the shop steward's own time and work. All these three are associated with higher occupational status. While the gender differences in some responses were small, in all cases a higher percentage of men than women indicated that their jobs helped with performance of union work.

When asked about conflicts between job and union work (see Table 3.2), a majority of both sexes agreed that there was a conflict of time demands, with fifteen women (68.2 per cent) and thirty-five men (83.3 per cent) agreeing. The fact that women appeared to experience less conflict in terms of demands on their time, may arise partly from the fact that women did more of their union work than men in out-of-work time. It may also arise from the lower degree of job flexibiliity that they enjoyed. When asked whether union work presented a threat to promotion prospects, 50 per cent of women and 59.5 per cent of men agreed. None the less, comments by female branch officers in interview suggested that women's promotion prospects were more likely than men's to be harmed by union activism.

Interviewees identified a problem of management discrimination against female union activists. They believed that managers saw union activism as an unfeminine activity, so that, whereas men were likely to be promoted as a result of union activity, women were likely to be discriminated against on account of it. Behaviour which was seen as assertive on the part of men was seen as aggressive when used by women. As one interviewee put it:

> I think women are discriminated against when they are shop stewards, because it is not seen as a feminine activity. If you are assertive, you are

Table 3.2   *Job conflicts with union work by gender*

	Male	*Female*
Informants agreeing that their job conflicted with their union work due to:		
conflict of time demands	35 (83.3%)	15 (68.2%)
threat to promotion prospects	25 (59.5%)	11 (50.0%)
problems of building up a backlog of work	26 (61.9%)	14 (63.6%)
inflexibility of work	4 (9.5%)	3 (13.6%)
conflict of responsibilities/ loyalties (wearing two hats)	19 (45.2%)	10 (45.5%)
	(*n* = 64)	

seen as being aggressive, whereas for men that's seen as being forceful and not aggressive. Men shop stewards tend to be promoted, whereas women don't.   (Female branch officer)

She noted that this discrimination could very well deter other women from taking on union office, if they believed it might damage their career prospects. Another interviewee reported three cases of women who had taken out grievances, because they had been discriminated against as a result of trade union activism. She noted that this discrimination contravened the Council's own code of practice on equal opportunities, which prohibited discrimination on grounds of trade union activity. Thus it appeared that a different response by the employer to union activism on the part of men and women was a factor discouraging women's involvement.

A majority of both sexes (63.6 per cent of women and 61.9 per cent of men) agreed that there was a problem of building up a back log of work. When asked about inflexibility of their job as a problem in carrying out their union work, 13.6 cent of women and 9.5 per cent of men agreed that this was the case, so this problem was only identified by a small number of both sexes. A sizeable minority of each sex agreed that there could be a conflict of responsibilities. In responses to questions about conflicts between job and union work, gender differences were small, except for the question about conflict of time demands, which was experienced by more men than women. The explanations to a number of these answers can be seen in Tables 3.3 and 3.4, which report time spent on union work and when union work was carried out. Under the union facilities agreement between the Council and NALGO in existence at the time of the research, branch officers and chief shop stewards were entitled to up to three days per week as time off for union work. For these union office-holders, cover for their own job was usually provided while they were away on union business. For other shop stewards the union facilities agreement provided that they could take as much time off for union work as was reasonably necessary, but there was no automatic provision of cover for their job. This agreement thus worked out better for shop stewards in some jobs than in others, depending on both the flexibility of the job and the extent to which it was possible to leave the job uncovered for a time. Hence, because of gender inequalities in employment, the agreement generally worked out better for male than for female shop stewards.

Table 3.3 shows that gender differences in the amount of time spent on union work were not particularly substantial. Table 3.4, however, indicates that there were important gender differences in the times when the union work was carried out.

Table 3.4 shows clearly that women used far more of their own time than did the men to carry out union work and this factor may explain the relative under-representation of women at shop steward level, since the inability to use facility time effectively may be a deterrent to taking on union office. This shows the importance of good facility agreements, providing time off for union work, for improving women's position within trade unions. It also explains why men experienced more conflict of time demands.

The issue of flexibility was further highlighted in interviews. A number of jobs were identified which made it difficult to be a shop steward. These included posts such as nursery nurse, typist, departmental secretary, reception/counter worker, data preparation worker and residential social worker. Apart from the last case, these were jobs in which women predominated. The differences in flexibility were clearly tied to occupational status. For instance, one former shop steward described how people in his department at senior officer level and above could just pick up a set of papers and say they were going to a meeting. This would not be challenged, and no one would enquire whether it was a union meeting or a work meeting. Staff on clerical and lower administrative grades, however,

Table 3.3 *Time spent on NALGO work, by gender*

	Male	Female	Total

'Approximately how many hours a week do you spend on NALGO work (including time attending meetings)?', by gender

	Male	Female	Total
0–5 hours	14 (33.3%)	6 (27.3%)	20 (31.3%)
6–10 hours	14 (33.3%)	10 (45.5%)	24 (37.5%)
11–15 hours	5 (11.9%)	2 (9.1%)	7 (10.9%)
16–20 hours	5 (11.9%)	2 (9.1%)	7 (10.9%)
over 20 hours	2 (4.8%)	2 (9.1%)	4 (6.3%)
missing	2 (4.8%)	0 (0%)	2 (3.1%)
			(n = 64)

Table 3.4 *Times when union work performed, by gender*

	Male	Female	Total
Mostly in work time	25 (59.5%)	7 (31.8%)	32 (30%)
About half in work time and half in own time	15 (35.7%)	12 (54.5%)	27 (42.2%)
Mostly in own time	2 (4.8%)	3 (13.6%)	5 (7.8%)
			(n = 64)

could not leave their desks in this way. This account shows real inequalities in the degree of autonomy experienced at work:

> In my opinion the only people who regularly work hard and consistently in the department are the clerk-typists. Everyone else comes and goes as they see fit, and so I tend to think that might be a reason why clerk-typists haven't got time to be shop steward. As a senior officer I never had any problems with time off when I was a shop steward. At senior officer level and above, it's quite easy to say 'I haven't been able to do that, I've had meetings', sort of ethereal meetings all day and not have to account for where those meetings were, with whom they were, when they were, what was the purpose of them. Clerk-typists cannot just get up and go out because someone would say 'What are you doing?', but above that level, everyone just picks up a load of papers and walks out.
> (Male former shop steward)

Another male shop steward recognised the way these occupational factors made it difficult for women on lower grades to become shop stewards and explained how in Family and Community Services, NALGO had attempted to tackle this problem by negotiating cover for union work. The issue of cover was a vital one for some workers. As one shop steward, who worked as a school clerk, commented:

> My own work piles up and has to be done, no matter what.
> (Education Department shop steward)

Some jobs were much easier to leave than others in order to do union work. For instance, some male shop stewards reported how computing analysis or planning applications were simply deferred or rescheduled. As one male informant put it:

> I have got such a flexible job that I don't have any trouble at all. If something's rescheduled, then something gets put back another week and we lose a week. The work piles up on my desk, but it just gets rescheduled.   (Male chief shop steward and former branch officer)

Some female shop stewards (and former stewards) interviewed had reached personal solutions to this problem by changing their jobs and moving into posts which allowed more flexibility in disposing of their time. For instance, one female branch officer, who had worked as a nursery nurse, was, at the time of interview, seconded to Personnel. This made it much easier for her to serve as a branch officer, since nursery nurses could not leave their work unless cover was provided.

Answers in interviews to questions about operation of the union facilities agreement showed both occupational and gender differences. Women were more likely than men to talk about feeling guilty when leaving work and colleagues, or to explain how they worked late to make up work when they had taken time off for union activities. For instance, one female former shop steward, a social worker in Family and Community Services, stated:

> It often meant I was working until seven or eight at night to attend to the demands of everything. So I suppose, if you think about only doing trade union work in work time, I worked a lot of overtime, but I never regarded it that way. I always regarded it that I would do a lot of trade union work in my own time.

Another female former shop steward who had worked in the Rates Office described the pressures of the work, which made it difficult to take union facility time:

> I did feel guilty if I had to go to a meeting and the Rates Office was packed out, taking twenty minutes for people to get through the queue to pay their rates. I'd feel guilty about having to go to a meeting.

These observations about feeling guilty when leaving the job to do union work suggest that the problems women experienced in effectively using the union facilities agreement arose from gender role socialisation in addition to occupational inequality.

The majority of both sexes reported in the questionnaire that they did not encounter formal difficulties in taking the time off for union work that they were entitled to take under the local union facilities agreement. The absence of cover, however, meant that individuals sometimes had to manage doing both their job and their union work. Nine women (40.9 per cent) and twelve men (28.6 per cent) reported that they encountered difficulties in taking the time off that they were entitled to take for union work.

Informants were then asked to rank which was the source of most difficulty, from a number of choices, including 'pressure from managers', 'pressure from colleagues' and 'pressure from service users' and 'workload'. Answers to this question suggested that slightly more stewards did encounter difficulties than the numbers who had initially reported doing so.

For women who encountered difficulties in taking facility time, pressure from managers was clearly as large an obstacle as the problem of work accumulating. An equal number (five, 22.7 per cent) ranked each of these factors first. For men who encountered difficulties in taking facility time, pressure from managers was only about half the degree of problem that accumulation of work was. Four men (9.5 per cent) ranked 'pressure from managers' first, four (9.5 per cent) ranked 'pressure from service users' first and eight (22.7 per cent) ranked 'workload' factors first. This may reflect variations in men's and women's jobs or maybe managers found it easier to pressurise women than men (which may be a gender role or an occupational seniority factor). On the other hand, it should also be borne in mind that maybe men experienced more of a problem in terms of accumulation of work, because they did more of their union work in work time than women did (see Table 3.4).

These research findings concerning the operation of the union facilities agreement show the interaction of occupational and gender role inequalities. More women than men worked in lower status jobs in which it was harder to take time off for union work, because the job was less flexible and subject to closer supervision. Women were also more likely than men in interview to express feelings of guilt about leaving their work uncovered. Some men, but no women, were quite cheerful about the prospect of work piling up or being rescheduled. These men were working in areas such as planning and computer analysis, but not in areas such as social work, so the clients were slightly more remote and rather less needy. This suggests that, to some degree, both gender role factors and occupational factors made it easier for male shop stewards to use the trade union facilities agreement more effectively than female shop stewards.

PERSONAL–SOCIETAL–CULTURAL FACTORS AFFECTING UNION ACTIVISM

In the questionnaire survey informants were asked about marital status and presence of children. A majority of female shop stewards (59.1 per cent) were not currently married, whereas 56.1 per cent of male shop stewards were currently married. A high proportion of single women (including divorced, separated and widowed) among female shop stewards has been found in many studies of women and trade unions (Roby and Uttal, 1988, Rees, 1990). These results are similar to the patterns found for male and female NALGO shop stewards by Rees and Read (1981) in their national survey of NALGO members.

Table 3.5   *Age of youngest child of shop stewards, by gender*

Age of youngest child (years)	Male	Female	Total
Under 5	9	0	9
5–11	6	1	7
11–14	2	0	2
14–18	2	1	3
Over 18	5	6	11
No children	18	14	32
Total	42	22	64
			(*n* = 64)

Noticeable gender differences emerged in relation to the presence of children (see Table 3.5). Fourteen women (63.6 per cent) had no children, as did seventeen men (40 per cent). Thus a majority of male stewards had children, while a majority of female stewards did not. Of the eight women who had children, six had two and two had three children. Of the men who had children, ten men had one child, eleven had two children, three had three children and one had seven. Presumably some of the male stewards were in the early stages of family formation. Most, possibly all, the women stewards who had children had completed their families. Of the eight women who had children, in six cases all the children were aged over eighteen, and in one case all over fourteen. There were no women stewards with children under the age of five.

Nine men, however, had children under the age of five, six had children aged five to eleven, four had children aged eleven to eighteen and five had children all aged over eighteen. There was a clear and sharp gender difference in ages of children, which suggests that men, but not women, were finding it possible to combine the shop steward role with being a parent of young children. This factor can partly be explained in terms of the fact that men performed more of their union work in work time than women did, but it also indicates gender inequalities within the household. Clearly the presence of young children was a major barrier to women's union activism. This was recognised in interview by both male and female informants. As one male chief shop steward stated:

> If I think about it, most women who are active in NALGO haven't got kids or have grown up kids.

One female branch officer, whose children were grown up, stated clearly that it would be impossible for her to be a branch officer if she had young children. The presence of children also had some impact on union activism of male stewards. For instance, one male branch officer had stepped down from any major union office for one year following the birth of twins, although he had resumed union office thereafter. Another male shop steward reported that he found it difficult to attend the Branch Executive on Thursday evenings, because he needed to go home and help his wife with childcare, since she had been alone with the children all day and deserved a rest. Thus for men who were taking a genuine share in childcare the presence of young children limited, but did not prevent, union activism. For women, the impact of childcare responsibilities was more marked, tending to remove the women from union office-holding altogether while the children were young.

The impact of union activism on other aspects of personal life, besides childcare responsibilities, was also explored in interviews. Some informants, particularly at branch officer level, recognised that union activism could take a heavy cost on personal life and relationships. For instance, one male chief shop steward defined union activism as 'bad news' for people's personal lives, because of the way that union work spilled over into evenings and weekends, leaving little time for personal relationships, leisure activities and maintaining contact with friends.

One male branch officer remarked:

> A lot of people in senior positions in the branch, although not all, are often people who are divorced, separated, or who have got very understanding partners, or who cannot stand the sight of their partners, rather than people who have so called normal relationships. In my opinion that runs through the hierarchy of lay officials at district and national level, so it's much more difficult for a so-called normal married relationship to be able to function.

The fact that male as well as female informants identified the personal costs of union activism as a problem is perhaps a positive factor in terms of the ability of trade unions to address such issues. None of the interviewees took a traditional macho trade union attitude, such as that reported by Cockburn (1991) or Heery and Kelly (1988, 1989), which glorified the hardships of activism and saw trade unionism as 'hyperactive and elitist and vanguardist' (Cockburn, 1991, p. 123).

In interviews a number of women informants described various strategies for coping with the pressures of activism. These included the company of union friends, which legitimated union and political activism as an appropriate activity for women, support from other union activists within the branch and the importance of periods of solitude. For instance, one female branch officer commented:

> I do need a lot of time on my own, to recover from the stresses, otherwise you just start suffering from burn-out and you don't want to pick anything up and you start getting sloppy. I'm fortunate that I can go home and be on my own, when lots of people can't.

This comment reflects a different perspective on women living alone from the conventional social view which often treats single women as a case for pity, emphasising instead the positive qualities of solitude.

UNION-RELATED FACTORS AFFECTING UNION ACTIVISM

The questionnaire survey uncovered some gender differences in the process of shop steward selection. Informants were asked a rank order question about how they became elected as a shop steward in the first place, with options such as 'asked by work colleagues', 'interest in trade unionism' and 'no one else was prepared to do the job'. Of the fourteen who ranked first that they were asked to stand by their colleagues at work, only two were women. Of the twenty who put this answer second only five were women. This suggests that perhaps women are less likely to be asked to stand for election and that the union members were less likely to think of women as potential shop stewards. Given the fact that most shop stewards begin as reluctant representatives (Nicholson, 1976; Moore, 1980) and the importance of sponsorship in developing a union career (Ledwith et al., 1990), this lack of encouragement from work colleagues to take on union office may be an important factor contributing to women's lower levels of union office-holding.

The question about being the only volunteer, however, scored a higher proportion of first and second choices from women. This raises the possibility that while a high proportion of both male and female stewards are reluctant representatives, there is some gender difference in the process of shop steward selection, in that women have to put themselves forward initially while men receive more encouragement.

There were no gender differences noticeable in response to involvement as a shop steward as a result of interest in trade unionism. Nineteen informants (seven female and twelve male) ranked this factor first and fourteen placed it second (five female and nine male). This was the most popular response, along with being the only volunteer, and suggests that interest in trade unionism was a strong motivating factor for both sexes.

Patterns of office-holding on departmental shop stewards' committees were examined to see how factors affecting union activism might operate at different levels of the union structure. This was done to see whether barriers and enablers of women's union office-holding varied with the level of the trade union. Within each department there was a departmental shop stewards' committee and for many shop stewards this was the most important representative body they attended. In the better organised departments the shop stewards' committee met weekly and dealt with a wide range of issues, functioning sometimes semi-autonomously from the branch.

A majority of the female shop stewards (54.5 per cent) held some post of responsibility on their departmental shop stewards' committee: a minority of the men (38.1 per cent) did. This suggests that once a woman had become a shop steward it was fairly easy for her to take on other union posts at departmental level. Five women and five men were chief shop stewards, that is the senior shop steward in their department. Becoming a shop steward was one of the important levels at which there was a problem about women's union representation, particularly since in the NALGO structure being a shop steward was the entry route to most other union offices. Once women were shop stewards, however, they seemed to participate fairly equally within the departmental shop stewards' committees.

Another important level of participation studied was involvement in the Branch Committee. The Branch Committee met monthly in the evening and functioned as an executive committee for the branch. It had a number of sub-committees: Education, Equal Opportunities, Finance and General Purposes, Publicity, Service Conditions and Welfare. In some departments all shop stewards were members of the Branch Committee, although not all attended; in others a distinction was made between executive and non-executive shop stewards. Involvement at Branch Committee level gave shop stewards a wider perspective on union affairs beyond their own department. It also provided the opportunity to move on to union office at district and national levels.

Of the shop stewards who answered the questionnaire, nine women and twenty-two men reported that they were members of the Branch Committee: 52.4 per cent of male shop stewards and 40.9 per cent of female shop stewards were members, so women were under-represented at this level. Most shop stewards who were on the Branch Committee held posts on it. This was the case for eight of the nine women and sixteen of the twenty-two men. So once women were members of the Branch Committee, they had a good prospect of holding positions of responsibility on it.

Five women and four men were members of the Finance and General Purposes Committee, the most powerful of the branch committees. Four women and six men were members of the Service Conditions Committee, the committee which advised on matters of local negotiations. Two women and three men attended the Equal Opportunities Committee, and two women and four men attended the Education, Publicity and Welfare Committees. Thus once women were members of the Branch Committee they were at least as likely as men to serve on the various sub-committees. In many unions during the 1980s and beyond, individuals who were willing to stand for union office had a good chance of being elected, often in uncontested elections, and it can be argued that women often enjoy a far greater degree of equal opportunities in trade unions than in employment. None the less, the large majority of female stewards, like their male counterparts, served as shop steward for only one or two years and so did not serve long enough to establish a union 'career'. The average length of office as shop steward, according to the study of branch records, was two years and was the same for both men and women.

The NALGO branch had attempted to promote women's union participation, as had NALGO nationally. It had a well organised system of shop steward training, with a high take up rate of courses by both sexes. Union training courses included substantial coverage of equal opportunity issues and it was the branch policy that the basic training course for shop stewards had to include an item on equal opportunities. Childcare expenses could be claimed for union work. One of the branch officers had also organised assertiveness training courses for women members. She described the results which had been identified at a recall day:

> Three of the women in the group had changed their jobs and two had left their husbands. It certainly empowered them to take decisions that they had been wanting to take for some considerable time.
> (Female branch officer)

Overall, the situation in terms of union-related factors affecting participation was that there was a problem in recruiting women as shop stewards and onto the Branch Committee, but when recruited to these levels women participated more or less equally with their male colleagues. Interviewees recognised that probably the most effective measure the branch could take to increase female union participation would be to negotiate an extension to the union facilities agreement to provide cover for shop stewards when taking time off for union work. They were also aware of the difficulties of negotiating such an agreement at a time when the City Council had severe financial difficulties and was introducing a number of budget cuts.

CONCLUSIONS

The research findings indicate both similarities and differences in the work and union experience of male and female shop stewards. Perhaps the most significant research finding is the gender variation in the time when union work was performed, which shows that the majority of male shop stewards were able to carry out their union work within working hours, while female shop stewards used more of their own time to perform their union work. This was related to gender differences in the work situation, particularly regarding seniority and job flexibility. It meant that male shop stewards experienced more conflict in terms of demands on their time at work than female shop stewards, although presumably less conflict with demands on family and personal time. On the other hand, the nature of the job overall supported union activity by male shop stewards far more than it did female shop stewards, particularly in respect of job flexibility. These findings help to explain the under-representation of women as shop stewards.

In studying the position of women in unions, it is necessary to take into account both similarities and differences with male workers. Both differences and similarities are relevant to feminist research, and to feminist projects within trade unions. It is also important when studying gender differences to distinguish carefully between those gender differences which arise from differences in socialisation and the social roles of women and men and those which arise indirectly as a result of occupational differences. This is obviously important in terms of strategies for increasing women's participation and representation in unions, which need to include better quality jobs for women workers, and increased access to time off for union work at all levels of the union structure. The development of sociologically adequate models of women's union activism and office-holding requires serious attention to women's work situation and experience, as well as to gender role factors and the interplay between work roles and gender roles.

References

Boston, S. (1987), *Women Workers and Trade Unions* (London: Lawrence & Wishart).

Briskin, I.. and McDermott, P. (1993), *Women Challenging Unions: Feminism, Democracy and Militancy* (Toronto: University of Toronto Press).

Cobble, D. S. (1990), 'Rethinking Troubled Relations between Women and Unions: Craft Unionism and Female Activism', *Feminist Studies*, vol. 16, no. 3, pp. 519–48.

Cockburn, C. (1991), *In the Way of Women: Men's Resistance to Sex Equality within Organizations* (London: Macmillan).

Dubin, R. (1973), 'Attachment to Work and Union Militancy', *Industrial Relations*, vol. 2, no. 1, pp. 51–64.

Feldberg, R. L. and, Glenn, E. N. (1979) 'Male and Female: Job versus Gender Models in the Sociology of Work', *Social Problems*, vol. 26, no. 5, pp. 524–38.

Fryer, R. H., Fairclough, A. J. and Manson, T. B. (1978), 'Facilities for Female Shop Stewards: The Employment Protection Act and Collective Agreements', *British Journal of Industrial Relations*, vol. 14, no. 2, pp. 160–74.

Gordon, E. (1991), *Women and the Labour Movement in Scotland 1850–1914* (Oxford: Clarendon Press).

Harrison, M. (1979), 'Participation of Women in Trade Union Activities: Some Research Findings and Comments', *Industrial Relations Journal*, vol. 10, no. 2, pp. 41–55.

Heery, E. and Kelly, J. (1988), 'Do Female Representatives Make a Difference? Women Full-time Officials and Trade Union Work', *Work, Employment and Society*, vol. 2, no. 4, pp. 487–505.

Heery, E. and Kelly, J. (1989), 'A Cracking Job for a Woman' – A Profile of Women Trade Union Officers', *Industrial Relations Journal*, vol. 20, no. 3, pp. 192–202.

Joyce, P., Corrigan, P. and Hayes, M. (1988), *Striking Out: Trade Unionism in Social Work* (London: Macmillan).

Lawrence, E. (1994), *Gender and Trade Unions* (London: Taylor and Francis).

Ledwith, S, Colgan, F., Joyce, P. and Hayes, M. (1990), 'The Making of Women Trade Union Leaders', *Industrial Relations Journal*, vol. 21, 112–125.

Lipset, S. M., Trow, M. and Coleman, J. (1956), *Union Democracy: The Inside Politics of the International Typographical Union* (Glencoe: Free Press).

Moore, R. J. (1980), 'The Motivation to Become a Shop Steward', *British Journal of Industrial Relations*, vol. 18, no. 1, pp. 91–8.

Nicholson, N. (1976), 'The Role of the Shop Steward: An Empirical Case Study', *Industrial Relations Journal*, vol. 7, pp. 15–26.

Nicholson, N., Ursell, G. and Blyton, P. (1981), *The Dynamics of White Collar Unionism* (London: Academic Press).

Perline, M. and Lorenz, V. (1970), 'Factors Influencing Participation in Trade Union Activities', *American Journal of Economics and Society*, vol. 29, pp. 425–37.

Purcell, K. (1979), 'Militancy and Acquiescence among Women Workers', in Burman, S. (ed.), *Fit Work for Women* (London: Croom Helm).

Rees, T. (1990), 'Gender, Power and Trade Union Democracy', in Fosh, P. and Heery, E. (eds), *Trade Unions and their Members* (Basingstoke: Macmillan).

Rees, T. and Read, M. (1981), *Equality? Report of a Survey of NALGO Members* (London: NALGO).

Roby, R. and Uttal, L. (1988), 'Trade Union Stewards: Handling Union, Family and Employment Responsibilities', in Gutek, B. A., Stromberg, A. H. and Larwood, L. (eds), *Women and Work: An Annual Review*, vol. 3 (Newbury Park, CA: Sage).

Spinrad, W. (1960), 'Correlates of Trade Union Participation: A Summary of the Literature', *American Sociological Review*, vol. 25, pp. 237–44.

Stone, L. (1984), *Positive Action Report* (Sheffield: Sheffield City Council).

Wertheimer, B. M. and Nelson, A. H. (1975), *Trade Union Women: A Study of their Participation in New York City Locals* (New York: Praeger).

4 The Gendering of Marketing Activities: An Example from the Computer Industry

LEE CHALMERS*

INTRODUCTION

In this paper, I draw on interviews with the marketing department personnel in a computer systems organisation to explore two issues: First, how gender is entering into the construction of marketing work at the firm level as marketing personnel seek to carve out a distinguished position for themselves in the corporate hierarchy; and, second, what implications these processes hold for the marketing work that women and men do. More generally, I address the debate concerning how gender impacts on work organisation and practice.

The issue of how gender is 'at work' in creating, maintaining and/or disrupting patterns of segregation has remained contentious. Here I argue for the view that gender plays a constitutive role in the 'crystallisation' process by which work tasks are consolidated into jobs. In contrast to Walby's view that 'the ideology of specific occupations as masculine or feminine follows on after the economic and political struggles over which gender shall occupy these job slots' (1990, p. 108), I emphasise that gender is a discursive resource that may be used in efforts to lay claim to particular areas of expertise and authority, and to disavow others, in struggles over occupational boundaries. This argument builds on recent research developments in the area of gender at work.

In her study exploring the politics of occupational closure among various health professions, Witz (1992) has elaborated the neo-Weberian concepts of social closure specifying various strategies that groups of workers employ to secure and limit access to scarce organisational

*My heartfelt thanks for the support I have received while conducting this research from both the Fuller Fund and the Department of Sociology, University of Essex. Also fond thanks to my sister, Jane Chalmers, for all her support during the write-up of this research.

55

resources and opportunities. Specifically, she has drawn attention to the closure practices involving not only struggles to exclude or be included in already clearly demarcated jobs, but also struggles over the creation and control of boundaries between related occupations. These latter demarcationary and dual closure practices embody the notion that struggles over job closure and crystallisation are interpenetrating.

According to Witz, demarcationary closure strategies are aimed at controlling the demarcation of boundaries, and hence the division of labour and relevant skills, with 'neighbouring' occupations. As such, these strategies are the prerogative of dominant social or occupational groups. In response to demarcationary strategies, subordinate groups may deploy dual closure strategies which involve both usurpationary claims to protect and enhance their areas of expertise and exclusionary efforts aimed at consolidating their position by relegating some subsection of their group to lesser valued areas of activity.

In addition, Witz's research has indicated that the eventual success of these closure efforts may depend in part on appeals to particular understandings of gender. Through the concept of 'gendered discursive strategies,' she has illustrated that groups of workers may draw on equivalences already established between, for example, femininity and caring tasks and masculinity and technical work, to distinguish their claims to particular areas of expertise and to draw boundaries around particular configurations of work activities. With this, Witz has shed light on the central role that gender discourses can play in the structuring of occupations.

In addition, a number of theorists have countered the tendency to use gender to refer simply to masculine and feminine attributes that become attached to males and females early in life and may be transmitted rather unproblematically to the work they do. They have emphasised that gender is an ordering principle that provides one means of organising, justifying and naturalising how different groups of people are positioned in power relations (e.g. Cockburn, 1985; Harding, 1986; Scott, 1986; Acker, 1992). This is so because gender discourses, as frameworks of meaning that construct what it means to be a man or a woman and pattern relations between them, are typically expressed through hierarchical dualisms contrasting a masculine with a feminine term (e.g. masculine authority with feminine service and support) and privileging the former. This understanding of gender allows that gender's entry into the struggles surrounding occupational closure and crystallisation does not depend on the presence of both men and women.

Marketing provides a useful focal point for this research. As a self-defined 'business philosophy' concerned with identifying and satisfying customer needs profitably (Baker, 1985), marketing is an aspiring management discipline that has been assuming greater importance through the 1980s and 1990s in some management circles as a means of dealing with increased competition. Nevertheless, in many industries its sphere of activity and authority remains ill-defined and a matter of some dispute (Piercy, 1986) – it has yet to crystallise into a clearly defined form. In addition, it is not clearly sex-typed as men's or women's work. Although men have been numerically dominant in the past, women have been increasingly entering the field (Cooper, 1992). Thus, given the apparent 'fluidity' of its current situation, marketing provides potentially fertile ground for exploring questions of how gender is at work in the processes through which a management discipline articulates its claim to manage.

In the next section, I introduce the case study firm and its marketing department personnel, and provide a short history of its marketing department. I then turn to explore how particular gender meanings have figured in the efforts of the marketing personnel to secure and extend the boundaries of their activity. Specifically, I argue that the senior male marketing personnel have drawn on masculine notions pertaining to technical competence, breadwinning honour and entrepreneurial drive to construct a new 'business management' role for themselves and to distinguish what they do positively from marketing and sales. The main point I develop here is that, as these gender meanings have been invoked in the struggles to value and lay claim to particular areas of expertise and to devalue and distance others, they have shaped the construction of business management along masculine lines and marketing along feminine lines. In drawing together the threads of the analysis, I point to the possible though not assured consequences for sex segregation.

AN INTRODUCTION TO INFOTEC COMPUTER SYSTEMS[1]

InfoTec Computer Systems (ICS) employs about 150 people and is one of three self-accounting business units comprising InfoTec Business Systems (UK). Business Systems is a division of InfoTec International (UK) based in London and serving as a distributor for InfoTec International which has its Head Office and Product Division in Europe. Founded in the last century, InfoTec International has developed a reputation as an innovator in electronic equipment design. Its product success has helped to instill in Head Office management the view that continued prosperity hinges on a centrally directed product development policy committed first and foremost to technical excellence and a network of national organisations devoted to distribution. As part of this network, ICS is largely engaged in 'project business', competing for the sale of large computer systems into a small number of targeted UK markets (e.g., government departments). Infotec's historical focus on product and sales has meant that national organisations like ICS have typically had both limited input into product development and a predominance of people with sales backgrounds in senior management positions.

At the time of the interviewing, the marketing department was headed by a marketing planning (marplan) manager with direct responsibility for a marketing services manager, a demonstration centre manager, an exhibitions manager and a secretary. A graduate trainee reporting to the personnel director was working full-time assisting the exhibitions manager. Formally outside the department, though physically located with it and indirectly reporting to the marplan manager, were three marketing, or business, managers. All nine personnel were white and British. The marplan manager and the three marketing/business managers, all men, held the senior marketing positions. The marketing services manager, exhibitions manager and demonstration centre manager were presented at a level below that of the four senior managers and roughly equivalent to each other. The graduate trainee and the secretary were portrayed as holding the more marginal marketing positions. The demonstration centre manager and secretary posts were held by women.

According to the marketing personnel, marketing initially emerged informally in ICS in the early 1980s through the efforts of a group of technically trained men to improve the competitive performance of their business. Despite this informality and the software design backgrounds of its founders, the activities comprising the fledgling marketing function reflected textbook marketing concerns with matching product to identified market requirements. Thus these ICS marketing pioneers devised 'product management' procedures to coordinate and control more efficiently when and how products were released and sold into the UK. They began actively to assess the needs of their target markets and to source and adapt appropriate product, turning increasingly to third-party suppliers to supplement InfoTec product offering, so as to meet those needs satisfactorily and profitably. They started to use 'marketing' in some job titles and to formulate 'marketing plans' to guide their activities. However, this movement towards assuming greater responsibility for product policy and the local sales process was ended under demarcationary pressure from Head Office and the local sales function aimed at concentrating marketing activity more exclusively on promoting InfoTec product in support of the sales effort. With the creation of a formal marketing department and a new marketing director position in 1987, marketing was shifted in focus from independent product sourcing to a more circumscribed function of introducing and adapting InfoTec product with a strong emphasis on promotional activities (e.g. product exhibitions, public relations).

For Andrew, the current marplan manager and one of the marketing pioneers, there is an associated sense of loss:

> [T]hat's been part of an important culture change in InfoTec in part, and it's also affected a lot of the way in which marketing has developed here, because marketing has moved from being a much more pure sort of marketing in the sense of looking at the needs of the local market and saying what do we need to go out and get in order to meet local requirements. It's moved from that to being how do we implement the international policy. And in some ways that's a more challenging marketing job because it's much more about the promotion and the execution end of things. In some ways it's a less challenging marketing job because it's less about the understanding requirements and sorting products and the upstream end of marketing.

Judging from all accounts, the loss of the 'pure', marketing-orientated activity of finding opportunities for their markets has been a permanent one. Andrew and the three marketing managers acknowledged that they have not been as successful as they would like interpreting market requirements back into product development, nor have they been given the time or the directive to repromote existing products by looking for additional markets.

Yet these activities of sourcing appropriate product, providing marketing input into product design and finding new market opportunitites for existing products are precisely those that they identified as comprising the strength of a marketing orientation. That they experience the marketing they have been left to do as somehow emasculated in comparison is evident in Andrew's comment that they have had to be 'whorelike' at times, using promotional activities to search for business they could 'turn around quickly' to compensate for shortfalls in orders or to clear old stock without hurting the unit. 'It's not strategic, it's not long-term, but it pays the wages.' Hardly at the 'pure' end of developing marketing plans to match product to market requirements. Rather the image is of the marketing managers having to prostitute themselves to meet the (product-orientated) objectives of international policy.

By the end of 1989, a general downturn in the computer industry and disappointing economic results for ICS saw a further round of restructuring and the loss of the marketing director position. The marketing personnel subsequently reported to the sales director (renamed sales and marketing director), with Andrew heading the marketing department from his marplan manager position. By June 1990, continued losses led to the decision to re-organise InfoTec Business Systems (UK) into three self-accounting business units, centred on different product areas. The Computer Systems unit was divided into two sections, each with its own director. The sales and marketing section consists of three 'sales teams', each focused on a particular project area market, and the marketing department. The product and project managers moved to the operations section which also houses technical support, logistics, purchasing and finance/ administration. In the spring of 1991, the three remaining marketing managers formally moved onto the sales teams and began reporting directly to their respective sales managers rather than to Andrew in his marplan manager capacity.

Generally, the five more junior people remaining in the department under Andrew's supervision thought that the loss of the marketing director position and marketing's closer alignment to sales signified a loss of autonomy and status for the marketing function. However, neither Andrew nor any of the three marketing managers made any attempt to intervene as marketing progressively lost people and position from 1989. Rather, by their own accounts, they have supported the changes, citing the need to be closely aligned with sales 'at the front end' to 'get the business'.

None the less, far from proposing to dissolve the marketing manager role into some subordinate support activity to the sales function, Andrew and the other technically trained men occupying the remaining marketing manager positions have begun to carve out a new position for themselves, distinguished from both marketing and sales, and based on asserting guardianship over the broader concerns of the business. Two aspects of the restructuring into a self-accounting unit catalysed the marketing managers' move towards such a 'business management' role. First, as much of the technical requirement of the job moved with the product and project managers into operations, the marketing managers' formal product responsibilities have become focused more on commercial issues and less on technical concerns than they were formerly. Second, the shift to self-accounting came at a time when InfoTec was experiencing losses. This environment, with fiscal responsibility at a premium, provided a ripe opportunity for the marketing managers to emphasise the importance of their commercial responsibilities to the unit's success, and so to redefine their work away from promotional activities. Andrew observed:

[T]he focus of the business moved very strongly onto being profitability-led rather than any other attribute of the business. And so the marketing managers were the focus if you like of the integrity of the business, their individual bits of business overall. So their work then started to become much more about how do we keep the stocks down, how do we get the debtors down, how do we balance our cash flow. They became much more business managers, and much less how do I run an advertising campaign and how do I create a whole load of sales leads. So it caused a change of shift from promotion to business management.

Indeed, the redefinition of their work away from promotional activities was marked by a change in terminology – they began to use 'business teams' synonymously with sales teams and substituted 'business manager' for 'marketing manager'. Andrew explained that 'business management' better describes what they do, their involvement in the 'non-promotional aspects of marketing' which he identified as management of the gross margins and of profit, 'ownership' of the commercial relations with suppliers, and business monitoring activities (evaluating business opportunities and formulating business plans to ensure that the business teams realise a profit in accordance with Head Office strategy).

Thus, rather than champion their marketing activity, Andrew and the marketing/business managers have fragmented it through a process of 'horizontal fission' (Armstrong, 1985). In this they have relegated their promotional and more routine tasks, bequeathed the marketing label to the more junior personnel remaining in the marketing department, and have claimed their non-promotional activities, centred on product sourcing, pricing and planning, as the basis for a new business management role. In specifying this role as the basis for a more influential position on the sales teams and a potential route into top management, they have in fact claimed activities that are easily encompassed by textbook definitions of the marketing concept (Baker, 1985). However, they have done so with considerable emphasis on their product management experience and their business acumen, not with any reference to marketing expertise, and they have done so in the name of business management, not marketing. As the next section details, they have used gendered discursive strategies to help to draw the boundary between the promotional and non-promotional aspects of their marketing activity and to privilege the latter under the banner of business management.

GENDERING BUSINESS MANAGEMENT HEROIC BLUE AND MARKETING PASSIVE PINK

In constructing a business management role that contrasts favourably with marketing and sales, Andrew and the marketing/ business managers have employed three interwoven gendered discursive strategies to bathe their usurpationary claims in a heroic masculinity and to challenge the masculinity of the traditional marketer and salesman. In the three parts of this section, I highlight how these strategies have been used to establish an equivalence between certain positively valued masculine associations (an idea of potency and credibility associated with technical expertise, a notion of honour and integrity connected to delivering results for the business, and an image of aggressive, driving entrepreneurship) and particular areas of expertise pertaining to product sourcing, business monitoring and planning. I indicate with reference to each strategy how the four senior marketing men are constructing business management so as to distinguish it from marketing and sales. In addition, I explore the potential implications that these gendered constructions hold for job segregation by sex.

(a)   Flexing Technical Muscle

Possession of technical expertise remains a central defining feature of hegemonic masculinity, conferring on men a competence that signals masculine prowess and so distinguishes them from women and 'lesser' men (Cockburn, 1983, 1985). Roper (1991) has highlighted how, in many firms, the power structure and the construction of activities like marketing, and management more generally, have been based on a 'deep-seated connection between masculinity and technical creativity', on an intimate understanding of product (p. 201). Although marketing at ICS developed with little control over product hardware design, clearly it was constructed with a focus on product sourcing and adaptation that privileged the possession of product knowledge. Pointing to the technological sophistication of their industry, Andrew and the marketing/business managers have continued to affirm a need for technical expertise to market their computer systems and manage their business areas successfully. However, Martyn, one of the marketing/business managers, acknowledged that, with the product expertise now located in the operations section, he and the three other senior marketing managers are all more technical than they need to be for their jobs. Indeed, judging from their accounts, they have continued to build a strong technical requirement into the business manager role as a means of claiming the pleasure, credibility and affirmation of heterosexually defined manhood that such expertise signifies and of distinguishing the business manager from both the traditional marketer and the salesman.

Retaining a hands-on connection to product may have been particularly important to these men because, as John, another of the marketing/business managers, noted, marketing has 'no machismo about it'. Christopher, one of the marketing-trained young men working on exhibitions, and Peter, the third marketing/business manager, explained that, although marketing skills, in their view, have general applicability and are transferable across industries, marketing is an attractive occupation for some men only in areas where they can achieve a masculine identification with the product. As Christopher observed, some men do care whether they market 'bulldozers or cosmetics'. Peter was particularly clear outlining the reasons why it matters:

> Being very sexist, I would say men are probably attracted to marketing jobs where they're not likely to be thought of as a pouf or a pansy. Um, and because of that, there'd be more opportunities for women in the industries where that label might attach to a man. . . . I think that if you're marketing ladies' knickers, I think you're probably going to be a woman. Yeah? Ladies' underwear and things. Um, cosmetics. You can just imagine, you know, the guy in the bar, in the pub, and somebody says 'What do you do?' And he says 'Oh, I'm marketing manager for ladies' cosmetics.' OH! Ho, ho, ho, ho, ho! You know. Chuckle, chuckle! And they all walk away thinking 'Oh well, is he one of those?'

Key to men's discomfort with marketing cosmetics, however professional their marketing expertise, is imagining that moment in the pub, that notorious male bastion, with all those male faces questioning one's heterosexually defined masculinity.

Andrew and the marketing/business managers used the affinity between technical expertise to distance themselves from promotional activities and to claim a 'more than marketing' role. Contrasting himself with the marketer 'putting together promotions for new lines of washing powder', Peter observed that his involvement 'on the software side and on the project management side' meant that his role was 'a lot more other than straightforward marketing' and that 'people don't look at me in the same light as they would do a traditional marketing manager.' Similarly, John observed that his life would no doubt be easier if he were into 'white goods' or 'baked beans'. At one point, he identified himself as a technologist rather than a marketer, noting that his technical expertise allowed him to cope more easily than would someone with a marketing background in such an engineering-driven industry:

> [I]t must be frustrating for anybody who's in traditional marketing, say sort of consumables . . . [to] think 'Oh, I'll have a crack at computers,' and suddenly come into this great technical environment where you're just sort of measured as much as by your marketing knowledge as by the amount of engineering knowledge you can apply. That comes back again to the fact that are we really marketing jobs?

Underscoring their 'more than marketing' role, both John and Peter portrayed the traditional marketer as a less capable figure, one better suited to the softer, cleaner and easier worlds of white goods and washing powder marketing than to the more rigorous demands of the computer industry.

Technical expertise has helped them to measure up in a way that they believe traditional marketing cannot. As Martyn explained, such expertise gives them credibility on their teams, an ability 'to know when the technical guys are spinning us on, you know, spinning us a real yarn'. Indeed, there is a sense in which technical competence marks for these men a rite of passage, signifying to the other men on their teams that they are not inexperienced boys who can be easily tricked, but masterful men.

Clearly, the credibility conferred by possession of technical know-how trades on its association with masculine prowess. In his comments on the difficulties women have establishing a marketing career in IT, Christopher pointed to the exclusionary effects of constructing the marketing/business manager positions in this way:

> I think there's a problem sort of within the IT industry in that there is this belief that you've got to have an IT background if you're in marketing. Now I haven't, so I would say that, wouldn't I? But the sort of technology snobbery, that you've got to be up on the latest, know all the latest acronyms, and there's a lot of sparring takes place. You know, amongst marketing managers. So, flexing technical knowledge muscles if you like. And actually if you go into the sort of basics of marketing, that's actually quite irrelevant to what you're doing. That's why you have sort of product marketing people, they've got a technical knowledge, but the business marketing, it's not really necessary. But all the guys . . .I am sure get a great deal of respect because they have a heavy technical background. They don't use it, because they deal purely with business issues. . . . I'm sure if (you're) in (the) baked bean industry, you don't have to know the composition of a baked bean! You're

purely marketing. And, you know, marketing managers within the car industry or whatever, and a car is a fairly technical product, they're not expected to know how they're built and how they're put together They're expected to know how to market them. Whereas in a computer industry, you're expected to know how the bloody computer works, and it's very – , it's still technical snobbery. And I think that's – , I don't know if that's being used (*Chuckles*) as a barrier to stop sort of non-technical people coming in, and unfortunately at the moment that means women. It's very difficult. It's difficult for me as a marketer.

Christopher recognised in the technical knowledge requirement more a display of virility to other men than a necessary skill for an effective marketing/business manager. Indeed, he believed that having less technical expertise and being less product identified work to a marketer's advantage, as it allows the marketer to communicate to potential customers in 'sensible language' and to evaluate product features from the customer's perspective.

As Christopher's remarks make clear, marketing-trained women, and men, will be at a disadvantage as long as they lack the technical knowledge deemed necessary for marketing/business management in ICS. The point remains that the marketing/business manager role could be constructed differently, for example, by focusing more exclusively on commercial and promotional issues and relying more on the technical expertise housed in operations to assess the adaptability of product to local markets. In the IT industry, the issue is in part whether technologists will consult formally trained marketers or whether the marketers will be technologists who dabble in marketing. That the marketing/business manager positions in ICS have included a strong technical component is in part a reflection of the masculine value attached to such competence by the technically trained men currently holding them. It is also a reflection of the credibility conferred on their role by association with a masculine status of such potency. Including this component has helped Andrew and the marketing/business managers to claim a role beyond the confines of a washing-powder-like marketing activity limited to promotions and communications. In addition, against a technically inexperienced sales function, it has provided them with a means of justifying their continuing to have primary responsibility for product introduction and pricing decisions now that they are under sales direction.

(b) Performing with Honour

Andrew and the three marketing/business managers also distinguished their business management role from marketing and sales through an appeal to the honour of their wealth-generating activity. Such an appeal trades on the notions of masculine pride and independence, as well as heterosexual potency, that are attached to a male breadwinner role (Barrett, 1980/1988; Cockburn, 1983). Collinson *et al.*(1990) and Roper (1991) have already provided evidence indicating that different groups of managers find the image of 'corporate breadwinner' (and its contrast with consumption and domestic support) a useful resource to substantiate usurpationary claims to various areas of activity and to relegate competing groups to 'lesser' activities. In contrasting the breadwinning business manager with the less productive and less manly marketer, Andrew and the marketing/business managers have laid claim to an active role in their project area markets centred on their product and profit-and-loss responsibilities, and have distanced themselves further from the promotional and desk-bound duties of the traditional marketer.

Peter expressed the strongest scepticism about marketing's integrity, voicing the view that as a discipline it has tended to be 'run by a lot of conmen' who have got jobs 'for doing not a lot'. Marketers, he noted, are frequently guilty of making extravagant gestures, like expensive advertising campaigns, that add to their own pleasure or prestige and consume a firm's resources but 'fail to deliver anything for the business'. In contrast, what he valued about his own role was the chance to be on the 'front-end of commercial activity', involved in the 'proactive, pre-event work' of going out with the sales force and 'actually impacting on' and improving the profitability of individual transactions or business lines.

John offered a similar contrast between his role and marketing work. He indicated that he fell into, rather than chose, a marketing role, and that he finally had the marketing title attached to what he did. His image of marketing work when the label was first attached?

> Oh, I was in shock. I think marketing has generally got quite a bad image. I know very few of my friends in marketing actually tend to own up to it too much (LAUGHS). . . . I think it's better, it's more honest to be an engineer than a marketing guy. Or more honest to be a salesman than a marketing guy. I think a marketing guy's a sort of half-way house, he has a very undefined role in people's opinion, so it's a strange role. . . . [E]verybody who's in marketing in different companies does different things. You get people involved in marketing who are just in charge of brochures and pamphlets. There are other people in marketing who are in charge of pricing strategy, others in charge of corporate data bases and so on and so forth. They all have this marketing label. But the

engineer makes things. Salesman sells things. And a street cleaner sweeps up the roads. But what does a marketing person do?

Here John touched on two problems he has with marketing's status. First, because marketing encompasses a range of activities, the marketing guy with pricing and profit-and-loss responsibilities can be easily confused with the marketing guy who simply orders and distributes brochures. Being a marketer does not connote a distinct occupational status.

Second, compared to other, predominantly male activities (notably the standard of comparison in John's account), marketing work lacks a clear, visible deliverable. It is less obviously productive. Indeed, for John, there is something dishonest about a man being in a job where he is not clearly identified with making things, selling things, getting out there and sweeping up the roads. Being a marketer connotes a less valued masculine status. So does John identify himself as a marketer?

> Well, I guess so. I actually own up to it when people ask me, so I suppose I must be there now. It's like coming out of the closet I suppose, isn't it? (*chuckles*) But I don't think I'm a typical marketing – what is a typical marketing – ? It's difficult to actually relate, when Mr A is in marketing and so is Mr B and Mr C, and the three of you are talking around the table, you're doing completely different things. It's difficult to feel part of the great marketing culture.

As a heterosexual male, John associates his reluctance to admit he is a marketer with how he imagines it would be to 'come out' and acknowledge being gay. Being seen as a typical marketer, with one's heterosexually defined manhood called into doubt, is not the image John has of himself. Again, for him, the typical marketer lacks some of the potency, the virility, to which the productive engineer, the wealth-generating salesman and the physically active street cleaner can lay claim.

Across these responses, John positioned marketing as a rather soft and ineffectual role compared to what he does. Marketing is not a particularly honest endeavour, not the sort of manly occupation you are proud to claim for yourself. It is ill-defined and less practical. Indeed, he observed that marketing journals typically rely on 'high' sounding jargon, with their 'talk about branding, talk about positioning and various methodologies, the delivery of products, the segmentation', activities which John and his colleagues do but which are 'such a trivial part of our job compared to the main activity which is the business'.

That marketing is gendered in feminine terms for John was revealed as he discussed whether there might be advantages to men and women working together in marketing:

Well, actually, there was one lady, . . . [marketing] manager, first class, very clever lady. And she's interesting because she used to think of her key role in the organisation as being to do something completely different to actually what I did. Now we're in nominally exactly the same jobs, we're running different business areas. But she saw her focus as being somewhere completely different to where I focussed on my part. And there was a lot of overlap, but she spent more time at the high end say, rather than at the low end or whatever. [*Sorry, she spent more time at the high*?] For example, she was more worried about the general positioning and the general overall feel for the products out in the market, and not very much down at the product, you know, that can worry about itself. Whereas I'm down here, trying to generate the business down at the dirty end with the sales guys. So that shows you an immediate difference in approach, and whether that was because she was a lady, or whether it's because she just thought differently, we never had enough people in the organisation to actually measure whether it was a common trend. But you could see it straight away. A completely different way of thinking.

In John's account, there is a blurring between the way a woman thinks and the way those high-sounding marketing journal guys understand marketing, between being a woman and being a marketer. Again, while this woman, with a marketing-based MBA, spent time at the 'high end', worrying about positioning (a 'trivial' part of his job) and getting a general 'feel' for products in the marketplace, John was down at the dirty end, actually dealing with the product and generating business with the sales guys. She got a feel for things, and worried about position. He got dirty and got the job done.

This contrast between getting down to business and being concerned with more trivial issues appears to have informed the construction of Pat's demonstration manager job. In large part, what Christopher and Robert do outside for the exhibition stand, Pat does inside for the demonstration centre. However, in Andrew's account, the boundaries of the two young men's jobs remain flexible, allowing room for growth and new responsibilities and promising that they will not be limited to being hosts on exhibition stands. However, he portrayed Pat's job as more circumscribed. The 'requirements of the role' are such, Andrew noted, that he was 'basically looking for a hostess', 'for somebody who runs a tea shop', for someone with 'a measure of empathy'. Pat indicated that, although she is at a point in her life where she welcomes less job pressure, she does find the job boring, and far less satisfying than her previous job in training where she had more responsibility in relation to the customers. She too saw the job as being 'a glorified tea lady' role, observing that all they have forgotten to do is to give her a hat and a frilly apron.

References to an empathetic hostess running a tea shop indicate that the requirements of the demonstration centre manager role have not been defined in gender-neutral terms. Indeed, Andrew expressed the view that women would be more likely than men to be recruited into marketing roles that have to do with corporate hospitality and which are 'really souped-up hostessing roles'. However, the point emphasised here is that gender dualisms contrasting male breadwinning with female domestic support play a significant role in the decision to combine these tasks into hostessing roles that are then delegated to one (female) person. Would a male marketing manager feel comfortable assigning another man to a role informally designated as a souped-up hostessing role? Or would he feel compelled not only to award the position higher status (emphasising its 'corporate relations' aspects) but also to leave room to add in additional responsibilities to challenge and develop the man? (cf. Cockburn, 1991). That jobs are constructed which are centred on comforting and relaxing (predominantly male) customers and stimulating their interest in the product offering, jobs that are then allocated to women and trivialised as souped-up hostessing roles, reflects more a particular discourse on masculine heterosexuality than any intrinsic logic to how tasks are best consolidated into jobs.

(c) Entrepreneurial Leadership

Notions of confronting the opposition in some form of combat, meeting the challenge of competition and aggressively pursuing opportunities all signify valued aspects of hegemonic masculinity. In business, they find expression in the image of the entrepreneur, the man able to unite a masterful command of his business with thrusting ambition, to combine calculative and combative masculinities, in the heroic pursuit of competitive success (Connell, 1987; Roper, 1989). Underwriting their claims to business management with references to their entrepreneurial drive and their 'ownership of the totality of their businesses' provided Andrew and the marketing/business managers with another means of distinguishing their work from marketing and sales. The appeal to entrepreneurial spirit lays claim to a planning and leadership role with reference to a capacity to drive the unit aggressively to commercial success. A recurrent theme here contrasts an image of forceful endeavour with one of 'sitting' outside the action, intellectualising rather than doing. It is a theme that trades on masculine associations with activity and feminine associations with passivity, as well as the greater masculine value acccorded practical activity over desk-bound intellectual work.

Contrasting his role to that of the 'marketing man sitting there strategising and theorising all day', John argued that '[t]here is no way you can sit there behind a desk and just theorise about things, you've got to go out and get kicked in the teeth'.

Similarly, Martyn observed that people in a job like his 'need to be forceful, a little arrogant in their view', and not 'sit back and let the world go past them'. Noting that there are some very poor marketers around, he commented:

> [T]hey sit back and let it happen a little bit. There isn't the killer instinct there, it's cosy. . . . They're doing a mechanical job rather than an entrepreneurial job, and I think that's in some ways causing some of the problems in some of the computer companies we've got today. The hunger's not there.

Andrew and the marketing/business managers used this image of aggressive entrepreneurialism to distinguish themselves from sales. Here, they acknowledged that the salesmen are combative and competitive, but portrayed themselves in the leadership role. Andrew observed:

> [I]t is a combination of . . . strong leadership, or we talk about a product championing role. [The marketing/business managers are] the people who will very often drive that product forward. . . . [T]here is this strong championing role, even to the extent that a very strong marketing man will be out there in the customer's dragging salesmen along behind him, if he's convinced that his solution is the right solution for the customer, he'll use a salesman effectively to create the situation where he goes and promotes product. . . . And he'll be in there explaining the benefits of his product and the salesman will be sitting there hopefully taking some notice of what's going on. And very often a marketing man will be the person who's sort of pushing the sales activity forward.

Clearly the image of an entrepreneurial champion dragging the salesman along to commercial success privileges the marketing/ business manager's combination of technical and commercial expertise and strengthens a claim to leadership. Indeed, it is the salesman who 'sits there' as the marketing/business manager pushes the business forward.

Drawing on gendered imagery to construct the business manager as an aggressive champion pushing the business forward and the marketer as someone content to sit cosily at a desk working on less practical matters genders the two activities at the same time that it helps to demarcate their areas of claimed expertise. In addition, this gendering process has implications for how women are received into these work activities and points to the lines along which segregation by sex may occur. Invoking a military metaphor, Andrew portrayed the marketing/business managers as adopting an aggressive stance in order to direct activities in a manner and language the salesmen can understand:

> All marketing is combative to a certain extent in that most of the time marketing is not about creating markets, it's about taking market share. . . . [I]t's probably a rather male thing, I think, I mean I find it a useful analogy. . . . [T]here are helpful analogies if you then bring them out into things that people can then translate into useful decision-making tools, like do your reconnaissance. Make sure your logistics is sorted out. Make sure your troops are equipped for the thing that you're asking them to do. . . . [I]n this particular role you're working in support of a sales force. And you're working quite closely with a sales force. And they are extraordinarily competitive! And combative. Because it really is him or me, one of us is going to get the order. . . . And they behave in a very male, aggressive manner, even the women do. . . . But the sales activity is very combative and they appreciate and can understand things that are put to them in those terms.

Indeed, it is more than an analogy that eases communication between marketing and sales. It is a construction that portrays both the sales process and marketing/business management leadership as naturally combative and competitive, requiring a male aggressiveness, and male bonding, even from the women.

However, when Andrew further explored what it might mean for a woman to remain feminine and be successful, the contradictory expectations women face become clear:

> I think generally speaking people underestimate, particularly in the business environment, the emotional content of decision-making. And people, particularly in business to business, believe that it's all an intellectual process. If there's a weakness that women have coming to that, and it is perhaps a reaction of trying to move away from their femininity – I mean

there are some feminine values. If we say feminine values tend to be the human things, they tend to be the caring things, the constructive things rather than the confrontational things, then I actually believe that those are tremendously useful qualities in a marketing person. Because . . . getting consensus to a point is by far the best way of ensuring that it's carried through. And that I can relate to. Those qualities I think are important and I have seen women bring those qualities to the job.

Women need to be forceful and push ahead with their ideas like men. Yet they need to retain their feminine values, the ability to build consensus around different points of view and the sensitivity to the too often denied emotional content to business decision-making. This is not an easy balance for anyone, man or woman, to maintain. The exclusionary potential resides in the constitution of two separate areas of job activity, a decision-making realm claimed to require a masculine combativeness, and a supportive, communications realm where women might be left to pick up the pieces and do the corporate 'emotional work' (cf. Hochschild, 1983).

Just as 'being forceful' is a gendered concept used to represent business management in valued masculine terms, 'sitting back' is a gendered image used to position marketing activity as feminine and passive. This was evident in the concerns the two marketing trained young men expressed about their marketing work. Though Robert was attracted to the opportunity his work affords 'to get out of the office' and meet customers, his job satisfaction was qualified by the status he and Christopher have as 'backroom boys' to sales. Reflecting on what he least enjoys about his job, he noted:

> [W]ell in this company certainly it's the backroom boys [to] the sales team. . . . [I]t's a sales support role here. So we put in quite a bit of sometimes (very) hard work to help a sales guy out, and say he makes a sale or whatever, he gets all the recognition and very little comes back to us. There's not a lot of recognition for what we do here.

Christopher presented a similar view. He noted that his experience to date has taught him that a good marketer has to be able to 'sit back' and be a 'backroom boy' rather than be 'upfront'. Otherwise:

> You'll have immense conflict with the sales guys. You can't go into a customer and because you're the marketing guy take over. The relationship is between the salesman and the customer, and you can support in whatever way, but it's got to be seen as being support, I think. And

that's what I mean by being sort of backroom. You're there to aid sales, not necessarily to take over. Sometimes I think that's difficult to do.

To fit into the organisation without conflict, Christopher accepted that marketing needs to be positioned in a backroom support role. But his feelings were mixed:

> [S]ometimes I find it difficult to sit back. You know, sometimes you want to burst out and say 'Look! (TAPPING HIS FINGER AS-SERTIVELY ON THE TABLE) That was bloody well me that did that, you know,' and yeah, there's a tension. Sometimes I get a bit frustrated. . . . I sometimes get upset by the fact that we don't get recognition. And that contradicts with what my view of what one of the qualities of the marketing guy is, that he's got to be able to sit back and maybe sort of sit behind. . . . And sometimes I don't find that easy.

Not only did sitting back and being a backroom boy mean a lack of recognition for one's accomplishments. It meant being/becoming passive. Commenting on the qualities he would like to develop to help him with his job, Christopher cited a need to be more assertive:

> When you're perceived as being in a support role, you're assisting somebody, there is sort of, a power differential there, you know, 'You're helping me.' And sometimes the activities I get involved in I would like to say no. I do, but I need to be able to do it better. I need to say 'No, this is wrong, we'll do it some other way,' or 'You shouldn't be doing this at all,' or 'Sod off,' you know. And when your role's being perceived as being support, it's very easy to start to become passive, and I think I would benefit really if I stamped me big boot a bit.

Christopher understood that being positioned as support places him in a less powerful position. It is a structural position that encourages him to become passive and it is a position where, like a woman, he has difficulty getting his 'no' accepted as meaning 'no'.

That the marketing work left in the marketing department is becoming women's work, even though men still dominate, is evident in Christopher's comments on whether men or women are better suited to any marketing tasks. Initially he said no, but then added:

> I sometimes think that some of the sales guys would be easier, feel more comfortable if I was possibly a woman because I'm providing a

supporting role, and I think sometimes on a few occasions I do tell them to go take a running jump. It's possible, yeah, that they would feel a woman would maybe acquiesce whereas I wouldn't. Yeah, I mean I think there are grounds, certainly a perception of a lot of men is that women are very good in supporting roles, and therefore they'd be good in marketing. I think that's a misconception on both women and marketing, but never mind, that is a perception.

In Christopher's account, marketing has become a support role that commands little recognition from other men. It is a role suited to passive acquiescence, not assertion. It is women's work, suitable for women and the backroom boys who are not yet men.

GENDER AND HORIZONTAL FISSION: SUMMING UP

In responding to demarcationary pressures, the four senior marketing personnel have drawn on gendered discursive strategies to support their usurpationary and exclusionary efforts. In making their usurpationary claims, they have appealed to various masculine identifications to construct a unique and valued business management role. As technically literate product champions, they have substantiated a claim to continue to have the final word over sales on product introduction and management decisions. As honest men dedicated to delivering for the business, they have supported their claim to a planning role from which to guide the activities of the other functions. As self-motivated entrepreneurs relying on their killer instincts to drive the business to prosperity, they have laid the foundation for a claim to a strategic planning and leadership role within the unit. Together, these themes have helped to crystallise business management as an occupation concerned with the technical aspects of assessing product adaptability and actually adapting product, with evaluating the commercial viability of product and determining pricing, and with assessing business opportunities, planning business activities and monitoring performance.

These usurpationary claims have been complemented by exclusionary efforts that have constructed traditional marketing as a pottering, ineffectual activity more concerned with advertising campaigns, promotions and positioning than with the front-line activity it takes to generate business results. This construction has underwritten a process of 'horizontal fission' (Armstrong, 1985) whereby the men with technical product management experience have carved out a separate and non-promotional business management role and have relegated those with marketing and sales backgrounds in the department to a marketing services role focused on promotions. As Armstrong has argued, relegating routine activities to subordinates within a business discipline helps to strengthen the usurpationary claims of the more elite group by focusing their activity on those areas of work and expertise that are more likely to form a solid basis for a claim to manage and by establishing an internal hierarchy that helps to portray and position the elite as managerial material. By joining with sales 'at the front-end', the four senior managers have been able to solidify a boundary between the promotional and non-promotional aspects of marketing and dissociate themselves from those aspects that threatened to limit them to a sales support role offering less challenge and pleasure.

Where business management requires a masculine forcefulness, technical competence and breadwinning prowess, marketing demands, and is experienced as demanding, a feminine acquiesence. This suggests that business management and marketing within ICS have the potential to become sex-typed occupations, male and female respectively. Moreover, the ICS experience indicates that it is not necessarily the case that the sex-typing of an occupation follows from the sex/gender of the holders of already crystallised jobs. Rather, it can be because gender meanings are used as a resource in such dual closure struggles that jobs crystallise into forms that lend themselves to sex-typing. Indeed, even though exhibition work is currently performed by men within ICS, it is already being experienced as women's work. Thus this analysis extends Witz's work by emphasising that gendered discursive strategies are available for use by same-sex groups who are in competition and that the gendering of jobs cannot be read off in some straightforward fashion from the sex/gender of those seeking to establish closure.

Note

1   To preserve anonymity, I have changed the names of both the firm and the individuals with whom I spoke.

References

Acker, Joan (1992), 'Gendering Organizational Theory', in Mills, Albert J. and Tancred, Peta (eds), *Gendering Organizational Analysis* (London: Sage) pp. 248–60.

Armstrong, Peter (1985), 'Changing Management Control Strategies: The Role of Competition between Accountancy and other Organisational Professions', *Accounting, Organizations and Society*, 10:2, pp. 129–48.

Baker, Michael J. (1985), *Marketing: An Introductory Text* (Basingstoke & London: Macmillan).

Barrett, Michele (1980/1988), *Women's Oppression Today: Problems in Marxist Feminist Analysis* (London: Verso).

Cockburn, Cynthia (1983), *Brothers: Male Dominance and Technological Change* (London: Pluto Press).

Cockburn, Cynthia (1985), *Machinery of Dominance: Women, Men and Technical Know-how* (London: Pluto Press).

Cockburn, Cynthia (1991), *In the Way of Women: Men's Resistance to Sex Equality in Organizations* (Basingstoke & London: Macmillan).

Collinson, David, Knights, David, and Collinson, Margaret (1990), *Managing to Discriminate* (London & New York: Routledge).

Connell, R. W. (1987), *Gender & Power: Society, the Person and Sexual Politics* (Cambridge: Polity Press).

Cooper, Helen (1992), 'Merit Rises for the Wise Guys', *Marketing Week*, January 10, 14:42, pp. 22–9.

Harding, Sandra (1986), *The Science Question in Feminism* (Ithaca & London: Cornell University Press).

Hochschild, Arlie Russell (1983), *The Managed Heart: Commercialization of Human Feeling* (Berkeley, CA: University of California Press).

Piercy, Nigel (1986), 'The Role and Function of the Chief Marketing Executive and the Marketing Department: A Study of Medium-sized Companies in the UK', *Journal of Marketing Management*, 1:3, 265–89.

Roper, Michael (1989), *'Masculinity and the Evolution of Management Cultures in British Industry, 1945–85'*, unpublished PhD dissertation, Department of Sociology, University of Essex, Colchester, England.

Roper, Michael (1991), 'Yesterday's Model: Product Fetishism and the British Company Man, 1945–85', in Roper, Michael and Tosh, John (eds), *Manful Assertions: Masculinities in Britain since 1800* (London & New York: Routledge), pp. 190–211.

Scott, Joan W. (1986), 'Gender: A Useful Category of Historical Analysis', *The American Historical Review*, 91:5, 1053–75.

Walby, Sylvia (1990), *Theorizing Patriarchy* (Oxford: Basil Blackwell).

Witz, Anne (1992), *Professions and Patriarchy* (London & New York: Routledge).

5 Strategy, Sexuality and the Stratosphere: Airlines and the Gendering of Organisations*

ALBERT J. MILLS

The study of strategic management focuses upon the relationship between strategy and organisational outcomes (Chandler, 1966; Rumelt, 1986; Kantrow, 1983) but rarely on interpersonal outcomes, such as self-esteem and gendered identity. Following on the recent work of Acker (1991) and the UMIST studies (Knights and Sturdy, 1987; Morgan and Knights, 1991; Kerfoot and Knights, 1993), this chapter examines the relationship between the dynamics of corporate strategy and the gendered nature of work.

Using Acker's (1992) 'gendered processes' framework and Mintzberg et al.'s (1986) distinction between emergent and deliberate strategies, the chapter traces the development of selected strategies in the British and North American airline industry and how those strategies influenced the gendered character of airline jobs. In particular the chapter focuses on developments within British Airways and its forerunners and documents how the company's changing passenger recruitment and flight services strategies are associated, over time, with different recruitment patterns and gendered images.

It is argued that while there is evidence of a number of cases where strategies were deliberately premised on the exclusion of women (e.g. from piloting) or on the selling of female sexuality (e.g. the erotic female flight-attendant image) it is the less conscious, emergent, aspects of strategy which play a key role in the discriminatory division and presentation of jobs in the airline industry.

The study is part of a broader analysis of selected British and North American airlines that seeks to understand how organisations develop gendered processes (Mills, 1994b, d), how those processes are influenced

*Supported by a General Research Grant from the Social Sciences and Humanities Research Council of Canada (no. 92–0476).

by organisational and social discourses (Mills, 1994a, c; Mills and Helms Hatfield, 1994) and how discriminatory processes change over time (Mills, 1993a, b). The investigation involves extensive archival research and a number of in-depth interviews with employees and former employees of four airlines – Trans World Airlines (TWA), Pacific Western Airlines (PWA), Air Canada (AC), and British Airways (BA). To-date, content analysis of over 3000 corporate documents (including in-house journals, annual statements, memoranda, etc.) belonging to British Airways, PWA, and Air Canada has been completed. A series of interviews is currently underway.

THEORETICAL FRAMEWORK

Sexuality is something which society produces in complex ways. It is a result of diverse social practices that give meaning to social activities, of social definitions and self-definitions, of struggles between those who resist. Sexuality is not given, it is a product of negotiation, struggle and human agency. (Weeks, 1986, p. 25)

This chapter examines how dominant notions of gender – 'the socially imposed dichotomy of masculine and feminine roles and character traits' (Warren, 1980, p. 181), and of sexuality – 'the social expression of or social relations to physical, bodily desires, real or imagined' (Hearn and Parkin, 1987, p. 15) are reproduced and maintained in the workplace and the role played by strategic thinking in those processes. The airline business is an interesting area of study because of its noted sexual imagery (Kane, 1975; Neilsen, 1982; Hochschild, 1983) and because it has been the subject of several studies of strategy (Mintzberg *et al.*, 1986; Arnold and Brown, 1986; Lasserre and Putti, 1990).

The recent work of Acker (1992) provides a useful framework for the analysis of the gendering of organisational arrangements. She (1992, p. 252–4) contends that 'gendered organisations can be described in terms of four sets of processes which are components of the same reality' and that, 'sexuality, in its diverse forms and meanings, is implicated in each of these processes'. Thus, to analyse how organisations develop discriminatory practices, we need to focus on (i) the production of *gender divisions* (i.e. the organisational practices which produce the gender patterning of jobs, wages, hierarchies, power and subordination); (ii) the creation of *symbols, images and forms of consciousness* that explicate, justify, and more rarely oppose, gender divisions; (iii) *interactions* between individuals, women and men, women and women, men and men, in the multiplicity of forms that enact dominance and subordination, and create alliances and exclusions; and (iv) the *internal mental work* of individuals as they consciously construct their understandings of the organisation's gendered structure of work and opportunity and the demands for gender-appropriate behaviours and attitudes.

For Acker (1992) the gendering of organisations occurs as a result of largely mundane, sometimes deliberate, processes. In contrast, strategy, as it is usually defined in the management literature, refers to a narrow set of *conscious* and *rational* decision-making processes. This definition suggests a focus on the deliberate framing of discriminatory actions and how they might be changed and avoided but, as Mintzberg *et al.* (1986) contend, this is to assume that intentions always lead to behaviour or that behaviour is largely the result of deliberate intentions. Mintzberg and his colleagues (1986, p. 4) deal with the issue of intended and unintended actions by defining strategy as 'a pattern in a stream of action':

> By contrasting this definition – essentially strategy as realized – with the usual one of intended – we were able to contrast what we call deliberate strategies (patterns realized as intended) with emergent strategies (patterns realized despite, or in the absence of, intentions).

This definition provides a useful refinement of the concept of strategy and allows a fuller exploration of its relationship to the mundane reproduction of discrimination in the workplace. That relationship is explored through a focus on two broad, interrelated, strategies – passenger activity and service provision (Arnold and Brown, 1986) – and their impact on the recruitment of flight crews.

PASSENGER ACTIVITY AND SERVICE PROVISION STRATEGIES AND THE RECRUITMENT OF FLIGHT CREWS

Historically, the recruitment and marketing of flight crews has gone through several broad stages: (i) the employment of male-only flight crews; (ii) the employment, in an already male-dominated profession, of female 'nursing' flight attendants; (iii) the large-scale employment of female flight attendants and the creation of a 'feminised' profession;

(iv) the eroticisation of the female flight attendant; and (v) the professionalisation of the flight attendant, and (re)hiring of a substantial minority of men into the profession, and the recruitment of female pilots.

Each of the broad phases occupied a different time frame or juncture (Mills, 1994c) and to understand how they developed and why they changed over time we need to examine some of the major influences on the policy makers of each time.

The Dawn of Commercial Aviation and the All-Male Flight Crew

The development of commercial aviation began in Europe immediately following the First World War with the establishment of airlines in Britain, the Netherlands, France, Belgium and Germany. From the beginning, in 1919, the recruitment practices of the new airlines established certain jobs as male preserves within the industry. All-male flight crews were hired to fly and navigate the aeroplanes and very few women were hired in any other capacity. In Air Union (the forerunner of Air France), for example, only a handful of women was employed in minor clerical and secretarial roles before the mid-1920s (Bamford, 1986). It was 1922 before a British airline hired its first female employee – in a secretarial capacity.

So strong was the view that women had no place on the crew of a commercial aircraft that in the mid-1920s two newly formed international aviation bodies – the International Commission for Air Navigation (ICAN) and the International Civil Aviation Organisation (ICAO) – both decreed that women be excluded from employment as flight crew members (Penrose, 1980; Cadogan, 1992). Thus, when airlines first created the job of the air steward in the late 1920s there was no question that the new position should be staffed exclusively by males. Even though a limited experimentation with the recruitment of female air stewards did begin in the US in 1930, the job remained a male preserve until well into the war years, continuing thus in Britain until the late 1940s.

Emergent and deliberate strategies

In terms of deliberate strategies, the earliest issues for airlines involved safety and luxury service. Safety was an issue because, for good reason, it was hard to convince potential passengers that flying wasn't dangerous. Provision of a luxury service was an issue because the airlines had to compete with first-class rail and luxury liner services for the upper-class elite who, due to aviation costs, were the mainstay of commercial airline passengers: while speed was the major competitive selling point of the airlines it was soon realised that they would also have to compete in terms of service. In regard to both issues, airlines developed strategies premised on male recruitment and the selling of forms of masculinity. The forerunners of British Airways, for example, were concerned in the early years (1919–24) to project an image of heroism and courage. Company advertising, designed to reassure passengers of the safety of its operation, featured biographies of its pilots – drawing particular attention to the Air Force record of the individual involved. This strategy seemed to be aimed at assuring potential passengers that the pilot knew his aeroplane but that in the unlikely event that something went wrong he would keep his cool and come through in heroic fashion. This strategy changed over time (1924–39) as the airlines sought to emphasise reliability and service by focusing on the number of commercial flights, hours flown, and company years put in by individual pilots: the projected image moved from the 'Flying-Ace' to that of company pilot, from rugged individualist to steady, but senior, organisational man (Imperial Airways Newsletters, 1927–39; Harper, 1930). A similar process happened with airlines in the US and Canada where projected images moved from the rugged experience of pilots (the military ace, the mail flyer, the bush pilot) to ones that focused on company loyalty and reability (Keith, 1973; Serling, 1983; Condit, 1984; Sampson, 1984).

In regard to passenger service strategies, it was the pilot who played the central role. On British airlines, for example, the pilot carried the luggage onto the plane, made out the necessary documents and was required, in some cases, to point out things of interest to the passengers during the flight (Penrose, 1980). As pressure on service grew, so British airlines began to hire passengers' affairs agents to take over from the pilots in attending to passengers' needs on the ground. In common with the practice of their competitors in the first-class rail and liner businesses, the airlines employed men to take on this new position.

One of the first attempts to introduce on-board service was by Instone Air Lines (a forerunner of British Airways) in 1922, who employed bellhops from luxury hotels to serve as 'cabin boys'. The employment of these young boys on board the planes was also designed to serve safety considerations as the airline hoped that their presence would reassure fearful adult male passengers (Penrose, 1980). The limited number of seats in aeroplanes and a fatal crash, which killed one of the boys, put an end to this experiment.

Towards the end of the 1920s, as aeroplane seating capacity improved, airlines began to introduce a more developed on-board service –

introducing 'stewards' on their planes. Lufthansa were the first to do so in 1928, followed shortly by Imperial Airways (a British Airways forerunner), and the American airline Pan Am. The service involved a straight replication of the white-coated male stewards used by competitors in other first-class transportation.

It may hardly seem surprising that airlines failed to hire more than a handful of female secretarial staff during the first decade of commercial aviation (1919–29). Yet, in Britain at least, the airlines were established in an era of important changes for women, some of which had a direct bearing on aviation. During the Second World War the large-scale recruitment of women into the Metal Industries and the Wood & Aircraft Trades and the establishment of the Women's Royal Air Force meant that some women, albeit a minority of recruits, acquired aircraft maintenance and allied skills (Escott, 1989). The skills and abilities of these women were clearly known to the airline heads who were drawn from the ranks of the aircraft manufacturers and the Royal Air Force (RAF). The fact that these airline heads did not exercise strategic choice (Child, 1972) in the recruitment of female labour gives some indication of an early perception of certain jobs as (male) sex-typed before those jobs had actually become sex-typed (see Mills, 1994b).

The recruitment of all-male flight crews, on the other hand, required little conscious thought, as the process was heavily influenced by prior decisions made by air forces. In Britain, the US, and Canada, air force policy restricted piloting and allied 'combat' roles to men and, thus, effectively determined the post-First-World-War labour supply of pilots (Nielson, 1982; McCafferty, 1988; Escott, 1989). The labour supply alone, however, does not fully account for the exclusion of women from commercial piloting. Many of those in charge of the new airlines were recruited from the top ranks of the very air forces that had prevented women from becoming pilots and it is likely that their attitudes would have carried on into commercial aviation.

The pattern of recruiting former air force flyers became common across airlines and national boundaries and served to reinforce the practice of restricting commercial piloting to men. What may have begun as the unconscious reproduction of gendered practices developed into deliberate policies of exclusion as witnessed by the ICAN and the ICAO decisions in the 1920s, and the failure of airlines to recruit female flyers in the face of mounting and irrefutable evidence of women's ability as pilots: the record breaking successes of women flyers in the 1930s and the contribution of women pilots to the wartime Air Transport Auxiliary, for instance, did little to break the male hold on commercial piloting.

Symbolism and strategy

The gendered recruitment practices in the development of commercial aviation were simultaneously encouraged and sustained by a series of symbols drawn from two male-dominated sources – the military and the first-class transportation industry.

In many ways the early airlines were reproductions of the air forces which had trained most off their top personnel and pilots. In Britain's airlines, for example, ex-RAF officers commanded former-RAF pilots, flying converted wartime bombers from former air force bases. The reproduction was often complete down to the uniforms and ranks. At the beginning it was not unusual for pilots to wear their old RAF flying suits. This gave way to uniforms influenced by other military imagery. For example, in the early 1920s Instone Air Lines (a British Airways forerunner) and Air Union both introduced uniforms of navy design – designed to achieve an 'air of masculine difference' (Bamford, 1986, p. 44; see also Learmoth *et al.*, 1983).

The links between the RAF and the development of British commercial aviation were so strong that when Colin Marshall took over as chief executive of British Airways in 1983 he found a culture rooted in RAF images, with pilots in 'navy blue uniforms with patterns of scrambled egg indicating their rank and role', 'military attitudes', and a 'Senior Manager's Mess' (Hampden-Turner, 1990, pp. 84–5).

From the first-class transportation industry the new airline companies adopted the practice, dress and title of the job of stewarding. But this symbolism proved less enduring than the military imagery.

Passenger Service and the Female Flight Attendant: From In-Flight Nurse to Flighty Flight Attendant

At its inception in 1928 the job of flight attendant was seen as a male occupation but that reality was to last for little more than fifteen years. As early as 1930 a US carrier – Boeing Air Transport (BAT) – successfully 'experimented' with the use of female flight attendants and slowly but surely the idea caught on to the point that the job was feminised by the mid-1940s. The next fifteen years saw a similar turn around in the imagery of the flight attendant. This time the changes were in the airline's use of female sexuality. The now standard image of the flight attendant as the wholesomely feminine, in-flight nurse steadily gave way to a variety of more eroticised images.

Emergent and deliberate strategies

Like their European counterparts, US airlines were concerned with the twin issues of safety and first-class service as they began to develop passenger-carrying flights towards the end of the 1920s. Competitive pressures from the railways was certainly a problem to overcome but a general fear of flying was an even greater restriction on the potential passenger base of the new American carriers. On both fronts airlines attempted to deal with the issue by strategies which depended on the hiring of male stewards.

On the issue of service, US carriers simply adopted the existing pattern within European airlines (and their own first-class rail services) of hiring male stewards. Safety was dealt with through references to pilot experience and the technical efficiency of the planes but at least one airline – BAT – was considering addressing the issue through the recruitment of cabin boys.

In 1930, BAT (a forerunner of United Airlines) was faced with declining passenger numbers and an image of flying as unsafe and felt that by hiring Filipino boys as cabin attendants they would reassure fearful passengers (Nielsen, 1982). In the end they decided to embark upon an even more radical strategy of employing young, American women: that year on an 'experimental basis', BAT hired eight female flight attendants according to criteria which would influence recruitment patterns across the industry for several decades. Female recruits were required to be from 'respectable', white, middle-class backgrounds, to have nursing qualifications, and to conform to a series of age (twenty-five), weight (one-hundred and fifteen pounds) and height (five feet, four inches) limits.

BAT's strategy was influenced by several competing factors. On the one hand, they had become convinced that hiring young, demure women would be a great 'psychological punch' in being able to simultaneously shame and attract grown men into flying (Nielsen, 1982, p. 7). On the other hand, the company faced sharp resistance across the industry to the employment of women, in particular they were faced with a moral panic over the sexual propriety of adding women to flight crews.

By hiring registered nurses (from a certain class of women) BAT company chiefs felt that they would get recruits who were trained to obey orders, to put people at ease and to be pleasant to them (Hudson and Pettifer, 1979), and to deal with anxiety and (air) sickness. In this way the company were able to advertise a unique service strategy which, through a focus on nursing qualities, helped to deflect moral concerns.

BAT's 'experiment' slowly but surely spread to other airlines. In the US Eastern (1931) and American (1933) were the next carriers to introduce female flight attendants – followed by TWA (1934), Western and National

Airlines (1935), Braniff (1937), Delta (1940), Continental (1941) and Pan Am (1943). In Europe, Air France began employing female flight attendants in 1933 and they were followed by Swissair (1934), KLM (1935), and Lufthansa (1938).

BAT's requirements of nursing qualifications and age, height and weight limitations became standard practice throughout the industry as the job of flight attending was transformed into a female occupation (Nielsen, 1982; Serling, 1983).

One of the last major airlines to employ female flight attendants was BOAC who stuck very firmly to a policy of female exclusion from the flight deck. The determination to employ male-only flight crews could be seen very clearly during the Second World War when, to release adult males into the armed forces, the company opened up a range of jobs to women but hired fourteen to sixteen year old boys to replace adult male stewards (*BOAC News Letter*, November 1942). This resolve was partially weakened in 1943 when, influenced by the recruitment practices of US airlines, the company employed six female stewards on a limited basis to deal specifically with the North America market (*BOAC Newsletter*, December, 1943).

The Second World War made several contributions to the post-war development of the airlines which was to influence BOAC to change its service strategy. Technologically, planes were now bigger and faster, and several new international routes–particularly across the North Atlantic – had been developed. Air-mindedness had been instilled in a new generation of demobilised soldiers. The old, pre-war social hierarchy had undergone dramatic change and a new generation of passengers – the businessman – replaced the upper-class elite as the mainstay of airline business as passenger numbers and competition grew rapidly.

In the immediate post-war period BOAC was still employing boys for training as 'Air Stewards' (*BOAC Newsletter*, no. 72, January 1946) but were beginning to experience pressure from Pan Am (their direct competitor on the transatlantic routes) who had begun recruiting female flight attendants (Wright, 1985). By the start of 1946, BOAC yielded to selected market pressures by hiring a limited number of female stewardesses for their North Atlantic routes. This was quickly extended to other routes.

Rapidly it became normal to see female flight attendants on British airlines, including the newly created British European Airways (BEA) which was an offshoot of BOAC. BEA and BOAC had both been anxious to deflect any suggestion that female flight attendants were being employed for their feminine charms. To that end, both companies embarked on a publicity campaign which utilised an employment equity theme – stressing 'the intelligence and hard work that goes into making a good stewardess' (*BEA Magazine*, no 4, September, 1947).

Two decades after the introduction of female flight attendants, BOAC (and BEA), in common with many other airlines in Europe and North America, was projecting an entirely different image. Gone was the equity look and in its stead were a series of images selling the sexual attractiveness of the female flight attendant. Form the late 1950s and well into the 1960s most US and British airlines adopted a strategy of selling a more eroticised form of female sexuality to gain new passengers. In the face of growing competition and over-capacity, airlines looked for new ways to attract customers. Price wars represented one form of strategy, but eventually many airlines felt that they could get an edge if they engaged in some form of sexual selling. The new strategy was evidenced in a number of practices which included explicit advertising and slogans, recruitment based on physical appearance, and the presentation of the female flight attendant through ways of dress and make-up (Nielsen, 1982; Hochschild, 1983; Sampson, 1984).

Symbolism and changing strategies
To understand how airline service strategy changed over the years we need to look at internal, organisational factors as well as the social context of the time.

When BAT launched their strategy of the female flight attendant it was premised on contradictory strands. On the one hand, there was the respectable nursing image – which the company reinforced through appropriate symbols, including nursing uniforms for in-flight use and wool twill suits with capes and berets for ground duty. On the other hand, there was the image of the demure, young women – which the company attempted to capture in the term 'sky girl'. Eventually, this latter image became the focus of company advertising and symbolism and in 1939, now operating as United, the company launched its new uniform which stressed a new type of femininity. Gone was the nursing uniform to be replaced by the image of the young hostess. By now other airlines had followed suit and were openly trading on images of femininity rather than nursing qualifications.

When BOAC and the new BEA began to employ female flight attendants they were concerned to avoid the 'glamour hostess' associations that were already popular throughout the industry. It was thought that the term 'hostess' would give off the wrong connotations in polite British society. Both companies deliberately set out to establish a 'desexed' image (*BEA Magazine*, no. 4, September 1947); a line followed in press handouts and reinforced through the provision of a uniform designed to make male and female stewards look very similar in appearance, and the use of a single job title for the male and female 'steward'. Sexuality was strictly controlled. BOAC, for example, carefully monitored the women's uniform hem lengths to ensure that they were not too revealing. Blouses were designed with an extra long shirt tail that tucked into skirts to ensure that, as the women bent across to the window passenger they wouldn't expose 'any enticing flesh' (Wright, 1985, pp. 7–8).

The strategy of desexualisation was undermined by several factors. To begin with, much of the imagery was built on existing male standards and this bought immediate pressure from women employees for changes in the uniform, forcing the company to recognise that:

> Nearly all existing women's uniforms are based on men's. But a woman's build being entirely different from a man's, the result can never be entirely satisfactory. (*BOAC Newsletter*, no. 7, October 1946)

In terms of work practices, the employment equity claims were far from real. At BOAC the woman steward was seen as an *assistant* to the male steward, helping the sick and feeding babies; she was not allowed in the galley or on the flight deck. The female steward at BEA was a 'housekeeper in the air – tending to all the housekeeping arrangements for the journey, washing up, and ensuring that crockery is stowed away' (Wright, 1985, pp. 6–7).

The in-house journals of both airlines reflected a growing tension between a policy of desexualisation and concerns with the projection of femininity. Towards the end of 1940, the in-house journals of BOAC and BEA began, for the first time, to feature images of uniformed female staff. At first this was to indicate that the company was now employing female flight attendants, but eventually this gave way to a series of images designed to 'add glamour' to the magazine. Both the *BOAC Newsletter* and the *BEA Magazine*, for example, regularly carried pictures of a uniformed female staff member and a furry animal of some kind. Increasingly throughout the 1950s and into the 1960s these images became more focused on sexual attractiveness. The staff journals started using photographs of female staff in swim-suits; cartoon images appeared which presented the ideal-typical woman as curvaceous and large breasted and the typical female steward as sexually promiscuous; and routine descriptions of female staff moved from the matter-of-fact to include reference to hair and eye colouring and figure measurements.

Beauty competitions became a standard feature of the organisational life of BOAC and BEA and uniform hem-lines, in common with current fashion trends, moved upwards. Recruitment and training practices moved from an emphasis on personality to one of glamour, with BOAC and BEA dropping 'technical knowledge' from their female stewards' training programmes and substituting sessions on deportment, make-up application, and personal hygiene (*BEA Magazine*, no. 237, March 1969).

By the late 1960s, in the face of sharp competition and the development of sex-selling strategies, it was no great leap in the dark for BOAC and BEA to transform emergent strategies of eroticism into new sales strategies.

In this era, across the industry, the symbolism of sexuality was often crude: uniforms ranged from Continental Airways' Playboy Bunny outfits, PWA's revealing cowgirl dresses, and a series of TWA paper dresses in the style of the serving wench, the Roman toga, the gold lamé cocktail dress, and the Manhattan lounging pajamas (Serling, 1983); and advertising included Continental's unsubtle, 'We really move our tail for you'. It was not, however, these crude examples that symbolised the era so much as the routine practices of recruiting young and 'pretty' women to be flight attendants; of dressing them in ways that stressed a certain kind of sexuality; and of advertising them as a part of the 'glamour' of flying.

The Professionalisation of the Female Flight Attendant

The selling of overt sexuality began to wane in the mid-to-late 1970s to be replaced by broader service strategies and price-war campaigns. A number of airlines in Britain and North America resorted to a team approach, with campaigns presenting airline staff as a united body of men and women ready to serve the customer. Throughout the industry a number of discriminatory practices (e.g. limits on the age and marital status of female flight attendants) were dropped and there has been a steady increase in the hiring of male stewards (who now constitute 15 per cent of the profession). Airlines have begun to recruit and train women pilots and at least one major company – British Airways – has embarked upon a campaign to recruit more female senior managers. Price wars and frequent flyer programmes have tended to push eroticised images off the advertising pages. Within this more complex environment sexuality has not, however, been dropped but rather reframed and shifted from the flight deck to the reservation counter.

The changing service strategy is the result of several diverse factors. Many of the more overtly sexist practices within the industry were challenged and defeated by a coalition of unionised flight attendants and the advent of the renewed women's movement of the late 1960s (Nielsen, 1982; Hochschild, 1983). Technological (the advent of the jet), political (e.g. the 1973 oil embargo) and competitive (e.g. deregulation) pressures forced airlines into price wars and cost-cutting exercises, including speed-up of the work (with one flight attendant doing the work previously done by two); the (re)introduction of short-term (5–10 years) contracts; and the employment of a large number of part-time female employees (Gil, 1990).

The changing demographics of the airline business, with the growth of mass tourism, also encouraged airlines to rethink their service strategy. As the old airline entrepreneurs retired companies increasingly replaced them with a new breed of chief executive recruited from successful service enterprises. The new men (*sic*), such as Jan Carlzon of Scandinavian Airlines System (SAS) and Colin Marshall of British Airways (BA), saw a need for a new, all-embracing service strategy which involved cost-cutting and the extension of 'emotion work' (Hochschild, 1983). Both SAS and BA put their entire staff through a programme of emotion management. While this new strategy is mediated by an elaborate series of bureaucratic rules (O'Brien, 1983), female sexual attractiveness has been retained as an important element. A comment on the physical attractiveness of female flight attendants by the 'chairman' of BA (Lord King) indicates the relationship between cost-cutting and sexuality:

> We give 'em five-year contracts and after that we take a look at 'em and see what they're like. (Quoted in Sampson, 1984, p. 221)

While female flight attendants are still expected to 'display' a certain appearance, much of the overt sexuality has been shifted to the check-in operations 'where it is cheaper to maintain and may have a greater impact, especially in crowded airports' (Gil, 1990, p. 328). The sexual appearance of female ground staff is often used to smooth over problems between the customer and the airline:

> Passengers checking in at the airport can't fail to have noticed the warmth of the welcome from the smiling BA girls behind the desks, and the freshness of their looks, their complexions smooth, their make-up alive with colour and gloss. If – heaven forbid – there should be a delay or baggage hold-up, the girls are all smiling efficiency and sympathy. (BA in-house magazine, quoted in Sampson, 1984, p. 221)

This is already taking its toll on airline reservation staff (Saxton *et al.*, 1991).

Symbolism and strategy

The construction of sexuality in the airline industry today is taking place against a background of conflicting pressures and this is reflected in some of the symbolism of the day. British Airways' 'supergirl' advertising campaign of the 1980s, for example, combines the image of professionalism with sexuality. The advertisements imaged the female flight attendant as 'supergirl' – prepared to go to great lengths to serve the customer while retaining a sense of youth and beauty; an image of sexuality that combines a mixture of the old (nursing, sexually alluring) with the new (professional). By the 1990s, the combination of sexual attractiveness and professionalism was still be played out in British Airways advertising but this time in even more oblique ways: one series of advertisements focuses on the face of a female flight attendant (using soft lighting and make-up) under the heading 'The most important instrument on our aeroplanes'.

What is of central importance here is that many of the positive changes and directions in the airline industry remain unsupported – even undermined – by organisational symbolism. It is extremely rare, for instance, to find images of male stewards in an airline's advertising. Interestingly, the only recent example was run by British Airways to advertise a new first-class service! It is even rarer to find any corporate advertising which makes use of images of female pilots. Despite British Airways' commitment to increase the number of senior managers it is not often that a female manager or pilot is featured even in the company's in-house newspaper. The central focus of advertising remains the *female* flight attendant – it is an advertising mystique that seems hard to break!

It is too early to say yet whether the strategy of overt sexual display will make a come-back but it would seem that the highest airline traffic growth in the next period is expected to be in the Pacific Rim, where strong competition will come from Singapore International Airlines, Thai International, Cathay Pacific, Korean Airlines and Japan Air Lines – all of whom have incorporated the sexuality of female 'submissiveness' into their training and advertising (cf. Sampson, 1984).

SEXUALITY AND STRATEGY: REFLECTIONS

In view of the growth of interest in strategic management in recent years and the explosion of management literature on the subject, it is important to make the point that gender has been a neglected, yet crucial, aspect of the study of strategy.

An examination of passenger activity and service strategies in the airline industry indicates that strategic management can have serious implications for the gendering of jobs. Conscious and deliberate actions to achieve a strategic end are key factors in the life of an organisation.

Strategic actions are usually developed and enacted by powerful members of the organisation and, as such, serve to propel and direct organisational members. Given that strategy leads to changes in organisational tasks and processes and given that organisations consist of people, strategic outcomes can rarely be gender-neutral. In the airline industry one set of strategic decisions led to the exclusion of women from flight attending for almost fifteen years and from piloting for more than fifty years.

If we are to understand strategic decision-making it is important to know something about the processes through which it developed. Here Mintzberg' *et al.*'s (1986) concept of the emergent strategy throws some light on the subject. An examination of the change from an equity to an erotic strategy in the airline industry, for example, indicates that strategic decisions may emerge out of a series of smaller (apparently mundane) actions.

It is also important to understand strategic decision-making in context and here Acker's (1992) framework encourages examination of how organisational symbolism serves to maintain a set of gendered practices. Acker (1992) helps us to see how the creation of a symbolic world, sustained through gender divisions, and enabled through a series of interactions and reflection, can influence a person's self-image. This is supported by several studies which have indicated the profound effect that the sex- and emotion-selling strategies of the airlines have had on the self-image of the women involved (Kane, 1975; Nielsen; 1975; Hochschild, 1983; O'Brien, 1983).

If there is to be a conclusion, it is that strategy can have a profound effect on the gendering of jobs and that the most profoundly gendered strategies are those which emerge from and are supported by the mundane life of the organisation.

References

Acker, J. (1991), 'Thinking about Wages: The Gendered Wage Gap in Swedish Banks', *Gender & Society*, 5, pp. 390–407.

Acker, J. (1992) 'Gendering Organisational Theory', in Mills, A. J and Tancred, P. (eds), *Gendering Organisational Analysis* (London: Sage), pp. 248–60.

Arnold, W. L. and Brown, J. L. (1986), 'Tracking Strategy in the Airlines: PWA 1945–84', *Canadian Journal of Administrative Science*, 3:2, pp. 171–203.

Bamford, J. (1986), *Croissants at Croydon: The Memoirs of Jack Bamford* (Sutton, Surrey: Sutton Libraries & Arts Services).

Cadogan, M. (1992), *Women with Wings* (London: Macmillan).

Chandler, A. D., Jr (1966), *Strategy and Structure* (Garden City, NY: Doubleday).

Child, J. (1972), 'Organisation, Structure, Environment and Performance – The Role of Strategic Choice', *Sociology*, 6:1, pp. 1–22.

Condit, J. (1984), *Wings over the West: Russ Baker and the Rise of Pacific Western Airlines* (Madeira Park, BC: Harbour).

Escott, Squadron Leader B. E. (1989) *Women in Air Force Blue* (Northamptonshire: Patrick Stevens).

Gil, A. (1990), 'Air Transport Deregulation and its Implication for Flight Attendants', *International Labour Review*, 129:3, pp. 317–331.

Hampden-Turner, C. (1990), *Corporate Culture: From Vicious to Virtuous Circles* (London: Hutchinson/Economist Books).

Harper, H. (1930), *The Romance of a Modern Airway* (London: Sampson Low, Marston).

Hearn, J. and Parkin, P. W. (1987), *'Sex' at 'Work': The Power and Paradox of Organisational Sexuality* (Brighton: Wheatsheaf).

Hochschild, A. R. (1983), *The Managed Heart: Commercialization of Human Feeling* (Berkeley, CA: University of California Press).

Hudson, K. and Pettifer, J. (1979), *Diamonds in the Sky: A Social History of Air Travel* (London: The Bodley Head/BBC Publications).

Kane, P. (1975), *Sex Objects in the Sky* (Chicago, IL: Follett).

Kantrow, A. M. (ed.) (1983), *Survival Strategies for American Industry* (New York: John Wiley/Harvard Business Review).

Keith, R. A. (1973), *Bush Pilot with a Brief Case. The Happy-go-Lucky Story of Grant McConachie* (Don Mills, Ontario: Paperjacks).

Kerfoot, D. and Knights, D. (1993), 'Management, Masculinity and Manipulation: from Paternalism to Corporate Strategy in Financial Services in Britain', *Journal of Management Studies*, 30:4, July, pp. 659–77.

Knights, D. and Sturdy, A. (1987), 'Women's Work in Insurance – Information Technology and the Reproduction of Gendered Segregation', in *Women and Information Technology*, ed. Davidson, M. J. and Cooper, C. L. (London: Wiley).

Lasserre, P. and Putti, J. (1990), *Business Strategy and Management* (Singapore: Times Academic Press).

Learmoth, B., Nash, J. and Cluett, D. (1983), *The First Croydon Airport, 1915–1928* (Sutton: Sutton Libraries & Arts Services).

McCafferty, D. (1988), *Billy Bishop: Canadian Hero* (Toronto: James Lorimer).

Mills, A. J. (1993a), 'Managing Subjectivity, Silencing Diversity: Organisational Imagery in the Airline Industry – The Case of British Airways', paper presented at the Eastern Academy of Management Annual Meeting, Providence, RI, May.

Mills, A. J. (1993b), 'Corporate Image, Gendered Subjects and the Company Newsletter – The Changing Faces of British Airways', paper presented at the European Group for Organisation Studies Meeting, Paris, July.

Mills, A. J. (1994a), 'Dueling Discourses – Desexualization versus Eroticism in the Corporate Framing of Female Sexuality: Images of British Airways, 1945–60', paper presented at the British Sociological Association Annual Conference, University of Central Lancashire, Preston, 28–31 March.

Mills, A. J. (1994b), 'The Gendering of Organisational Culture. Social and Organisational Discourses in the Making of British Airways', *Proceedings of the Women in Management Section, Administrative Sciences Association of Canada Annual Meeting*, Halifax, Nova Scotia, 25–28 June.

Mills, A. J. (1994c), 'Gendering Organisational Culture: From Theory to Analysis – Identifying Discriminatory Discourses in the Making of British

Airways', paper presented at the Business History Section of the Administrative Sciences Association of Canada Annual Meeting, Halifax, Nova Scotia, 25–28 June.

Mills, A. J. (1994d), 'No Sex Please, we're British Airways – A Model for Uncovering the Symbols of Gender in British Airways' Culture, 1919–1991', paper presented at the Conference on Organisational Symbolism, Calgary, 10–13 July.

Mills, A. J. and Helms Hatfield, J. C. (1994), 'Air Canada vs. Canadian: "Competition" and "Merger" in the Framing of Airline Cultures', paper presented at the Metaphors in Organisational Theory and Behaviour Conference, London, 28–30 July.

Mintzberg, H., Brunet, J. P. and Waters, J. A. (1986), 'Does Planning Impede Strategic Thinking? Tracking the Strategies of Air Canada from 1937 to 1976' in Lamb, R. and Shrivastava, P. (eds), *Advances in Strategic Management*, vol. 4 (Greenwich, CT: JAI Press), pp. 3–41.

Morgan, G. and Knights, D. (1991), 'Gendering Jobs: Corporate Strategies, Managerial Control and Dynamics of Job Segregation', *Work, Employment & Society*, 5:2, pp. 181–200.

Nielsen, G. P. (1982), *From Sky Girl to Flight Attendant* (New York: ILR Press).

O'Brien, G. (1983), 'Negotiating Order in the Workplace: The Case of the Air Hostess', *Journal of Irish Business and Administrative Research*, 5:2, pp. 3–13.

Penrose, H. (1980), *Wings Across the World: An Illustrated History of British Airways* (London: Cassell).

Rumelt, R. P. (1986), *Strategy, Structure, and Economic Performance* (Boston, MA: Harvard Business School).

Sampson, A. (1984), *Empires of the Sky: The Politics, Contests and Cartels of World Airlines* (New York: Random House).

Saxton, M. J., Phillips, J. S. and Blakeney, R. N. (1991), 'Antecedents and Consequences of Emotional Exhaustion in the Airline Reservation Service Sector', *Human Relations*, 44:6, pp. 583–95.

Serling, R. (1983), *Howard Hughes' Airline: An Informal History of TWA* (New York: St Martin's/Marek).

Warren, M. A. (1980), *The Nature of Women: An Encyclopedia and Guide to the Literature* (Inverness, CA: Edgepress).

Weeks, J. (1986), *Sexuality* (London: Tavistock).

Wright, C. (1985), *Tables in the Sky: Recipes from British Airways and the Great Chefs* (London: W. H. Allen).

Other Sources Used

Imperial Airways Monthly Bulletin, issues nos June 1926–May 1928.

Imperial Airways Weekly News Bulletin, issues no. 1 (24 March 1936) – no. 94 (1 April 1938).

Imperial Airways Staff News, issues no. 1:25 (29 May 1931) – no. 9:34 (25 August 1939).

Imperial Airways Gazette, issue vol. 4, no. 41 (January 1932) – vol. 11, no. 6 (June 1939).

B.O.A.C. News Letter, issues no. 5 (June 1940) – no. 73 (February 1946).
B.O.A.C. Speedbird (renamed News Letter) issues no. 1 (April 1946) – no. 51 (June 1950).
B.O.A.C. Review & Newsletter, issues nos July 1950 – August 1951.
B.O.A.C. Review, issues nos September 1951 – March 1967.
B.E.A. Magazine, issues no. 1 (December 1946) – no. 262 (April 1971).

6 Income Dependency within Couples

CLARE WARD, ANGELA DALE and
HEATHER JOSHI

*Liffey opened the letter and understood that she was no longer rich, that
she was to live as the rest of the world did, unprotected from financial dis-
aster; that she was pregnant and dependent upon a husband, and that her
survival, or so it seemed, was bound up with her pleasing of him. That she
was not, as she had thought, a free spirit, and nor was he: that they were
bound together by necessity. That he could come and go as he pleased;
love her, leave her as he pleased; and that domestic power is to do with
economics. And that Richard, by virtue of being powerful, being also
good, would no doubt look after her and her child, and not insist upon
doing so solely upon his terms. But he could and he might: so Liffey had
better behave, charm, lure, love and render herself necessary by means of
the sexual and caring comfort she provided.*

Fay Weldon, *Puffball* (1984)

It is commonly thought that the generation of women who have entered the
labour force since the 1970s no longer need social protection as their
husbands' dependants. Indeed, equality between men and women in the
labour force and the recognition of women as individuals in their own right
and not as the dependants of men is increasingly accepted as a desirable aim. Indeed, this philosophy underlies the European Directive 79/7
on the Equal Treatment for Men and Women in Matters of Social Security.
However, although improved opportunities have given some women greater
economic independence this does not apply in full to all women. Therefore
it is important to establish how many women are financially dependent on
their partners and the extent of this dependency. This chapter sets out to do
this for a generation of women leaving school and entering the labour
market in the mid-1970s.

The chapter begins by discussing women's financial dependence in broad
terms. It then considers the barriers which still exist to women achieving
economic independence in the labour market, in the state benefit system and

within the family. Alternative definitions of dependency are examined and the method of implementing the definition adopted here is explained. The paper concludes with the empirical results of implementing these definitions.

Throughout the paper, partners are defined as a woman and a man who are living as a couple. With the exception of entitlement to certain derived benefits in the National Insurance system and pension schemes, the theoretical discussion applies to all co-resident couples whether legally married or not. Whether cohabitees differ from legally married couples in the extent of their dependency must be tested empirically. The paper uses data from the fifth sweep of the National Child Development Study, NCDS5. The NCDS is a cohort study of all those born during the week 3–9 March 1958 and who are resident in England, Scotland and Wales. The fifth sweep was conducted when the cohort members were 33 years old; 11,407 cohort members were interviewed, representing an 85 per cent response rate (Ferri, 1993). It is important to remember that it represents a single cohort and, therefore, results will differ from those that might be obtained from a population with a wider age range.

THE INCOME DIMENSION OF WOMEN'S DEPENDENCE

Most people aspire to some form of independence, with its associations of autonomy and dignity. In contrast, the connotations of dependency include unequal distribution of power, a lack of alternatives and parasitism. This was pointed out by Arber and Ginn (1991) who also argue that there are a number of forms of dependence which are gendered and socially structured and which are evaluated by society in differing ways.

Broadly conceptualised, dependency should take account of all interdependencies within partnerships, including access to, and transfers of, all the couple's economic and emotional resources such as goods, time and energy as well as income. Whilst it is difficult to establish how much is transferred between partners in monetary terms, measuring the flows of other less tangible resources is even harder. One cannot assess who gains from transfers and exchanges, nor whether they are made freely or under coercion. Lazear and Michael (1988, p. 2) argue that 'since family members care about each other, what one member gains is not a total loss to the others'.

This paper concentrates on income dependence between partners within marriage or cohabitation. Although dependency between spouses is not just economic, we believe that the economic relations underpin most others. Since economic resources carry more value, more prestige and more marketability than domestic work, income dependency tends to be associated with powerlessness and inequality in other spheres.

There are two main sources of 'own income' for both men and women, the labour market and the state, whilst a few people have income from capital and elsewhere. Transfers between family members and sometimes from outside the family provide further income for some. If partners pool their income, and benefit equally from its use, purchasing power can be presumed to pass from the major to the minor contributor. In referring to this presumed flow as a transfer, we do not necessarily imply that it is a grant, unrequited by unpaid contributions (Davies and Joshi, 1994), nor that pooling is always perfect. In this chapter, income dependence is equated with this assumed transfer of income. If one partner contributes significantly less than the other, s/he is deemed to be dependent upon the other. Conversely, economic independence occurs when a partner's income is approximately equal or greater than that of the other.

For women, income dependency is strongly influenced by the primacy still given to domestic and childcare work and the consequence that this has for earning power. This can be seen as a two-way relationship, with a woman being economically dependent on her partner whilst her children, and also her partner, depend upon her for caring and domestic maintenance. The consequence of this arrangement for men is the requirement to maintain the family's income. Although 'trading' within families is seen as necessary by functionalist sociologists such as Parsons (1942) and as rational by economists such as Becker (1981), this interdependent relationship between women and men is not generally on equal terms.

Although the interdependent relationship of marriage has benefits for both partners, the negative consequences of women's income dependence are considerable. Indeed for feminist theorists, a married woman's economic dependence is crucial in maintaining her subordinate position in society (Hartmann, 1976; Barrett, 1980; Delphy, 1984), and has long-term influences on resources, and dependency (broadly defined) in old age (Arber and Ginn, 1991; Joshi and Davies, 1994).

IMPLICATIONS OF ECONOMIC DEPENDENCE FOR WOMEN

Female Poverty

Women's economic dependence on men leaves them vulnerable in the event of divorce, separation or widowhood. Divorced mothers in particular are far more likely to be on benefit and to be in receipt of a lower net weekly income than divorced fathers (Gregory and Foster, 1990). Elderly women, too, are particularly at risk of poverty, as a result of poorer pension provision for unpaid work.

Increased divorce rates, increasing numbers of births outside marriage and lengthening female life expectancy have resulted in growing numbers of female-headed households. This growth in female-headed households has meant that women's poverty has become increasingly visible in official statistics. Dependency on a man is, in many cases, exchanged for dependency on the state. Whilst female-headed households tend to be 'visibly' poor because of women's low earning power, married or cohabiting women may also suffer 'hidden poverty', irrespective of the family or household income. Mainstream poverty statistics take aggregated units such as households, families and benefit units as the unit of income receipt. Where women belong to a unit headed by a man their own income is masked by aggregation with his. If the couple's income is not pooled then women whose own income is low may suffer poverty hidden by official statistics. Later we develop the concept of 'self-sufficiency' to assess whether women have enough income paid direct to them to avoid this form of hidden poverty.

In conventional income distributions women are under-represented in the top income groups and over-represented in the low income bands. Female-headed households (lone mothers and single elderly women) are among those at the highest risk of measured poverty. Using the 1986 Family Expenditure Survey (FES), Davies and Joshi (1994, Table 4) found one-third of all single women (along with 27 per cent of single men and 15 per cent of married couples) in the bottom fifth of an income distribution which assumed that married couples pooled their incomes. If, however, pooling was minimal, then in addition to the 15 per cent of women from married couples in visible poverty, a further 37 per cent could have been in 'hidden poverty' (with own incomes below the poverty line) if their husbands did not share their resources.

Debt is another aspect of women's low income and, in low income families its managment is often a woman's responsibility (Ford, 1991). Ford also points out that 'where women need to seek credit . . . their social and economic dependence is likely to restrict their use of [formal] credit to higher cost credit sources' (1991, p. 79).

Citizenship

Marshall (1952) identifies civil, political and social rights as the three distinct elements of citizenship (Barbalet, 1988, p. 6). Although political and civil rights have traditionally been central to the status of citizenship, it is only since the war that citizenship has, in the eyes of many, come to embody social rights including the right to resources such as income, social security, education and health care (Plant, 1992, p. 15). A key aspect of social citizenship was seen by Marshall to be the right to a minimum level of welfare irrespective of the market value of the individual (Hindess, 1987; Lister, 1990). It has been argued that, 'Access to ones own money should be considered a minimum welfare requirement in a monetary economy' (Dahl quoted in Lister, 1992). This inability to receive an income in their own right, either from the labour market or the state, can leave women without Dahl's minimum level of welfare and therefore without the means to citizenship.

One of the main components of Marshall's conception of citizenship is that all citizens are equal in terms of their rights and duties (Hindess, 1987). Beveridge, however, perceived married women as individuals with different duties and hence rights to men and single women:

> all women by marriage acquire a new economic and social status, with risks and rights different from those of the unmarried.
> (Beveridge, 1942, para. 108)

> The attitude of the housewife to gainful employment outside the home is not and should not be the same as that of the single woman. She has other duties. (para. 114)

Since many women have not been able to contribute and benefit equally from the contributory insurance scheme developed by Beveridge, their rights as citizens are undermined. In the intervening years, changes to remove direct discrimination from the system have been made but the fundamental asymmetry of entitlement based on labour-force participation and the assumption that wives are the dependants of men still remains. Women tend to be excluded from some parts of the benefit system and treated as dependants in others.

TOWARDS ECONOMIC INDEPENDENCE

If women are to reduce their risk of poverty and also become equal citizens they need to gain greater access to independent sources of income. Such sources also bring a sense of independence and security, as illustrated in the following quotes. The first refers to earnings from paid employment and the second to income from Child Benefit:

> It gives you a feeling of independence – a feeling you're not absolutely reliant on your husband. You feel you are somebody – more confident.
>
> (Pahl, 1989, p. 130)

> It's my one thing I can fall back on, my bit of independence.
>
> (Pahl, 1989, p. 158)

Lister (1990) identifies three key aspects of economic dependence for women: a lack of control, a lack of rights and a sense of obligation. The receipt of income is almost always conditional; for example, earnings are conditional on working (Atkinson, 1989, p. 12). However, the nature of the conditions attached and the status conveyed by different sources of income differ considerably. As a result, the reality and experience of dependency is likely to differ according to the source of income. In addition, different types of income have different levels of accessibility and liquidity associated with them and vary in terms of regularity, reliability, liquidity and portability.

Earnings from employment are important both for the money that is generated and because of the independence and self-esteem that they bring (Pahl, 1989). Women are likely to play a greater part in the family's financial decision-making if they are in paid, particularly full-time, employment (Pahl, 1989; Vogler, 1989). More generally, position in the pay hierarchy conveys status and access to fringe benefits (such as an occupational pension, a company car and credit worthiness) which in turn help determine future levels of financial reward (Pond and Smail, 1987, p. 115).

State benefits are the other main source of a woman's 'own income' which confers independence, in the sense used here. Most social security claimants, particularly for non-contributory benefits, are women (Lister, 1992). Although many such benefits are means-tested, women receiving them often have much more control over their income after a partnership ends than was the case before (Pahl, 1985; Graham, 1987). Despite this, dependency on the state may carry considerable stigma and loss of self-esteem. Some benefits such as Child Benefit, however, are neither means-tested nor related to contributions and these represent a valued source of income for many women, even those in households with a relatively high income (Pahl, 1989).

Income received from a partner may be more volatile than either income from employment or from the state. The lack of any clear legal right to the money may also result in feelings of lack of control and insecurity and a sense of obligation towards the provider. For example, income transfers between partners may be conditional implicitly or explicitly, on supplying 'unpaid' domestic work and childcare.

> a wife's share of her husband's earnings or income does not give her true economic independence, because it is an indirect payment through another person for the work she does.
>
> (*Women's Bulletin*, 6 September 1943, quoted in Clarke *et al.*, 1987)

Whilst this may be a division of labour freely entered into, it also represents a choice which has long-term implications for women. By taking on domestic commitments, women lose earning potential and may find themselves trapped in a situation of dependency from which it is hard to escape.

BARRIERS TO WOMEN'S ECONOMIC INDEPENDENCE

Whilst legislation in the 1970s[1] and other improved opportunities[2] have given some women greater economic independence, this is not true for all. For many the basis of economic dependency is established, even before family formation, by societal expectations. Some women reduce their paid work hours on marriage (Ward and Dale, 1991; Marsh, 1991); more reduce them when responsible for children.

To achieve economic equality with men, women need to obtain equal access to paid employment, equality within the benefit and pension system and equal access to resources within the family (Millar and Glendinning, 1989). At the moment obstacles exist to all three.

Paid Employment

Despite the trend towards more paid employment for women, most of the observed increase in employment has been in part-time work. The ability of women with young children to enter the labour market is still hampered by a lack of childcare facilities (Dale and Joshi, 1992). Once in employment, their ability to earn equal amounts to men is reduced on two fronts. First, women work fewer hours than men. Although a majority of women today are economically active (71 per cent aged 16–59 in Britain in 1991) a large number work part-time at some time in their lives. In 1991, 51 per cent of married women employees were working part-time[3], as compared to 27 per cent of non-married women in employment and 4 per cent of male employees aged 16–64 (Watson, 1992).

Second, women get paid less per hour than men. In 1992 the gross hourly earnings of female full-time employees were 79 per cent of those of their male counterparts (Spence, 1992)[4]. For women working part-time, the gap is greater. Female part-time earnings per hour are 58 per cent those of male full-time earnings and 74 per cent of the earnings of women working full-time (Central Statistical Office (CSO), 1991).

Combined with a tendency to interrupt employment on the birth of their first child and return to part-time work, these factors mean that women's lifetime earnings are substantially less than those of men (Joshi, 1989, 1990; Joshi and Davies, 1992, 1994). Policies, public or private, that could maintain and improve women's earning power would include better child-care facilities and maternity benefits, greater flexibility of working hours, parental leave and leave for family reasons for **both** partners as well as access to training.

Benefit and pension system

Social security benefits in Britain fall into three main types, National Insurance benefits, means-tested benefits and categorical benefits. Two assumptions disadvantage women in the contributory benefit system. The first is that entitlement is linked to employment rather than to caring responsibilities and the second that a couple contains a breadwinner and his dependent (Roll, 1991). Failing to make full contributions to the National Insurance scheme affects current benefit entitlement and future pension provision: 2.25 million working women in 1991 were excluded from the contributory social security system because their earnings fell below the lower earnings limit for National Insurance (Lister, 1992).

Primary pension rights accrue through labour-force participation and income earned, whereas derived rights to a wife's or widow's pension are based on being legally married to a contributor. Many women still do not qualify for a full pension in their own right and their own contributions may count for nothing if they are not worth more than the wife's pension. A wife's expectations of an earnings related pension derived from her husband's contributions are dependent upon the marriage ending in death, not divorce. Even in the state pension system, income inequalities in the labour market between men and women are perpetuated after retirement. This effect is even more marked in occupational pension schemes.

Women who do not qualify for contributory benefits have to rely on the lower paying means-tested benefits. A couple's entitlement to means-tested benefits is calculated on the basis of their joint resources and benefit is paid to the claimant, usually the man, on the implicit assumption that resources are shared equally within the family. This affects women's ability to receive an independent income. For instance, if a woman's Unemployment Benefit expires, she cannot claim Income Support if her husband is employed (Lister, 1992). The reverse applies, but this is a much less common situation. Since 1983, women have been able to claim Income Support on the couple's behalf, and the proportion doing so by 1990 had risen to 1 in 20 (Lister, 1992). In addition, Family Credit is paid almost exclusively to mothers after government plans to pay it through the pay packet failed following pressure from employers, women's groups and the poverty lobby (Lister, 1989).

Women are the major recipients of categorical benefits which are neither means-tested nor dependent upon National Insurance contributions. These benefits fall into two categories, those that replace income, such as the Severe Disablement Allowance (SDA) and the Invalid Care Allowance (ICA), and those that meet costs, such as Child Benefit, One Parent Benefit and the Disability Living Allowance (Lister, 1992). Although these benefits represent an independent source of income for women, they have some conditions attached and some, such as the SDA, are less than their equivalent in the contributory scheme.

Although today's social security system has lost much of its overt sex discrimination following the European Directive 79/7 on 'Equal Treatment for Men and Women in Matters of Social Security', recent changes are still reinforcing the idea of women's economic dependence on men. For instance, the Child Support Act 1991 which became operational on 5 April 1993 for new social security claimants, includes a maintenance assessment formula that calculates the child maintenance payable by the absent parent. A lone parent in receipt of benefit who refuses to provide information on the identity and whereabouts of the absent parent is liable to a reduction in benefit. Enforcement of payments is likely to result in a woman's dependence on the father of her children whether or not she was dependent on him before (Lister, 1992).

The question of the individualisation of benefits has been raised by the European Community Draft Directives on the equal treatment of men and women in social security schemes and occupational schemes. The result of these has been to focus attention on the abolition of 'derived right' features, such as the Category B Wife's Pension and the Widow's Pension, in the current contributory benefit system. Although the retention of derived rights appears to constitute unequal treatment, their abolition, at least in the short term, would leave many women materially worse off. Allowances and disregards based on the assumption of women as dependants have led to a number of disincentives to women's employment. In the benefit system current in 1991, part-time work was more or less ruled out for wives of beneficiaries and lone mothers (Dilnot and Kell, 1987; Metcalf and Leighton, 1989). A system in which women could claim benefits in their own right may, however, produce other disincentives to earning an independent income from paid employment (Esam and Berthoud, 1991).

Within the Family

If money provides a source of power through which to command resources within the family, then women's income dependence and their restricted access to labour market income disadvantages them in terms of consumption within the family.

> Nothing, whether it be work, money, help from relatives, food or time, is shared equally among household members.
>
> (Brannen and Wilson, 1987, p. 16)

Both food and clothing are resources to which access is determined by the relative power and status of different family members (Charles and Kerr, 1987; Craig and Glendinning, 1990; Cohen, 1991; Sadiq-Sangster, 1991; Cohen *et al.*, 1992). What little evidence there is suggests that there is also unequal access among family members to space, warmth and light (Land, 1983; Graham, 1984).

There is also inequality within the family in the division of domestic work and childcare. Even in families where women work full-time, tasks are seldom equally shared (Brook *et al.*, 1989). In addition to domestic work and child related activities, women are often responsible for providing care for elderly and disabled relatives.

The provision of informal care has an impact on the employment patterns and earnings of carers (Nissel and Bonnerja, 1982; Finch and Groves, 1983; Baldwin, 1985; Glendinning, 1990; Baldwin and Parker, 1991; Brotchie and Hills, 1991). Fulfilling the caring role often increases the economic dependence of the carer, particularly if they are not in full-time work. It increases the dependency of married women carers on their husbands and the dependency of single women on the state (Glendinning, 1988). Invalid Care Allowance provides some alleviation but not a living wage.

A PRACTICAL DEFINITION OF 'INCOME DEPENDENCY' AND 'SELF-SUFFICIENCY'

In order to develop and operate the concept of 'income dependency', two assumptions are made. First, that income from all sources is shared equally between partners. We do not make the assumption that cash is necessarily handed from one partner to the other. Rather, we assume a joint income that is used to support the couple's lifestyle; the proportion contributed by each partner will vary. Although in reality the share of income consumed by each will also vary and is likely to be unequal, this assumption of sharing is necessary if we are to obtain a measure of dependency. Second, it is assumed that receipt and control go together: an assumption which has considerable support in the literature (Pahl, 1989; Vogler, 1989). Thus the minor contributor of income is deemed to be dependent on the major contributor for the resources which would bring her/him up to equal shares.

Income Dependency

'Income dependency' is said to exist when one partner in a couple contributes an unequal and smaller amount of the family income (defined below). Dependency may be partial if the contribution is positive but smaller than that of the other partner, and total if there is no contribution. As discussed, this definition makes the implicit assumption that family income is equally shared between partners. In practice an equal contribution is defined as between 45 and 55 per cent of family income, rather than exactly 50 per cent for each partner. Thus one partner is treated as 'income dependent' on the other if s/he is contributing less than 45 per cent of the family income. Equal contributors are contrasted with those who are partially and totally dependent. 'Partial dependency' occurs when a partner makes a contribution to the net family income which is less than 45 per cent. 'Total dependency' occurs when one partner makes no monetary contribution to net family income.

This concept of dependence is not related to the absolute level of income. It refers only to the relative amounts contributed by each partner. Thus two women with the same income may be defined as either partially dependent or partially independent, depending solely on the level of income of the partner.

'Self-sufficiency'

Given the relative nature of 'income dependency', a secondary absolute measure of level of income is also used, termed 'self-sufficiency'. This refers to the ability to meet minimum needs on the assumption that there is no sharing of income between partners. This measure addresses the issue of hidden poverty within partnerships. It assesses whether a woman has sufficient income in her own right to meet the minimum day-to-day needs of herself and her children. Children have been included in this calculation since, on the break-up of a partnership, the vast majority of women retain custody. To be truly independent the woman would need to be able to meet her child(ren)'s needs too. We have, however, assumed that housing costs within a partnership are met by the man. Any decision over how to treat housing costs is arbitrary, but the assumption made here allows us to identify the potential for hidden poverty in terms of day-to-day living costs.

Since this measure is designed to assess whether a woman has enough income, paid directly to her, to 'get by', we have set the 'self-sufficiency' level at April 1991 Income Support levels. The basic personal allowance for a single person aged 25 or over (or a lone parent aged 18 or over) was is £39.65 per week. The rates for children vary according to age, from £13.35 for children under 11 to £31.15 for those aged 18. So in this analysis the 'self-sufficiency' level is set at £39.65 plus an amount for children based on the number and ages of children in the family.

It will be evident that a woman may be income-dependent (by generating less than 45 per cent of the family income), but may, none the less, be above the 'self-sufficiency level'.[5] Such women must, in some sense, be less dependent upon transfers from their husband than if their own income was below the 'self-sufficiency' threshold. This may have implications for the part women play in financial decision-making in the family and the negative feelings associated with economic dependency, such as lack of control, lack of rights and a sense of obligation (Lister, 1990). It also gives some, although not an exact, idea of the immediate resources that would be at her disposal if she left the partnership.

Defining family income[6,7]

The following section considers how family income is defined and discusses the various components that are and can be included in such a definition. A complete definition of family income might include the receipt of all resources such as income from employment, benefit, maintenance, unearned income, fringe benefits such as a company car, pension scheme and goods in kind. However, the definition used here includes 'money' income only. Income variables in NCDS5 refer to different time periods and all amounts have been recoded to a weekly basis.[8]

The 'family' consists of the cohort member and partner. The definition of their income is a net figure made up of the following.

1. Current income from the main job of both partners, net of tax, national insurance, union dues and pension payments but inclusive of overtime, bonuses and commission or tips. Self-employed cohort members were asked to say how much a week they took out of the business *before* tax. Their answers were coded in bands, the midpoints of which have been taken as an estimate of their gross weekly earnings. Income from any other job of the cohort member (net of tax and other deductions) is also included. There is no information on any second job of the cohort member's partner.
2. Income from state benefits paid to the cohort member, her/his spouse or to them jointly. These payments are assumed to be net of tax.
3. Income from other sources paid to the cohort member, her/his spouse, and to them jointly. These payments are also assumed to be net of tax.

Thus the basic definition of family income gives a measure of the income entering the family before housing costs are met and is defined as:

family	=	net earnings of	+	benefit income	+	other income of
income		cohort member		of cohort member		cohort member
		and partner		and partner		and partner

Issues concerning the inclusion of the imputed value of owner-occupied housing and the deduction of housing costs from the definition of family income, are more fully discussed in NCDS Working Paper 36.

RESULTS

This analysis is carried out on 3374 women living as married with valid income and employment data. Eighty-two per cent (2783) have children; 32 per cent (1082) work full-time, 34 per cent (1148) work part-time, 30 per cent (1012) are looking after the home and family. Table 6.1 shows how children and employment status interact.

'Looking after family' refers to women who, when asked about their current employment status, said that they are looking after the home and family. The 'other' employment category covers those not included above,

Table 6.1 *Children and employment status*

	%
With children	**82**
Full-time	18
Part-time	32
Looking after family	29
Other	3
No children	**18**
Full-time	14
Part-time	2
Looking after family	1
Other	1
All	100 (3374)

Table 6.2 *'Income dependency' within couples and median net family income in £ per week*

	(a) *Family income*		(b) *Family income minus child benefit*	
	Col%	*Median*	*Col%*	*Median*
Not dependent	**22**	**348**	**21**	**343**
Equal contributors	12	390	12	384
Dependent male	10	279	9	278
Dependent	**78**	**308**	**79**	**294**
Total dependence	2	231	20	231
Partial dependence	76	310	59	308
n	3167		3167	

who are permanently or temporarily out of the labour force; this category is not included in the following analyses.

'Dependency' and 'Self-Sufficiency'

Despite the assertion that young women these days are less dependent on their partners than ever before, this analysis of 33-year-olds in 1991 shows that 'dependency' is still the norm for a majority of women (78 per cent) (Table 6.2(a)). Assuming equal sharing, this means that over 3/4 of the sample would receive income flows from their partner. Put another way, over 3/4 of the women in the sample contribute less than 45 per cent of the joint income. Of the 22 per cent who are not 'dependent' about half (12 per cent) have income levels between 45 and 55 per cent of the family income and are 'equal contributors'. The other half (10 per cent) have incomes which represent more than 55 per cent of the family income and so their partners are assumed to be dependent upon them. Figure 6.1 illustrates the percentage contributions that women make to net family income.

Just under half (46 per cent) of this cohort of women are below the 'self-sufficiency' level (Table 6.3(a)) and so if income is not shared by their partners they are at risk of hidden poverty. They are also likely to be at risk of poverty if their relationship breaks down since they would be unable to support themselves on their current income. These figures are very similar to those found for women of all ages by Davies and Joshi (1994) and Sutherland (1990) (cited in Atkinson, 1991).

A low level of 'total dependence' is recorded in Table 6.2(a) because most women who are not earning in the labour market are in receipt of Child Benefit and because income which is received jointly (e.g. some benefits) has been allocated equally between partners. The exclusion of the 'other' category (see above) will also reduce this percentage. Levels of women's 'dependence' alter dramatically when Child Benefit is removed from family income (Table 6.2b). Although the overall divide between 'dependence' and 'non-dependence' changes only slightly between the two definitions of family income, 'total dependence' rises from 2 to 20 per cent (Table 6.2). For those who are not in paid employment 'total dependence' rises from 6 to 65 per cent when Child Benefit is removed (data not shown), highlighting its importance as an independent source of income for non-employed mothers. In the United States, where there is no such universal benefit for mothers, 'total dependence' among white women of all ages in 1980 was found to be 31 per cent (Sorensen and McLanahan, 1987).

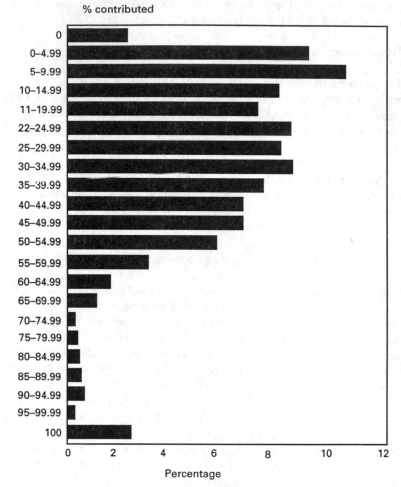

% contributed

Family income = combined earnings, benefits and other income.

Figure 6.1   *Wife's contribution to net family income (5% bands)*

Tables 6.2 and 6.3 also provide the income context in which 'dependency' and 'self-sufficiency' are located and show that considerable disparities exist. Where partners are 'equal contributors' median family income is highest, £390p.w., and where the woman contributes nothing in monetary terms, median family income is lowest, £231p.w. Although total female 'dependence' is associated with a relatively low median family

Table 6.3   *'Self-sufficiency' within couples and median net family income in £ per week*

	(a) Family income		(b) Family income minus child benefit	
	Col%	Median	Col%	Median
Self-sufficient	54	366	49	364
Equal contributors	12	393	11	398
Dependent male	9	312	8	301
Partial female dependence	33	368	30	364
Total female dependence	0	0	0	0
Not self-sufficient	46	254	51	255
Equal contributors	<1	130	1	87
Dependent male	1	84	1	64
Partial female dependence	43	259	29	251
Total female dependence	2	231	20	231
n	3167		3167	

income (£231p.w.) it is not as low as that of families in which the male partner is 'totally dependent' on his wife (£135p.w.). It is particularly noteworthy that women who are not 'self-sufficient' have lower median family incomes (£254) than those who are (£366). This means that women who are most at risk of hidden poverty are also in families with the lowest median family income levels.

The Effects of Employment Status and Children

As expected, levels of 'dependency' increase as attachment to the labour force decreases (Table 6.4(a)). Forty-nine per cent of married women working full-time are 'dependent' as are 90 per cent of those working part-time and 94 per cent of those not in paid employment and looking after children. 'Totally dependent' women are only found among this latter group and even then only at a very low level (6 per cent).

Table 6.4 *'Income dependency' of women living as married by own employment status (column percentages and median net family income in £ per week)*

	Full-time		Part-time		Looking after home	
	%	£p.w.	%	£p.w.	%	£p.w.
(a) 'Income Dependency'						
Not dependent	**51**	**385**	**10**	**235**	**6**	**116**
Equal contributors	30	410	5	280	2	203
Dependent male	21	338	5	150	4	109
Dependent	**49**	**398**	**90**	**300**	**94**	**252**
Total dependence	<1	351	<1	241	6	231
Partial dependence	49	398	90	300	88	254
n	1057		1135		975	
(b) 'Self-sufficiency'						
Self-sufficient	**96**	**396**	**55**	**325**	**7**	**306**
Equal contributors	30	410	5	293	1	225
Dependent male	21	338	4	203	2	132
Partial female dep.	45	408	46	328	4	414
Total female dep.	0	0	0	0	0	0
Not self-sufficient	**4**	**234**	**45**	**266**	**93**	**245**
Equal contributors	<1	177	<1	178	1	91
Dependent male	0	0	1	80	2	85
Partial female dep.		3238	43	271	84	249
Total female dep.	<1	351	<1	241	6	231
n	1057		1135		975	

Whereas the overall figures in Table 6.2 showed that women who contribute equally with their partners live in families with a higher median family income than those who are 'dependent', this pattern varies with employment status (Table 6.4(a)). Amongst 'non-dependent' women, median family income is much higher where women are in full-time work (£385p.w.) than where they are either working part-time (£235p.w.) or looking after the family (£116p.w.). Amongst women who are 'dependent' this differential by employment status is still present but less strong.

'Self-sufficiency' shows a similarly strong relationship with employment status (Table 6.4(b)). Almost all women who are employed full-time are 'self-sufficient' (96 per cent)[9]. Among part-time workers, however, only 55 per cent are 'self-sufficient' and among women not in paid work looking after their family a majority (93 per cent) are not 'self-sufficient'. There are marked differences in the median family incomes of women who are 'self-sufficient' and those who are not. Among those who are 'self-sufficient' there is a slight differential across employment status in terms of median family income, with 'self-sufficient' women working full-time in families with a higher median family income (£396p.w.) than 'self-sufficient' women at home looking after the family (£306p.w.). Among those that are not 'self-sufficient', this differential is reversed. Women working full-time who are not self-sufficient are likely to be on very low income and appear to have partners who also have low incomes.

The association of children with 'income dependency' is marked, although this is related to labour force participation (Tables 6.5(a and b)). Childless women are far more likely to contribute equally to or more than their partners (48 per cent) than those with children (17 per cent) (data not shown). Once employment status is controlled, however, it is apparent that the effect of children is largely removed. Amongst women working full-time, the presence of children makes little difference to the levels of 'dependence' and 'non-dependence' (Table 6.5(a)). Childless women working full-time are the only group in which a majority of women (54 per cent) are 'not dependent' on their partners; 23 per cent have a partner who is 'dependent' on them and 31 per cent are contributing to the family income on an equal basis to their partner. Amongst women working full-time with children a slightly lower percentage are 'not dependent' (49 per cent) although levels of equal contributors are very similar (30 per cent).

Median family income is higher among families in which both partners contribute. This is largely because income tends to be the outcome of a couple's joint employment status and confirms previous evidence that dual earning households are likely to have higher incomes than those with just one earner (Rimmer, 1988; Dale, 1990). Consideration of the sources of family income (reported in NCDS Working Paper 36) reinforces the fact that women's ability to earn their own income is influenced by their current domestic responsibilities and that their access to an independent source of income is reduced once they leave the labour market.

Table 6.5   *'Income dependency' of women living as married by employment status by children*

	No children			Children		
	FT	*PT*	*Looking after home*	*FT*	*PT*	*Looking after home*
(a) 'Income Dependency' (column percentages)						
Not dependent	**54**	**18**	**0**	**49**	**10**	**6**
Equal contributors	31	9	0	30	5	2
Dependent male	23	9	0	19	5	4
Dependent	**46**	**82**	**100**	**51**	**90**	**94**
Total Dependence	<1	2	46	<1	<1	5
Partial Dependence	46	80	54	51	90	89
n	477	54	24	580	1081	951
(b) 'Self-sufficiency' (column percentages)						
Self sufficient	**99**	**83**	**25**	**95**	**53**	**7**
Equal contributors	31	9	0	30	4	1
Dependent male	23	9	0	19	4	2
Partial female dep.	45	65	25	46	45	4
Total female dep.	0	0	0	0	0	0
Not self-sufficient	**1**	**17**	**75**	**5**	**46**	**93**
Equal contributors	0	0	0	<1	<1	1
Dependent male	0	0	0	0	1	2
Partial female dep.	1	15	29	5	45	86
Total female dep.	<1	2	46	<1	<1	4
n	477	54	24	580	1081	951

DEPENDENCY AND THE DOMESTIC DIVISION OF LABOUR

Earlier in this paper we argued that income dependency is likely to be reflected in the domestic division of labour. We would expect that women who are partially or wholly dependent on their partner will provide a greater share of domestic and child-care work than women who contribute a greater share of cash income. NCDS5 provides a limited amount of information about which partner is mainly responsible for a range of domestic tasks. Although it is not possible to report the full details, it is evident that there are some significant differences between women who are dependent and those who are contributing an equal or greater share of the family income.

Among couples with children, although about 50 per cent of women who are not dependent say they are mainly responsible for looking after a sick child, this rises to 70 per cent amongst dependent women. Similarly, about a third of the former group report being mainly responsible for general child-care compared with 55 per cent of the latter group. Both cleaning and shopping are considerably more likely to be shared in couples where the woman is an equal contributor or independent. However, household repairs and DIY still remain firmly a male province whilst laundry and ironing remain a female one.

CONCLUSIONS

These analyses confirm that married women's 'income dependence' is inextricably linked to their labour force participation, which, in turn, is affected by their domestic responsibilities, in particular by whether or not they have children. Thus childless women working full-time are most likely to contribute equally to the family income, whereas women not in paid work are least likely to either contribute equally or to be 'self-sufficient'. Half of the sample are at risk of poverty within their relationships if resources are not shared, or if the relationship were to break down. Although this may only be a transitory state for some women, for others it will be more permanent and for all it is likely to have longer-term implications for their position in the labour market and within the family.

Although dependency is strongly related to the presence of children, a substantial minority of childless women working full-time are also dependent on transfers from their partners if they are to have equal access to the family's income. It remains to be seen whether these differences in partners' incomes can be accounted for by age differences, differences in qualifications, the labour market disadvantage of being female and other factors. It is also the case that some mothers manage to escape dependency by working full-time while they have young children. The role of paid childcare in these situations is explained in NCDS Working Paper 38.

The presence of Child Benefit reduces levels of total female dependence and is of considerable importance in providing mothers in the UK, particularly those not in paid work, with some degree of independent income.

In summary, the results reinforce the importance of enabling women to participate equally in the labour force if they are to achieve economic equality with men. Women who retain full-time employment whilst having young children are heavily dependent upon childcare. These snapshots of family incomes portrayed for 1991 may or may not be representative of longer-term patterns of economic dependency. Some of the husbands who are dependent on their wives in this analysis may have been temporarily sick or unemployed giving a picture which was neither well established nor likely to persist. Similarly some instances of female dependency associated with maternity leave or somewhat longer breaks for childrearing may soon be redressed towards an earlier state of more equal contributions. These questions require further analysis.

The widespread asymmetry in the couple's contribution to joint incomes matches the asymmetry in the domestic division of labour. It suggests that, if income is indeed pooled, women's unpaid work in the home is still substantially supported by men's paid work in the labour market, and the features of social security which recognise this dependence are still needed. If the assumption of pooling is wrong, as the social expectations which reinforce it are weakened, our figures suggest that what is needed is better access to independent income for women, rather than reinforcing their claim on pooled income.

Notes

1. Equal Pay Act 1970 and the Sex Discrimination Act 1975.
2. In the 1960s, 1970s and 1980s these improvements included greater access to higher education for women. In the 1980s they also included employer initiatives, albeit on a limited scale, such as career break schemes, re-entry and retainer schemes, flexible working arrangements such as job-sharing, flexi-time and term-time working, and a few workplace nurseries.
3. The classification of part-time work is based on the respondent's definition of the job rather than hours worked.
4. This is true of gross hourly earnings before and after overtime.
5. In theory it is possible to be independent and not self sufficient but in practice this occurrence is rare.

6.   A family is defined as a couple living as married together with their own, adopted, foster and step-children. Children at boarding school and those away for less than 6 months are included but those in local authority care, foster homes, long-stay institutions and those being brought up elsewhere are not.

7.   Any definition of family income in NCDS5 must assume that all income is generated by the husband and wife and that none comes from other members of the family or household since there is no information about the financial contributions of other family members in NCDS5. The age of the cohort members means that it is unlikely that they will have children earning significant amounts although a few could have older step-children. The 'other income' category might include regular income from extended family members to the cohort members since it includes a category for cash from parents and one for cash from ralatives or friends.

8.   The cohort member is asked to give their usual take-home pay and that of their partners. They are then asked how long a period the pay covered; one week, a fortnight, four weeks, a calender month, a year or some other time. The self-employed gave grouped gross income data for a week. Information about benefits and other income is given for those currently in receipt and the period of the last payment covered is recorded: 1, 2 or 3 weeks, or 1, 2, 3, 6, or 12 months.

9.   Four per cent of women who are working full-time are not self-sufficient. All four are self-employed and are taking little or nothing out of the business for their own use.

References

Arber, S. and Ginn, J. (1991), *Gender and Later Life* (London: Sage).

Atkinson, A. (1991), 'Poverty Statistics and Progress in Europe', Welfare State Programme Discussion Paper no. 60, STICERD, London.

Atkinson, A. (1989), *Poverty and Social Security* (Hemel Hempstead: Harvester Wheatsheaf).

Baldwin, S. (1985), *The Costs of Caring: Families with Disabled Children* (London: Routledge & Kegan Paul).

Baldwin, S. and Parker, G. (1991), 'Support for Informal Carers: The Role of Social Security', in Dalley, G. (ed.), *Disability and Social Policy* (London: PSI).

Barbalet, J. (1988), *Citizenship* (Milton Keynes: Open University Press).

Barrett, M. (1980), *Women's Oppression Today: Problems in Marxist Feminist Analysis* (London: Verso).

Becker, G. (1981), 'Altruism in the Family and Selfishness in the Marketplace', *Economica*, vol. 48, pp 1–15.

Beveridge, W. H. (1942), *Social Insurance and Allied Services*, Cmnd 5404 (London: HMSO).

Brannen, J. and Wilson, G. (1987), *Give and Take in Families* (London: Allen & Unwin).

Brook, L., Jowell, R. and Witterspoon, S. (1989), 'Recent Trends in Social Attitudes', *Social Trends*, 19 (London: HMSO).

Brotchie, J. and Hills, D. (1991), *Equal Shares in Caring* (London: Socialist Health Association).

Central Statistical Office (CSO) (1991), *New Earnings Survey* (London: HMSO).

Charles, N. and Kerr, M. (1987), 'Just the Way it is: Gender and Age Differences in Family Food Consumption', in Brannen, J. and Wilson, G. (eds), *Give and Take in Families* (London: Allen & Unwin).

Clarke, J., Cochrane, A. and Smart, C. (1987), *Ideologies of Welfare: From Dreams to Disillusion* (London: Hutchinson).

Cohen, R. (1991), *Just About Surviving: Life on Income Support* (London: Family Service Units).

Cohen, R., Coxall, J., Craig, G. and Sadiq-Sangster, A. (1992), *Hardship Britain: Being Poor in the 1990s* (London: Child Poverty Action Group).

Craig, G. and Glendinning, C. (1990), *Missing the Target* (Ilford: Barnados).

Dale, A. (1990), 'Stratification over the Life-course: Gender Differences within the Household', in Payne, G. and Abbott, P. (eds), *The Social Mobility of Women* (Basingstoke: Falmer), pp. 139–58.

Dale, A. and Joshi, H. (1992), 'The Economic and Social Status of British Women', in Buttler, G., Hoffmann-Nowotny, H.-J., and Schmitt-Rink, G. (eds), *Acta Demographica* (Heidelberg: Physica Verlag), pp. 27–46.

Davies, H. and Joshi, H. (1994), 'Sex, Sharing and the Distribution of Income', *Journal of Social Policy*, 23 July, pp. 301–40.

Delphy, C. (1994), *Close to Home: A Materialist Analysis of Women's Oppression* (London: Hutchinson).

Dilnot, A. and Kell, M. (1987), 'Male Unemployment and Women's Work', in Dilnot, A. and Walker, I. (eds), *The Economics of Social Security* (Oxford: Oxford University Press).

Esam, P. and Berthoud, R. (1991), *Independent Benefits for Men and Women* (London: PSI).

Ferri, E. (1993), *Life at 33: The 5th Follow-up of the National Child Development Study* (London: National Children's Bureau and ESRC).

Finch, J. and Groves, D. (eds) (1983), *A Labour of Love: Women, Work and Caring* (London: Routledge & Kegan Paul).

Ford, J. (1991), *Consuming Credit: Debt and Poverty in the UK* (London: CPAG).

Glendinning, C. (1988), 'Dependency and Interdependency: The Incomes of Informal Carers and the Impact of Social Security', in Baldwin, S., Parker, G. and Walker, R. (eds), *Social Security and Community Care* (Aldershot: Avebury Gower).

Glendinning, C. (1990), 'Dependency and Interdependency: The Incomes of Informal Carers and the Impact of Social Security', *Journal of Social Policy*, vol. 19:4, pp. 469–97.

Graham, H. (1987), 'Being Poor: Perceptions of Coping Strategies of Lone Mothers', in Brannen, J. and Wilson, G. (eds), *Give and Take in Families* (London: Allen & Unwin).

Graham, H. (1984), *Women, Health and the Family* (Brighton: Wheatsheaf).

Gregory, J. and Foster, K. (1990), *The Consequences of Divorce* (London: HMSO).

Hartmann, H. (1976), 'Capitalism, Patriarchy and Job Segregation by Sex', *Signs*, vol. 1, pp. 137–68.

Hindess, B. (1987), *Freedom, Equality and the Market: Arguments on Social Policy* (London: Tavistock).

Joshi, H (1989), 'The Changing Form of Women's Economic Dependency', in Joshi, H. (ed.), *The Changing Population of Britain*, ch. 10 (Oxford. Blackwell), pp. 157–76.

Joshi, H. (1990), 'The Cash Opportunity Cost of Childbearing: An Approach to Estimation Using British Evidence', *Population Studies*, vol. 44, pp. 41–60.

Joshi, H. and Davies, H. (1992), 'Pensions, Divorce and Wives' Double Burden', *International Journal of Law and the Family*, vol. 6, pp. 289–320.

Joshi, H. and Davies, H. (1994), 'The Paid and Unpaid Roles of Women: How Should Social Security Adapt?', in Falkingham, J. and Baldwin, S. (eds), *Social Security and Social Change: New Challenges to the Beveridge Model* (London: Harvester Wheatsheaf), pp. 235–54

Land, H. (1983), 'Poverty and Gender: The Distribution of Resources within Families', in Brown, M. (ed.), *The Structure of Disadvantage* (London: Heinemann).

Lazear, E. P. and Micheal, R. T. (1988), *Allocation of Income within the Household* (London and Chicago: University of Chicago).

Lister, R. (1992), *Women's Economic Dependency and Social Security* (Manchester: Equal Opportunities Commission).

Lister, R. (1990), 'Women, Economic Dependency and Citizenship', *Journal of Social Policy*, vol. 19:4, pp. 445–67.

Lister, R. (1989), 'The Politics of Social Security: An Assessment of the Fowler Review', in Dilnot, A. and Kell, I. (eds), *The Economics of Social Security* (Oxford: Oxford University Press).

Marsh, C. (1991), *Hours of Work of Women and Men in Britain*, EOC Research Series (London: HMSO).

Marshall, T. H. (1952), *Citizenship and Social Class* (Cambridge: Cambridge University Press).

Metcalf, H. and Leighton, P. (1989), *The Under-Utilisation of Women in the Labour Market*, IMS Report No. 172 (Brighton: IMS).

Millar, J. and Glendinning, C. (1989), 'Gender and Poverty', *Journal of Social Policy*, vol. 18:3, pp. 363–81.

Nissel, M. and Bonnerja, L. (1982), *Family Care of the Handicapped Elderly: Who Pays?* (London: PSI).

OPCS (1992), *General Household Survey: Carers in 1990*, OPCS Monitor SS92/2 (London: OPCS).

Pahl, J. (1989), *Money and Marriage* (London: Macmillan).

Pahl, J. (1985), *Private Violence and Public Policy: The Needs of Battered Women and the Response of the Public Services* (London. Routledge & Kegan Paul)

Parsons, T. (1942), 'Age and Sex in the Social Structure of the United States', *American Sociological Review*, vol. 7, pp. 604–16.

Plant, R. (1992), 'Citizenship, Rights and Welfare', in Coote, A. (ed.), *The Welfare of Citizens: Developing New Social Rights*, ch. 1 (London: Rivers Oram Press), pp. 15–29.

Pond, C. and Smail, R. (1988), 'Wages and Salaries', in Walker, R. and Parker, G. (eds), *Money Matters: Income, Wealth and Financial Welfare*, ch. 8 (London: Sage), pp. 115–31.

Rimmer, L. (1988), 'The Intra-family Distribution of Paid Work, 1968–81', in Hunt, A. (ed.), *Women and Paid Work: Issues of Equality* (London: Macmillan).

Roll, J. (1991), *What is a Family: Benefit Models and Social Realities* (London: Family Policy Studies Centre).

Sadiq-Sangster, A. (1991), *Just About Surviving: Life on Income Support: An Asian Experience* (London: Family Services Units).

Sorensen, A. and McLanahan, S. (1987), 'Married Women's Economic Dependency', *American Journal of Sociology*, vol. 93:3, pp. 659–87.

Spence, A. (1992), 'Patterns of Pay: Results of the 1992 New Earnings Survey', *Employment Gazette*, Department of Employment, November, pp. 579–88.

Todd, J. and Jones, L. (1972), *Matrimonial Property* (London: HMSO).

Vogler, C. (1989), *Labour Market Change and Patterns of Financial Allocation within Households*, ESRC Social Life and Economic Change Initiative Working Paper no. 12 (Oxford: Nuffield College).

Ward, C., Joshi, H. and Dale, A. (1993), *Income Dependency within Couples*, NCDS Working Paper 36 (Lonson: SSRU).

Ward, C. and Dale, A. (1991), 'The Impact of Early Life-course Transitions on Equality at Work and Home', *The Sociological Review*, vol. 40:3, pp. 509–32.

Watson, G. (1992), 'Hours of Work in Great Britain and Europe', *Employment Gazette*, Department of Employment, November, pp. 539–77.

Weldon F. (1984), *Puffball* (London: Coronet).

7 Gender, Inheritance and Women as Testators*

JANET FINCH and LYNN HAYES

INTRODUCTION

The transmission of property and assets following a death should be of fundamental interest to sociologists, since it is one of the key mechanisms through which social and economic structures are reproduced over time, in a society based upon private ownership. It is also of particular relevance to sociologists of family life, since inheritance is so closely associated with the idea of passing assets down the generations, from parent to child. Engels recognised this in his influential, if somewhat flawed, discussion of nineteenth-century bourgeois marriage in which he argued that inheritance was a critical driving force in producing different family formations. He also saw the significant gender implications, in arguing that the bourgeois view of the family was dominated by the need to ensure the transmission of property from father to son, leaving married women in a position analogous to prostitutes, needed only because their bodies were necessary to produce sons, but otherwise excluded from the process of inheritance (Engels, 1985 edition, pp. 101–3).

It is therefore somewhat surprising that the analysis of inheritance patterns and processes has not occupied a more prominent place in sociology, the more so since the potential significance of inheritance has been further enhanced in the UK context in recent years, as rates of home ownership have risen. By 1989 two-thirds of houses were owner-occupied, double the number in 1961 (*Central Statistical Office*, 1993). This means, *inter alia*, that many more people now have something substantial to bequeath than would have been the case even in the recent past. So the significance of inheritance is now spread far beyond those wealthy families for whom it has always been a prominent consideration (Scott, 1982).

*The inheritance project, on which this paper draws, is funded by the ESRC (grant no. 000232035). The research team comprises Janet Finch, Jennifer Mason and Judith Masson as directors, with Lynn Hayes and Lorraine Wallis as research associates. This paper is co-authored by Janet Finch and Lynn Hayes, who would like to acknowledge the assistance of other members of the team in data collection and preparation, and for their helpful comments about earlier drafts of this paper.

In this chapter we look at some consequences of these changes at the micro level of family relationships, as opposed to macro-level questions on which most other researchers have concentrated (Forrest and Murie, 1989; Forrest *et al.*, 1990; Hamnett *et al.*, 1991). Our concern is with how questions of inheritance are now handled in families, given that they are relevant to many more people than in the past. This is the focus of an ongoing empirical study, on which this paper draws. In this paper we raise issues of gender in particular, following the lead not only of Engels, but also more recently of Delphy and Leonard (1986) who have argued that inheritance is a key element in sustaining and reproducing gender relationships in families. However, whereas these writers focus mainly on the respective positions of women and men as beneficiaries of inheritance, in this paper we have chosen to look at the other side of the process. Our specific focus is on women as testators.[1]

The work of historians suggests that there are some interesting issues about women's position as testators. Until a series of Married Women's Property Acts in the 1870s and 1880s introduced the right of a woman to retain property in her own name after marriage, the opportunity to be a testator was confined to two groups of women: those who had never married, and those who had outlived a husband but had not remarried. For the duration of a marriage, a woman had no effective legal right to determine the disposition of property after her death, including property inherited from her own family or brought into the marriage (Holcombe, 1983; Pahl, 1989). These Acts therefore represent a significant change in women's relationship to inheritance, though it is worth noting that married women were not put fully in the same position as single women, with respect to owning and disposing of property, until 1935 (Lewis, 1984, p. 78).

In the intervening century, we have seen not only the consolidation of a woman's right to hold property in her own name but also the growth of the concepts (both in a legal and a cultural sense) of joint property and shared ownership, especially of houses which represent most people's single largest asset. Thus a woman may now be the owner not only of any property which she herself has inherited or has purchased through earnings, but if married she will have a stake in property purchased as the matrimonial home (Cretney, 1992). Thus in principle we have a situation now where a woman should be on equal terms with a man regarding her capacity to make decisions about the disposal of property after her death, and its transmission to the next generation. But is this so? Do women and men act in parallel, and indistinguishable, ways when they are in the position of being testators? We know that there are gendered differences in other types of marital decision making about money and resources (Wilson, 1987, Pahl, 1989; Morris, 1990). Are these also reflected in the way in which decisions about disposal of assets are made?

This chapter is based on a study of inheritance in contemporary Britain, focusing not on the wealthy but on ordinary individuals and families, many of whom will not have had anything significant to bequeath in previous generations. Our inheritance project was conducted between 1990 and 1993 and incorporated three linked empirical studies, two of which are used here. These are first, an analysis of a random sample of 800 wills probated in four sample years (1959, 1969, 1979 and 1989) from testators living in the north west and south east of England at the time of their deaths. Second, a series of qualitative interviews with members of the public about their views and experiences of inheritance. Interviewees were selected for the study using a form of quota sampling where the quotas were defined in theoretical rather than representational terms.[2] The interview study includes individuals of all ages from 18 to 89, women and men, people of differing family circumstances and people of differing ethnic descent. Where appropriate, we interviewed more than one member of the same family. Of a total of 98 interviewees, 66 have at least one other member of their own family in the study and 46 have more than one.

WILLS, GENDER AND PATTERNS OF BEQUEATHING

The starting point for our discussion on women as testators comes from our wills study, which allows us to examine outcomes in terms of formal bequeathing patterns. The wills data indicate that there is little significant difference in the bequeathing behaviour of men and women either in the ways in which the estate is bequeathed (Table 7.1) or in the inclusion of key beneficiary categories in the descendant generation (Table 7.2). The data in these tables are confined to people who were married when they made their last will[3] because our wills data reveal a major difference related to the marital status of testators. This in itself has implications which are gender-related, since women (17 per cent) are much less likely than men (58 per cent) to be married at the time of making their last will. Of course, this is a consequence of a simple demographic pattern, namely women's tendency to outlive men. But it does mean that the actions of widows as testators is sociologically significant. Given the tendency of married people to bequeath the majority of their property to each other it is women, as the most likely survivors of any couple, who are the ones who will determine

Table 7.1   *Ways of bequeathing estate by gender of testator (married testators only)*

		Women		Men		Total	
		n	(%)	n	(%)	n	(%)
(i)	**Whether estate divided***						
	Total estate	47	(65)	155	(69)	202	(68)
	Estate divided	25	(35)	69	(31)	94	(32)
	Total	72	(100)	224	(100)	296	(100)
(ii)	**Specific gifts in divided estates†**						
	Cash	16	(64)	43	(62)	59	(63)
	Personal property	14	(56)	36	(52)	50	(53)

*This distinction referred to here, and in Table 7.3, denotes two different forms of will. In total estate wills, no specific items are mentioned. All the testator's property is rolled together and bequeathed as a single entity, either to one person or divided between several beneficiaries in specified proportions. In the other type of will, specific items are given to named individuals before the residuary estate is bequeathed to one or more beneficiaries. The most common specific gifts are cash sums and items of personal property.

†Percentages here, and in the equivalent sections of Table 7.3, refer to the proportion of testators who bequeath divided estates.

Table 7.2   *Inclusion of selected beneficiaries in wills by gender of testator (married testators only)*

	Women		Men		Total	
	n	(%)	n	(%)	n	(%)
Child(ren)	18	(25)	47	(21)	65	(22)
Niece/nephew(s)	6	(8)	5	(2)	11	(4)

the disposition of property to the next generation. Thus, the way in which women approach inheritance, especially women who no longer have a partner to consider, has potentially far-reaching social consequences. The

differences between married and widowed women testators also have implications for our study in terms of what they say about marriage and its effect
on women as testators, a point to which we shall return.

When we separate out the two categories we see that widows name their
own children as beneficiaries much more frequently than do married
women. To some extent this is expected, as children 'replace' a deceased
husband as the main beneficiaries of a widow's estate. What is more striking is that they also include siblings, nieces and nephews, and affines to a
much greater extent (Table 7.3). Significant differences are also evident
when we look at the way property is divided. The most common practice
amongst married women is to bequeath their estate in its entirety.
However, widowed women divide their property into a variety of gifts.
They include bequests of cash and personal property more frequently than
married women (Table 7.4).

Taken together, these patterns would seem to suggest that, once women
no longer have a partner they tend to use inheritance in a rather different
way. They acknowledge a wider range of relationships and do so in ways
which distinguish gifts more individually for each beneficiary. We do
acknowledge the possibility that the same pattern applies to widowers by
comparison with married men. Unfortunately we cannot make a direct
check on that since widowers are seldom identified as such in their wills.
However, our justification for focusing specifically on the actions of
widows as important rests upon women's greater longevity. For the majority of couples in Britain it is likely to be the widow rather than the widower
who makes the final decision about the disposal of the couple's assets.

Our wills data provide a starting point on which to base substantive
questions about gender, marriage and inheritance. However, we are aware
that wills represent only the formal side of inheritance, and arguably are
less important in understanding inheritance than is an analysis of informal
inheritance processes – embodied in spoken and 'understood' arrangements – since only a third of the population actually write a will (Law
Society, 1991). So we now turn to our interview data to examine more
informal outcomes and processes.

Our interview data demonstrate the importance of the distinction
between formal and informal means of passing on property in understanding women's distinctive approach to inheritance and, in particular,
women's use of inheritance as a means of acknowledging a wider range of
relationships as indicated by the wills data. When we look at what women
do from the perspective of our interview data, we see that they appear to
use informal means of distribution to acknowledge relationships in a way
that men do not. This is strongly reminiscent of the theme of kin-keeping,

Table 7.3 *Inclusion of selected beneficiaries in wills by women's marital status (comparing married women with widows)*

	Married women		Widows		Total	
	n	*(%)*	*n*	*(%)*	*n*	*(%)*
Child(ren)	18	(25)	95	(63)	113	(51)
Sibling(s)	5	(7)	27	(18)	32	(14)
Niece/nephew(s)	6	(8)	35	(23)	41	(18)
Affine(s)	2	(3)	33	(22)	35	(16)

Table 7.4 *Ways of bequeathing estate by women's marital status (comparing married women with widows)*

	Married women		Widows		Total	
	n	*(%)*	*n*	*(%)*	*n*	*(%)*
(i) Whether estate divided*						
Total estate	47	(65)	46	(31)	93	(42)
Estate divided	25	(35)	104	(69)	129	(58)
Total	72	(100)	150	(100)	222	(100)
(ii) Specific gifts in divided estates*						
Cash	16	(64)	75	(50)	91	(41)
Personal property	14	(56)	52	(35)	66	(30)

*See Table 7.1.

the long-observed phenomenon that women typically are more active than men in keeping alive contacts with family members, and in initiating actions which will lubricate and sustain kin relationships (Firth *et al.* 1969; Cheal, 1988; Finch and Mason, 1993). It would appear that kin-keeping is also reflected in matters of inheritance. In our interview data we can see this happening in two ways. First, in the passing on of property during a woman's lifetime and second, through women's actions in dealing with other people's property following the death of that person.

WOMEN AND LIFETIME GIFTS

Lifetime gifts are, by definition, excluded from wills since they have been passed on before the testator's death and, in some sense, in anticipation of it. Thus it is quite possible for the pattern of distribution of lifetime gifts to be different from the formal distribution of an estate as reflected in a will.

This indeed seems to be the case when we look at the data from our interview study. Where women had made a will, what they told us about its contents tended to be in line with our wills data. For example, hardly any married women were including anyone beyond their own line of descent, in addition to a spouse. But in talking about lifetime gifts, they brought in a much wider range. Women spoke frequently about wanting a niece or nephew to have something of theirs but they did not necessarily have a bequest in a will in mind. It appeared that they were thinking instead of informal arrangements, where property is passed on during the giver's lifetime. Of course it may be difficult sometimes to work out whether gifts to younger relatives are being seen as part of the process of passing on property, or as other types of gift. However, we found that our interviewees often were quite explicit. The passing on of property in this way seems to be a course of action characteristic of women in particular, but which men reported rarely. In our whole data set we only have one example of a man, Toby Wallace, a never married man in his late 60s, who frequently gives property to relatives. However, we have numerous examples of women passing on items of their own property and, in the case of widows, passing on property which formerly belonged to their husbands but which is now theirs.

The nature of these gifts, and the manner and circumstances under which they tend to be passed on, suggests that they represent a more personal way of passing on property for women than is the case with formal inheritance. Indeed, there are several unique characteristics to this kind of transfer: the giver is able to personally take part in the giving; there is room for negotiation in that the recipient may be offered a choice of gift; the items involved tend to be small and have a personal rather than a monetary value. Often these are gifts which do not fit common perceptions of 'inheritable property' but which, nevertheless, clearly have a value to those involved. It is this involvement of the two concerned parties which is important here, for such gifts can be seen to be a token of the affection between the giver and the receiver. Thus, the passing on of property during a woman's lifetime can be seen as a symbolic way of acknowledging relationships, particularly powerful since it entails symbolism of the continuation of family relationships over time and across generations. It seems to us to be both an important and a logical extension of women's kin-keeping role.

WOMEN AND OTHER PEOPLE'S PROPERTY

The second way in which women use inheritance informally relates to their handling of someone else's property, (after the death of a parent, for example). This occurs quite frequently, especially when someone has died without writing a will. Under intestacy laws a spouse and/or children will inherit the property in most cases, and this normally means that agreement needs to be reached on how different items will be disposed of. Our interview data suggest that women play a prominent role here.

Again, we see this as an extension of kin-keeping, in that the distribution of someone's property after their death can be seen as a way of confirming the relationship of the recipient to the deceased. The phrase 'keeping it in the family' has a symbolic as well as a material meaning here. Our study contains a number of examples of how women use inheritance in this way to hold the family together. Men's involvement in sorting out someone's affairs after their death tended to be limited to the practical arrangements of organising the funeral and dealing with banks and similar organisations. However, it was generally women who were taking decisions about what was to happen to specific items of property, decisions which were charged with responsibility to the deceased and to those left behind, as we have argued elsewhere (Finch and Hayes, 1994).

An example of this process is afforded by the experience of Shirley Scott-Parker. When Shirley's mother died it fell to her and her sisters to sort out their mother's property. Shirley's brothers did not get involved, however, her sister Sharon felt strongly that they ought to have something belonging to their mother and when they failed to say which items they wanted took it upon herself to put together a parcel of items for them:

Shirley: Well we asked them . . . 'Is there anything that you want?', and
     er no, there was nothing in particular that they wanted, so our Sharon
     insisted that they have something. So I think she just put two piles of
     things together, like, and 'Do you want that?' you know.

In dividing up and distributing someone else's property in this way these women were taking responsibility on themselves to see that things were done properly and fairly. Making sure that everyone received something, and employing concepts of fairness and equality in the process, served the dual purpose of defusing any potential family conflict and counteracting any feelings of exclusion which may have existed had the property not been shared out in this way. In distributing property amongst the family, women apparently seek to consolidate a sense of family unity and belonging. Their actions serve as a reaffirmation of the relationship between the deceased and the person receiving the gift, and a reaffirmation of the relationship between the distributor and the receiver.

So what we see from our interview data is how women are able to use inheritance informally to reinforce family relationships. The sharing of inheritance through the passing on of items of jewellery and other personal property by women underscores the notion that for women relationships are on-going and that inheritance is a way of extending and continuing that relationship, even after death.

THE ACT OF BEQUEATHING: GENDERED MEANINGS

The kin-keeping phenomenon which we note above suggests that women play a key role in operationalising the symbolic meanings associated with passing on property after a death. But we can go further than this. Our interview data demonstrate how women and men attach fundamentally different meanings to the act of bequeathing. Here we focus on the question: What is the core concern which women express when they talk about bequeathing in comparison to men? In order to draw out the gender differences in approach here we will concentrate upon those interviews in the study where husbands and wives (or partners) were included in the study but interviewed separately. We have eleven such couples. Our reason for focusing on these interviews in this section is that the dynamics of individual interviews are somewhat different to those where couples are interviewed together (a choice which we gave our interviewees). In the latter instances partners frequently prompt, remind or contradict each other. Separate interviews with each partner in a couple therefore demonstrate particularly well the different emphases which men and women in a similar position place on the need for, and purpose of, a will.

Although the reasons which men and women give for having a will are essentially practical, there are significant differences in what that means to men and women. Out of the eleven couples who were interviewed separately, seven contain clear examples of women who see inheritance in terms of their children's or grand-children's needs, and, importantly, in terms of their need for care as much as their need for material security. By contrast, their husbands spoke about inheritance as the disposal and division of property and referred to the problems which can occur if this is not properly organised through the mechanism of a will.

We will give one example from this sub-set of wills, where the contrast between husband and wife shows clearly. Wendy and Souresh Khan are in their early forties with two teenage sons. Wendy owns and runs a sweet shop and Souresh is a GP. Though Souresh is of Asian descent, and Hindu by religion, we found that his approach to inheritance was very much closer to the white men in our interview study than to some other interviewees of Asian descent. The Khans had written their first will about 10 years ago when their sons were 8 and 6. Wendy was quite clear that this had been prompted by concern for her children's welfare, in the event of her own and her husband's sudden death.

> The reason for doing it was that at that particular time if, like I say, if anything happened to us that the children should be looked after. . . . The thing that we thought most about was if anything happened to us what would happen to these two chaps?

By contrast Souresh, like other male interviewees, reflected different concerns in relation to making a will, principally financial, and focused on the disposal of his property:

Interviewer: Can you think back to your first will, can you remember why you decided to make a will in the first place?
Souresh: I think, I think mainly listening to, or reading the papers and erm, how people got into trouble. I think that something like that spurred us on.

The children/property contrast is reflected in other cases in our study, and in the majority where we can compare the separate accounts of married or cohabiting partners. This is not to say that our male interviewees lack concern for their children. Both men and women were clear that their children should have priority where inheritance is concerned. Rather it is to say that men appear to see the security of their children in different terms to that of their wives.

Exploring our data in this way indicates that seemingly straightforward patterns in the wills, which on the surface would seem to indicate similarities between men and women, are actually underpinned by substantial gendered variations in the meanings associated with bequeathing. Thus our interview data offer an insight into those aspects of inheritance which are not readily apparent from a study of wills alone. From the interview data, it appears that women and men associate fundamentally different meanings with the act of bequeathing. This applies both to the writing of a formal will and (as we showed in the previous section) to the way in which women use informal means of passing on property.

DISPOSAL OF PROPERTY: ISSUES OF OWNERSHIP AND POWER

At this point in the paper we have exposed something of a paradox. At the level of meaning it seems that there are clear differences between the ways women and men approach inheritance. This is most evident in relation to what we have called 'informal' methods of disposing of property. However, the formal method of disposing of an estate, through writing a will, typically results in very similar patterns of disposal for male and female testators. Herein lies the paradox: though we see significant differences between women and men at the level of meaning, those differences are not reflected in outcomes, at least not in formal outcomes.

In order to explore this paradox further, we return to the important insight from our wills, namely that there are some statistically significant differences between the wills of widows and those of married women, with widows tending to adopt a pattern of bequests which acknowledge a much wider set of relationships, more in line with patterns of informal disposal adopted by many women, whether married, widowed or single. This suggests that married women, in writing their wills, may be under some constraint to fall into line with the pattern of disposal favoured by their husbands whereas widows, freed from such constraints, write rather different types of wills. It may well be that, a century after having first gained the right to own and dispose of property, married women remain less than equal partners in such decisions.

The growing body of British literature on power in marriage, especially over the disposal of money coming into a household, can help us to generate some insights into how this works. That literature would lead us to expect that women and men are not necessarily on precisely equal terms when it comes to controlling how assets are used (Delphy and Leonard, 1986; Pahl, 1989; Morris, 1990). In particular, Jan Pahl's (1989) influential empirical work indicates that there are variations between different couples in the ways in which money is managed, and that some variations entail a greater degree of real equality in decisions about spending money than do others. Her work also confirms that of previous researchers, in linking those variations to the relative power of women outside the household. In crude terms, women who themselves had a job were much more likely to have real influence over the disposal of 'joint' resources than were women who were currently not in paid work.

With these findings in mind, we return briefly to our interview data. In this section we are going to use data from all nineteen cases in our study (representing thirty-eight individuals) where we have interviewed both partners in a married or cohabiting heterosexual couple. Eleven of these were interviewed separately and eight together, by their own choice. From these cases we can ask: Is there any evidence that decisions about the disposal of 'joint' property after death follow a similar pattern to that observed in studies of decisions over other aspects of money within marriages? We do not have the kind of sample which would enable us make statistical generalisations about predominant patterns. However, our findings are broadly in line with what one would expect to find in a larger sample. This is certainly true in the sense that there is – even amongst nineteen couples – apparently quite wide variation in the ways in which matters concerned with inheritance are approached.

We have examined these nineteen cases to see how far each couple's process of decision-making appeared to reflect gendered patterns of inequality, looking especially for whether men take the lead in practice. In nine cases the couple had not really tackled inheritance as a sufficiently live issue for them, to enable us to discern which would take the lead in practice. Two of those were couples who adhered to the Muslim faith, who indicated that their assets would be disposed of according to the guidelines laid down by Islamic law.

Of the other ten, we detected an interestingly varied pattern. There were four cases where a woman appeared to defer to her male partner, allowing him to take the lead in practice in decisions about inheritance. There was one case which was the mirror image of this, where a man appeared to allow his wife to take the lead. In four cases, we felt that the interview contained positive evidence to support the couple's claim to joint decision-making – the topic of inheritance had been discussed, views aired and a joint approach agreed. In the final case, a woman seemed to have acted rather independently of her partner, in that she had written a will but he had not. There was no obvious pattern linking these cases to whether the woman was in paid work, but perhaps that is not surprising in a relatively small sample.[4]

To illustrate something of the dynamics of inheritance decisions within couple relationships, we are going to examine in some detail the case of the Hiltons. This has distinctive features, and in some senses is the most extreme of the four cases where men clearly took the lead. Roy and Julie Hilton are a married couple in their mid-forties, both self employed, Roy as an electrician and Julie as proprietor of a craft shop. They have two sons and a daughter, all of whom are young adults, and one grandchild. Both are very interested in inheritance, which clearly has been a live issue in their own extended family at various points over the last few years.

From the perspective of this paper, the distinctive thing about them is that Roy's family has, apparently for several generations, had what amounts to a family policy on bequeathing. That policy is that assets should always pass down the blood line. He explains it this way:

Roy: My side of the family have always been very careful to ensure that the money stayed in the Hilton's hands. To clarify that, one of my uncles married but he didn't produce any children. So he left his money and his property – which was quite substantial in its day – to his family, which was my father and his brother, rather than go to his wife's family. . . . They've always made sure that it stayed in the blood line rather than go anywhere else.

The tradition of excluding wives from benefiting directly from inheritance extended also to their exclusion from any family discussion related to inheritance. Roy said that his own mother had been expected to leave the room whenever the matter was discussed and the wife of Roy's uncle (cited above) knew nothing about the terms of her husband's will until after his death. Roy explained:

Roy: She was most annoyed when the will was read thirty years ago.
Julie: Mind, I can understand that.
Roy: What he did, he left everything in trust to her . . . well, she had the interest for the rest of her life but after that it then passed back into our family. She was not happy about that.

Roy's own wife Julie obviously has some reservations about this, as is apparent from her interjection above ('Mind, I can understand that'). This is evident also in other parts of the interview. Roy's father had died intestate and during the interview the couple engaged in a lengthy disagreement about how he would have written a will, Roy insisting that his mother would not have been given full control of her husband's estate. Roy and Julie have not written a will themselves. However, Roy also intimated several times that he would like to follow the Hilton tradition, which would effectively mean that his assets would be bequeathed to his children, with Julie entitled to the income only from a trust established during her lifetime. Roy's style in the interview is one which can perhaps best be described as jokey provocation (of his wife *inter alia*), so it is difficult to disentangle how far his comments reflect the likely outcome in practice. But it is difficult to believe that comments such as the following have no bearing upon the dynamics of marital interactions over inheritance:

Roy: To me it is the right way to do it. I don't see why it should go to someone else's family. It is family money. In mean the nobility . . . make sure that it stays in their line. They're doing the same thing. it's the natural thing to do.

Roy   [referring to the way in which his grandfather had written his will]: There is no way it could ever go out of that [i.e. the family]. Marvellous. I would do the same thing.

Our conclusion is that there is indeed some sociological mileage to be gained by examining women's actions as testators in relation to the operation of power in marriage (and marriage-like) relationships. On the basis of our evidence, we would expect further exploration to show that the range of ways in which it is handled reflects a similar picture to that produced by studies of the management of money in marriage. If we are correct, the extent to which processes of deciding about inheritance are gendered is probably rather variable. Some women (like Julie Hilton) will be in a subordinate position in practice. Others would appear to be more able to operate as testators on the same terms as men, even when they are part of a heterosexual couple. However, we need to balance that conclusion with a recognition that, in terms of formal outcomes, our wills data suggest that women tend to fall into line with men if they are still married when their will is actually written.

CONCLUSION

We began this paper by exploring the question of whether women's approach to bequeathing their property is different from men's. In the course of exploring this question through our empirical data, we have found it important to make the distinction between formal and informal methods of disposing of property following, or in anticipation of, death. Our main conclusions are four-fold.

First, it would seem that women's ability in practice to act as testators on the same terms as men is by no means guaranteed, especially if they are living as part of a married, or cohabiting heterosexual, couple. As with all questions about power over the disposal of resources in such relationships, there is considerable variability in the way in which different couples approach inheritance. But the balance of our evidence, especially about the formal outcomes of inheritance decisions as expressed in a written will, suggests a tendency for married women to fall into line with a pattern of disposal which is similar to men's but different in significant ways from that which we find in the wills of widows.

Second, whatever happens in relation to decisions about how a will is written, it is clear that women take a strong and active lead in the informal ways of distributing property. They do this in advance of their own deaths, and they act as distributors of other people's property when, for example, a family member has died without making a will. Men appear to engage in these informal distribution activities much more rarely.

Third, the ways in which women approach inheritance suggest that they associate meanings with the act of bequeathing which are different from men's. Whereas men see it as an economic issue concerning the disposal of financial resources and material property, women tend to see inheritance in the context of close relationships, and use it as a means of consolidating these, and of acknowledging their practical and symbolic significance. For men bequeathing is about control of assets. However, for women it is much more subtle than that. It is about managing relationships, effected mainly through informal mechanisms of inheritance which reflect women's kin-keeping activities in other spheres of family life.

Finally, given that the meanings associated with bequeathing are strongly gendered and that widows, freed from the constraints of their male partners, appear to use their wills in a way more characteristic of women's approach to inheritance, it is important to remind ourselves of the differences in life expectancy between women and men. Since there is a clear tendency for women to outlive their male partners, and in a context in which the ownership of property is spread much more widely amongst the British population than ever before, clearly it is going to be widows who increasingly are deciding on the disposal of property to the next generation. As part of a couple, they may have had a less than equal say in decisions about inheritance. But many such women, none the less, will be able to have the last word.

Notes

1. We are aware that the feminine of testator is testatrix but use testator throughout the paper since that is the term which is more widely understood.
2. The sample was constructed on the basis of quotas which represent a range of life experiences. It is designed to enable us to compare women and men; people who do and do not have experience of will-making; being a beneficiary, executing a will; people who are first generation home owners and people whose families have owned property in previous generations; people who have experience of an elderly person buying residential care or sheltered housing.
3. It is not a requirement that the marital status of a testator be stated in a will and consequently many wills do not give this information directly. We therefore developed categories which separated out knowledge from presumed marital status. Of those testators that do state marital status clearly, the majority are women. Hence we were able to categorise known spinsters, married women and widows more easily than their male counterparts. Where marital status was not given, a number of clues in the will were used, for example a testator naming a spouse as a beneficiary (especially where it appeared that the spouse was to receive the major part of the estate) was categorised as married when the will was written. Alternatively, wills which included children and/or grandchildren but which did not bequeath to a spouse were placed into our 'presumed single/widowed/divorced' category.
4. As a small but important methodological point, it is also worth recording that there is no clear relationship between where a couple appears in this categorisation and whether they were interviewed together or separately. We cannot comment systematically on whether the approach which each of these couples took to decisions about inheritance reflected their management of money in general, since we did not ask questions about the latter topic. But where we do have some sense of this, there does seem to be such an alignment.

References

Central Statistical Office (1993), *Social Trends 23* (London: HMSO).

Cheal, D. (1988), *The Gift Economy* (London: Routledge).

Cretney, S. (1992), *Elements of Family Law,* 2nd edn (London).

Delphy, C. and Leonard, D. (1986),'Class Analysis, Gender Analysis and the Family', in Crompton, R. and Mann, M. (eds), *Gender and Stratification* (Cambridge: Polity).

Engels, F. (1985), *The Family, Private Property and the State* (Harmondsworth: Penguin; first published 1884).

Firth, R., Hubert, J. and Forge, A (1969), *Families and Their Relatives* (London: Routledge).

Finch, J. and Hayes, L. (1994), 'Inheritance, Houses and the Concept of Home', *Sociology*, vol. 28, pp. 417–33.

Finch, J. and Mason, J. (1993), *Negotiating Family Responsibilities* (London: Routledge).

Forrest, R. and Murie, A. (1989), 'Differential Accumulation: Wealth Inheritance and Housing Policy Reconsidered', *Policy and Politics*, vol. 17:1, pp. 25–79.

Forrest, R., Murie, A. and Williams, P. (1990), *Home Ownership: Differentiation and Fragmentation* (London: Unwin Hyman).

Hamnett, C., Harmer, M. and Williams, P. (1991), *Safe as Houses: Housing Inheritance in Britain* (London: Paul Chapman).

Holcombe, L. (1983), *Wives and Property* (Oxford: Martin Robertson).

Law Society(1991), 'Taking Wills to Market', *Law Society's Gazzette*, vol. 88:39, pp. 4–5.

Lewis, J. (1984), *Women in England 1870–1950* (Brighton: Wheatsheaf).

Morris, L. (1990), *The Workings of the Household* (Cambridge: Polity).

Pahl, J. (1989), *Money and Marriage* (London: Macmillan).

Wilson, G. (1987), *Money in the Family: Financial Organisation and Women's Responsibility* (Aldershot: Avebury).

Part II
Domesticity and Intimacy

8 Can we Research the Private Sphere?

Methodological and Ethical Problems in the Study of the Role of Intimate Emotion in Personal Relationships

JEAN DUNCOMBE and DENNIS MARSDEN[*]

In the classic discussion from which this conference took its title, C. Wright Mills (1959) argued that the sociological imagination works on the distinction between 'the personal troubles of milieu' and 'the public issues of social structure', giving as one of his examples marriage. Our paper takes up this theme, describing some of the sociological, methodological, philosophical and ethical problems raised by research including our own (Duncombe and Marsden, 1993a, 1993b, 1995a, 1995b) on intimate couple relationships. Our research is in line with the recent theoretical shifts which have focused attention on the nature of interpersonal relationships in contemporary society and have emphasised the need for a greater understanding of the interconnections between the 'public' and the 'private' spheres of social life. There is a new urgency in attempting to research intimate personal experience, in order to resuscitate and re-theorise areas such as changing family bonds and other newer forms of close relationships (Morgan, 1985, 1990; Clark and Haldane, 1990) but also as an essential contribution to broader theories of society (Cheal, 1991; Giddens, 1991, 1992).

It is a cliché that modern marriage is in a state of crisis, with increasing rates of marital breakdown and divorce, more cohabitation prior to, but also as an alternative to, marriage, and an increase in births outside wedlock. Tensions have arisen because the move from an emphasis on the institutional framework of marriage to a stress on the couple's personal relationship (Morgan, 1990), and women's increased participation in the labour market, have brought a sharper feminist scrutiny to traditional inequalities in the domestic division of labour and finance.

*We gratefully acknowledge ESRC funding (grant no. R000 23 2737) for our study of couple relationships. There is a description of the pilot stage of our research in Duncombe and Marsden (1993)

141

However, recently a number of writers have pointed to a deeper crisis in the emotional basis of the modern heterosexual couple relationship. For example, Giddens has argued that increasingly in late modern society people (especially women) are seeking the ideal of 'the pure relationship' characterised by an intimacy achieved through emotional openness and disclosure (Giddens, 1992). He suggests that such relationships were pioneered by women with women, but women are now seeking similar relationships with men, only to be frustrated by men's unreconstructed dominative and coercive sexuality. Rubin too identifies a gulf between the all-pervasive media image of sexual and emotional fulfilment through relationships, and the lived reality of men's and women's everyday experience of coupledom (Rubin, 1991). She points to the contradictions and tensions inherent in the ideal of *self-*fulfilment through a relationship *with another*. And of course currently we are in the middle of several interlocking moral panics concerning the 'selfishness' of individuals who renege on their duties to their partners or offspring: for example, marital breakdown, absentee fathers, and single and working mothers are all being identified as causes or evidence of major failures in private morality which threaten to undermine not only public morality but the very stability of society (Murray, 1990; Dennis and Erdos, 1992).

Clearly, in order to gain a greater understanding of how the private troubles of heterosexual couples contribute to the public issues of marital and family breakdown, we need to probe beneath the couple's public image and attempt to enter the private sphere of the intimate couple relationship. In this paper, we pose questions as to how far it is practically possible and ethically desirable to explore the role of intimate emotion in close personal relationships. And we show how such explorations will require a more complex conceptualisation of the private sphere than the conventional view that it consist merely of 'secrets' to which people in close relationships are privy but which they are reluctant to disclose to outsiders.

As part of our exploration of the private we will also seek a deeper understanding of the nature of the stories or narratives which couples and individuals construct about their relationships, and we aim to throw some light on current debates as to the validity of narrative material gained via interviews (Denzin, 1989; Atkinson, 1990; Stacey, 1990).

INTERVIEWING TACTICS TO PROMOTE DISCLOSURE

Such is the intimacy and privacy of family life in complex industrial societies that (with several notable exceptions – see Stacey, 1990) researchers have usually taken the view that it is scarcely possible to participate in and directly observe private family life (Larossa *et al.*, 1981). Indeed, Henry claimed that as an onlooker rather than a participant, he was better able to observe and interpret what was going on than family members themselves (Gubrium and Holstein, 1990). Accordingly, until comparatively recently sociologists have viewed the problems of researching the private sphere rather conventionally and tactically in terms of interview method: how to establish a degree of trust and rapport sufficient for respondents to disclose personal information of which they are fully aware but which they would normally prefer to keep to themselves. However, in relation to couples, we need to discuss not merely what are the best techniques for persuading people to disclose sensitive personal information, but also how the process of interviewing affects what is disclosed and whose subjective reality we are interested in.

Some researchers have favoured repeated interviews (Bott, 1957; Burgoyne and Clark, 1984); for example, Burgoyne and Clark describe how Clark went to considerable lengths to get to know the stepfamilies in their study, through making several visits, dropping in for tea, buying the children birthday cards and so on. On the other hand, Brannen makes the case that people are more likely to disclose personally sensitive information if they know that the interviewer will remain a stranger, so that it is best to reassure interviewees that the in-depth disclosure, whilst elicited through a fairly lengthy interview, will be strictly a one-off occasion with no embarassing follow-ups (Brannen, 1988).

Opinions also differ as to how far, in the pursuit of informality, interviews themselves need to be totally informal and unstructured. Some earlier family researchers favoured a semi-structured approach (Bott, 1957; Voysey, 1975), Bott in particular describing how her initial attempts to keep the interview sessions completely unstructured seemed to make her respondents puzzled and suspicious as to what she was after: they became happier when she began to ask her questions more formally and to write down their answers openly. However, less-structured approaches need not seem aimless, and there are strong advocates of informal approaches which seek to make the interview non-directive yet, nevertheless, like an extended 'conversation with a purpose' (Weiss, 1975; Brannen, 1988). Oakley has further argued that to gain any degree of insight into people's lives, rather than being unequal and one-sided interrogations, interviews must be interactive, with an equal exchange of personal views and information (Oakley, 1981). Although Oakley argues the case specifically for women *not* formally 'interviewing' women, there seems to be a convincing argument that more generally where researchers – women or men – are looking for disclosures from people's private lives, interviews need to be as interactive as possible. However, while this approach seems likely to promote greater disclosure among women, as Wise has pointed out, the fact of shared womanhood does not necessarily transcend barriers of social class, colour, circumstance and power over the material produced by the interview (Wise, 1987).

We would also note that it does not automatically follow that to gain personal information from men the interviewer must be male. Men may be more willing to discuss the intimacies of their sex-lives with another man, but the literature on male non-disclosure suggests that men have relatively more difficulty than women in recognising and labelling their feelings, and also in discussing those feelings with male friends (Brannen and Collard, 1982; Ingham, 1984; Brannen, 1988; Mansfield and Collard, 1988; Duncombe and Marsden, 1993b, 1994). Indeed men may disclose their emotions more to female confidantes with whom they associate the emotional side of life – although, as McKee's work shows, the situation of women interviewing men can sometimes bring its own distortions, difficulties or even dangers (McKee and O'Brien, 1983).

Where, as in our work, we are interested in couples, the key question is how best to promote disclosure about the couple relationship itself. Some earlier work assumed that where couple relationships were basically 'conjugal' (Bott, 1957), 'companionate' (Berger and Kellner, 1970) or 'symmetrical' (Young and Willmott, 1973), the private sphere was the personal experience of the relationship which the couple shared. This view would imply that it is sufficient to interview the couple together (Bott, 1957; Voysey, 1975) or even to interview only one partner. However, recognition of a possible conflict of views came with the rise of feminism, a greater interest in the causes of divorce, and Jessie Bernard's proposition that every marriage (or close relationship) may in fact be regarded as two, 'his' and 'hers' (Bernard, 1972). Research into the private sphere of emotion must therefore face the possibility that couples do not merely share secrets which they wish to conceal from outsiders, but that as individuals they may have quite different perspectives on their relationship, even to the extent of each holding secrets or views which they wish to conceal *from the other.*

To some extent this problem of differing individual views or secrets may be skirted by interviewing the couple separately with assurances of confidentiality, and indeed most work on the family has been carried out by means of individual interviews, albeit partly from an unquestioning stance that the individual is the basis of research (Allan, 1980). In these circumstances it might be suggested that couples with more segregated relationships will be more truthful about their private lives (Allan, 1980) and, indeed, this practice pays off where separate interviews reveal rather different accounts of the domestic division of labour or household finance (Brannen and Wilson, 1987; Pahl, 1989; Morris, 1990). However, paradoxically, it may sometimes be middle class couples with outwardly more conjugal relationships who are prepared in private to acknowledge their different perspectives, and Morris comments that in her research, working-class couples were more likely to use the joint interview to air disagreements, whereas in separate interviews each partner appeared to censor what they said on the basis of loyalty to their partner.[2] And, of course, the relationship between the interview situation and disclosure may vary depending upon *what* is to be disclosed.

The issue of whether to conduct joint or separate interviews therefore seems far from cut and dried. Indeed Allen advocates deliberately interviewing couples together, on the grounds that if the primary focus is the couple's *relationship* rather than their individual stories, 'the interaction of the couple as they create their accounts . . . provides the researcher with material he [*sic*] would not otherwise obtain . . . one spouse can contradict the idealised statements of the other and deny the reality the latter is trying to signify' (Allen, 1980, p. 207). Allen argues that by being aware, as one partner speaks, of what the other spouse is saying or doing, of expression, gesture and noises off, the interviewer may gain insights into the private marital relationship and how the couple deal with disagreements.

Faced with this dilemma of joint or separate interviews, in our own research we felt it best to adopt a flexible strategy. We began with the intention of conducting quite a short joint interview before splitting the couples for separate individual same-sex interviews, to be followed by a brief reunion and winding down (whose purpose we will describe in more detail below). However, we were so impressed by the amount of information gained in some of the joint interviews that we decided to adopt a more flexible approach so as to let the joint interview run longer if it seemed likely to be fruitful. It is difficult to generalise about which interviews benefit from such an approach, but we would suggest that the most fruitful involve couples where one or both partners are committed to a degree of 'truth-telling' about the relationship (Duncombe and Marsden, 1995).

Finally, we may also report our own experience with pilot group discussion, which suggests that the private sphere may not always be quite as private as one might suppose. As far as possible our discussion groups were kept below ten in number, with a predominance of women – who otherwise tend to get swamped by men, but who are also more used to discussing emotion and relationships and disclosing to one another (Duncombe and Marsden, 1993b). We need to maintain the usual caution concerning the way that groups tend to express majority and strongly-held views whilst those in a minority or with weakly-held views tend to stay silent (Banks, 1959;

Morgan, 1990). Nevertheless, the group situation seemed helpful in encouraging or giving permission for individuals to talk about quite intimate details of their emotional and sexual lives, revealing to the women that what they had previously thought were their own private troubles (of emotional loneliness in heterosexual relationships) were actually fairly widely shared.

However, confirmation that groups may develop powerful and not always benevolent dynamics of their own was provided by several incidents where a group tended to ridicule or pillory its more 'sentimental' or 'romantic' members, and the ethical problems of our research came dramatically to the fore when one participant first became silent and distressed, then attempted to speak but burst into tears and had to be led away from the discussion weeping. Clearly, for group discussions as well as individual interviews there may on occasion be a need for the researcher to engage in more active intervention and guidance, and the discussion should end with a 'therapeutic' period (see below).

ETHICAL ISSUES IN DISCLOSURE

Unfortunately, the more effective the interview in persuading respondents to disclose their private secrets, the greater the ethical problems posed for the interviewer. For example, Wise argues that the goal of equal interaction in interviews is illusory because ultimately the interviewer retains the power to walk away with information from which – perhaps partly to further her own research career – she will shape and publish a version of the respondent's life, with consequences which cannot be fully known and controlled and which may not be beneficial to all respondents who do not necessarily have shared interests (Wise, 1987; see also Kelly, 1992; Stacey, 1990). This problem cannot be dealt with by the negotiation of 'informed consent' since, even with the best will in the world, the interviewer cannot provide enough information about the purpose and processes of research and publication to bring respondents fully within her or his frame or reference.

Larossa has pointed to the further obstacles to the negotiation of informed consent, inherent in the exploratory character of qualitative research which constantly changes focus in the interview itself as information is disclosed, and which (we would add) changes focus again in ways the researcher cannot anticipate during the later processes of data analysis (Larossa *et al.*, 1981). As a result, the researcher will inevitably pick up or be told things not covered in the original formal request or interview 'contract', yet it is not practicable to provide informants with a full description of the purposes of the research (some of which will be unrecognised, covert or yet to be discovered) at the outset of the interview, or for consent to be continuously renegotiated as the interviews and the interviewer's perspective develop.

There are also situations where unstructured or qualitative research interviews may take a form or direction that leads respondents to betray more of their private selves than they would upon reflection wish to expose to the gaze of an interviewer or indeed their partner. Larossa suggests that there are particular dangers in joint interviews because, although couples may have a formal or tacit mutual agreement about what they will reveal or conceal, in a freely-ranging interview an unforeseen turn of discussion may bring about disagreements which expose private tensions. Although researchers tend to worry about protecting the identity of informants from recognition by outsiders, as the discussion by Larossa *et al.* points out, a worse betrayal of confidence may arise from the exposure of the family or the couple *to themselves*. These authors agree with Barnes's comment that, 'We know almost nothing about the effects of research on our respondents' and they quote one women who said that she had merely wanted 'a little light to see by' but instead felt 'pounded by a thousand suns' (Larossa *et al.*, 1981, p. 310). Larossa *et al.* suggest this means that subjects' rights to maintain silence or to evade certain areas should be respected, and the interviewer should not probe further or bring inappropriate pressure to bear if the subject is clearly reluctant or uncomfortable with a particular line of questioning. But whether researchers will follow or breach such a self-denying ordinance will depend on how far they persuade themselves that individual revelation will serve some notion of professional integrity and responsibility to uncover deeper layers of experience.

Similar, sometimes more severe ethical problems may arise from the way that interviews have a tendency to turn into therapy sessions where one or other partner forgets or mistakes the purpose of the interview and opens up emotional chasms which cannot then be resealed. Laslett and Rapoport have advocated that the research should consciously seek to become like a therapeutic exercise, with full explanations aimed at enlisting collaboration, repeated interviews, and analysis of the interviews undertaken with the help of an outsider who notes the input of the interviewer and the therapeutic nature of the exchanges (Laslett and Rapoport, 1975). However, these procedures do not escape the ethical problems identified above since, unlike the consensual (or imposed) therapeutic relationships, sociological interviews do not have the sanction from their subjects, their training or society at large to engage in therapy, nor a full appreciation of its possibly disturbing outcomes.

In fact, Clark and Haldane recommend that interviewers in this field of intimate relationships should have training in therapy or counselling skills

(Clark and Haldane, 1990), and in Burgoyne and Clark's study of step-families, Clark undertook the interviewing while Burgoyne remained apart in order to provide a detached view of the interviews (Burgoyne and Clark, 1984). Brannen and Collard took care to try to explain to their respondents the distinctions between interviewing and therapy, but also sometimes used two interviewers, one of whom remained detached and able to intervene if the interview threatened to cross the boundary into therapy (Brannen and Collard, 1982). Brannen also recommends that joint interviews end on a neutral note, where a deliberate attempt is made to return the relationship to the point from which the interview began (Brannen, 1988), although (for reasons we explore below) this outcome seems scarcely attainable. And Larossa also warns of the dangers that the interview may suggest to families who think they're healthy that they need therapy, so that interviewers have a responsibility to provide a debriefing at the end to distance the role of therapy (Larossa *et al.*, 1981). Kelly argues that interviewers have a duty to take on board the possibility that the interview may raise disturbing emotions, and for this reason she advocates follow-up conversations to assist respondents in talking through the aftermath of the interview (Kelly, 1992). Clearly, we are working here with a number of very different ideologies concerning the nature of the researcher's involvement with and responsibilities towards participants in the research process.

Finally, another seldom-described aspect of intensive work with couples, is that not only interviewees but also interviewers may themselves need access to therapy, because if the research process probes at all deeply it is likely to unearth issues germane to problems in their own personal lives (Mansfield and Collard, 1988). And certainly in our work with couples it took us some time to realise and accept that what seemed like an inordinate amount of exhumation and discussion of our own relationships should be seen as an integral and necessary part of understanding the relationships of others.

IS THERE AN AUTHENTIC PRIVATE SPHERE TO BE KNOWN – AND IS IT KNOWABLE?

Gubrium and Holstein have recently questioned what they see as the commonly held view upon which much research is based, that family members have privileged or private knowledge about the family (Gubrium and Holstein, 1990). This view, they say, arises because only family members are direct witnesses to the area where the family is supposedly at its most authentic, in its private moments protected by the physical barriers of closed doors and the normative barriers of public belief in the sanctity and inviolacy of the private sphere. As a consequence, the public image of the family is seen as unreal, but it is suggested that a true picture may be obtained if only we can find the key – the research techniques to encourage full disclosure. As a counter to what they regard as this somewhat benign view that family members merely lack awareness, objectivity or insight into the workings of family life, Gubrium and Holstein cite the perspectives of Laing and Jackson, who argue that families operate tacit conspiracies of silence and create a 'fog of family fictions'.

If we were to take these comments fully on board, we would be left with the view that the real private sphere is actually at the level of individuals' pathological or unresolved psychic experiences, distorted by complex patterns of denial or secrecy. Attempts to conduct sociological research by conventional interview methods may merely obtain for the researcher access to another layer of stories, more secret but essentially no more valid than people's public presentation of their lives. From such a perspective, critics of sociology would argue that while there are secrets of the private sphere to be known, the tasks of obtaining access and interpretation would require the techniques and skills of psychotherapy rather than sociology.

An alternative view is retained by those like Skolnick who argue that family members *do* know what occurs backstage behind closed doors. However, each individual family keeps its secrets because family members only see what other families choose to present frontstage and so believe themselves to be unusual: 'One of the discoveries of recent family research is that families have myths, secrets and information processing rules that determine the kind of communication that goes on, what can be said and more important, what can't be said' (Skolnick, 1983).

Faced with these alternative views – that the inner processes of the private sphere are unknown to some or all of the family, that they are pathologically distorted or denied, or that they are known but kept secret because perceived as socially deviant – the question arises whether there is a *sociological* level at which family (or couple) secrets or stories can be explored.

A SOCIOLOGICAL VIEW OF COUPLE STORIES CONCERNING EMOTIONAL LIFE IN THE PRIVATE SPHERE

Our concern to understand the meanings of couples' stories about their relationships intersects with some of the wider current methodological issues in relation to the ethnographic collection of people's accounts of their lives. There has rightly been a move away from earlier realist ethnographies which 'unreflexively, and thus dishonestly, assume the voice of an omniscient, invisible author who neutrally reports the objective reality of an exotic "other"' (Stacey, 1990, p. 36). The furthest reaction is to treat interview material as stories or fictions which have no privileged status compared with actual works of fiction (for discussion see Denzin, 1989; Atkinson, 1990). However, along with other writers we find this position too 'relativistic and solipsistic' (Stacey, 1990, p. 36). We recognise that ethnographic subjects construct narratives in a dialogic process with the interviewer. Yet we want to argue for a connection between the narrative life as constructed and the life as lived by the subject (Stacey, 1990, p. 37; Stanley and Morgan, 1993, p. 3).

The outermost layers of the public–private divide appear in how couples or families present an image of their intimate relationship to various audiences of kin and friends, and here we can see one overarching story pattern. Burgoyne and Clark have observed, 'even private testimonies given in research interviews are themselves publicly-scripted' (Burgoyne and Clark, 1984, p. 33) and earlier Voysey offered pioneering insights as to how families shaped their interview responses in order to conform to an ideal of the normal family (Voysey, 1975). The key influence in couples' stories appears to be the desire to conform to the model of the happy, sharing companionate relationship – perhaps not always Giddens's 'pure relationship' but at least the ideal of companionate marriage (Mansfield and Collard, 1988). Other researchers have noted that in the interests of presenting such an image, women in particular have been prepared to misreport their husbands' pathetically small input to the household (Brannen and Moss, 1991; Coward, 1992; Duncombe and Marsden, 1993a).

This kind of story, which entails women's collusion in the unequal domestic division of labour, clearly reflects and helps to reproduce gender inequalities of power in the wider society. But can we go any further in understanding the character of the stories that couples construct about their relationship either for one another or for themselves? A fruitful sociological approach to the study of intimate emotion in close personal relationships appears to be offered by the model of the 'social management' of emotion (Hochschild, 1983). Hochschild points out that feelings are to some extent controlled by ideologies operating through 'feeling rules' which prescribe how people *ought* to feel in different social and emotional situations. In accordance with these feeling rules, individuals, may try to 'act' the emotions appropriate to particular situations, an effort which Hochschild calls 'emotional labour' or 'emotion work'.

The best discussion of story-construction by women is Hochschild's account of how working wives come to terms with the failure of their husbands to take into account women's double shift by assuming their fair share of domestic chores (Hochschild, 1990). She argues that in most relationships, couples (but especially women) come to live by a 'family myth', a 'mild delusional system' which functions to obscure the women's feelings of resentment at their husbands' lack of participation in housework and childcare (Hochschild, 1990, p. 44). Women's active maintenance of the family myth, through strenuous emotion work *on themselves*, is the best they can manage in the face of 'the stalled revolution' of modern feminism, and the myth permits them to hold together a number of very contradictory views on feminism, egalitarian relationships between the sexes and respect for their husbands despite their selfish behaviour. Hochschild comments that women's maintenance of the family myth may be regarded as denial, or alternatively as an act of 'intuitive genius' (Hochschild, 1990, p. 46).

Some women have observed to us that *acting* the family or couple myth actually makes them *feel* more companionable; that is, the ritual public celebration of their coupledom may serve to revivify their private relationship. But how far do individual women come to *believe* the couple myth and persuade themselves that it is true – in effect helping to reproduce the conditions of their own continuing exploitation? Here we can draw further on Hochschild's work, where she distinguishes between different levels of acting in the furtherance of changing emotional states. While they are 'surface acting', people still retain a sense of what their 'real' feelings are. But there are some powerful situations which call upon 'deep acting', where (Hochschild argues) people may no longer recognise whether they are acting or not, and 'deep acted' feeling may substitute for 'authentic' emotion.

In relation to our research, Hochschild's insights may be combined with Vaughan's description of couple relationships at various stages of 'uncoupling' (Vaughan, 1987). According to Vaughan, the first hint of uncoupling comes at the point where one of the couple allows himself or herself to recognise a critical thought concerning the partner. Such a recognition will have been difficult because of powerful impulses to suppress it (impulses stemming, we would say, from the operation of ideologies concerning how love and coupledom *should* feel in this particular relationship). Prior to such a recognition, any adverse thoughts about the relationship will have been handled in various ways so as to deflect criticism from the partner. And even after acknowledgement of the criticism, it may remain as a guilty secret, not to be dwelt on or revealed to the partner, until some further development or incident causes the process to ratchet on and the emotional gap to widen, possibly eventually to the point of breaking up.

To make matters more complex, Vaughan argues that the process of uncoupling which allows one partner to recognise and dwell upon the other's shortcomings, actually leads to a *rewriting* of earlier feelings and experiences. Thus, whilst couples who have broken up will often talk more readily about their feelings towards their partners, researchers should not be fooled into thinking that they are able to recapture how they 'really' felt at the time. In an earlier study, Brannen and Collard describe a similar process among the couples they interviewed, in the way that marital 'difficulties' changed to become defined as marital 'problems' (Brannen and Collard, 1982). Initially, couples 'placed considerable importance on presenting to others, and more importantly to themselves, an apparent consensus, for fear that recognition or definition of an underlying conflict or rift in their relationship might threaten the little security they had in their lives, namely one another' (Brannen and Collard, 1982, p. 102). Difficulties were at first accommodated within the relationship by deflecting blame onto external circumstances, but once the relationship became defined as problematic in the light of later developments, frames of meaning changed and there was a reappraisal (although not necessarily always a complete rewriting) of significant events. Patterns of friendship networks (for example having friends who were happy or, alternatively, troubled) also affected how the couple defined and described their relationship.

If we attempt to follow through how individual or couple myths or stories may change with the decay of love, we might suggest a sequence something like the following (Duncombe and Marsden, 1993a, 1994, 1995). While there is the initial perception of 'being in love' or 'loving', this feeling serves to block out perceptions of any imperfections in the partner or dissatisfactions with the relationship. And even as relationships lose something of their earlier intimacy, women's performance of emotion work seems actively to obscure, both from themselves and from others, any dissatisfaction or exploitaion in the relationship. At some stage in the transformation of the relationship, they may no longer be able to sustain *for themselves* the illusion of happy coupledom, yet they may continue to shallow act for outsiders and even for their partners. Finally, it is only in the later stages of change in the relationship that individuals begin to leak to their partners and to outsiders (not necessarily in that sequence) their recognition of their feelings of exploitation and unhappiness.

In conclusion, we will draw together the implications of what we have been saying for a discussion of the private sphere. Such a multilayered conceptualisation of the stories that individuals tell about their intimate feelings poses severe problems for ethnographic research. Our discussion has made it even clearer that, ultimately, the interviewer who undertakes the task of researching the private must be prepared to carry a burden of responsibility or guilt, to the extent that the research process may persuade – or betray – participants into articulating to their partners or themselves doubts about their relationship which may help to push the process of un-coupling along its course towards break-up.

But as we explore the private sphere, we are also faced with dilemmas concerning *which* layers of stories and feelings we are interested in, and how we are to know whether our informants are offering the conventional couple myth, 'authentic' feeling or (shallow or deep) acting.[2] Rather than the apparently simple public–private dichotomy from which we began – where the private appears to be merely the couple's experience shared behind their closed front door – we need to conceptualise the private sphere as like a Chinese box. The task of the ethnographic interview may then become to determine how many layers of stories there are, what purpose each serves, when do the stories change, and how do the different layers interlink.

There is the external, protective story layer – 'we're so happy really' – which couples present to kin and friends until the story becomes unsustainable. But within that, one or both partners may also act, yet not believe, the story for the other's benefit: that is, *within* the couple relationship there lies a realm that is kept private from one partner by the other. And further, even within the complex layers of an individual's daily presentation of self, there may ultimately lie a sphere which is private – suppressed from conscious thought during the whole of the waking time when others are present – yet not to be completely escaped. As one of our respondents put it:

> There is no private me, well, almost never. I suppose you could say I'm 98% social. But the moment I hate, when it hits home to me, is those few minutes, you know, after getting into bed, looking at the 'close', but 'separate' (if you know what I mean) body of John – those few minutes before you go to sleep. That's the *real* me, and that's really scary. I shut my eyes quick and will the thought to go away!

Notes

1.   Personal communication.
2.   The full complexity of the search for feeling which is truly authentic is caught in Cohen and Taylor (1992).

References

Allan, G. (1980), 'A Note on Interviewing Spouses Together', *Journal of Marriage and the Family*, February, vol. 42, pp. 205–10.

Atkinson, P. (1990), *The Ethnographic Imagination: Textual Constructions of Reality* (London: Routledge).

Banks, J. (1959), 'Research Note on the Use of Group Discussions in Research', *Sociological Review*, vol. 7.

Berger, P. L. and Kellner, H. (1970), 'Marriage and the Construction of Reality', in Dreitzl, H. (ed.), *Recent Sociology No. 2* (New York: Macmillan).

Bernard, J. (1972), *The Future of Marriage* (New York: World Publishing).

Bott, E. (1957), *Family and Social Network* (London: Tavistock).

Brannen, J. (1988), 'Research Note: The Study of Sensitive Subjects', *Sociological Review*, vol. 36, pp. 552–63.

Brannen, J. and Collard, J. (1982), *Marriages in Trouble: The Process of Seeking Help* (London: Tavistock).

Brannen, J. and Moss, P. (1991), *Managing Mothers* (London: Unwin Hyman).

Brannen, J. and Wilson, P. (1987), *Give and Take in Families: Studies in Resource Distribution* (London: Allen & Unwin).

Burgoyne, J. and Clark, D. (1984), *Making a Go of It: The Study of Stepfamilies* (London: Routledge & Kegan Paul).

Cheal, D. (1991), *Family and the State of Theory* (London: Harvester Wheatsheaf).

Clark, D. and Haldane, D. (1990), *Wedlocked? Intervention and Research in Marriage* (Oxford: Polity).

Cohen, S. and Taylor, L. (1992), *Escape Attempts*, 2nd edn (London: Rouledge).

Coward, R. (1992), *Our Treacherous Hearts: Why Women Let Men Get Their Way* (London: Faber).

Dennis, N. and Erdos, G. (1992), *Families without Fatherhood* (London: IEA Health and Welfare Unit).

Denzin, N. K. (1989), *Interpretive Interactionism* (London: Sage).

Duncombe, J. and Marsden, D. (1993a), '"Workaholics" and "Whingeing Women": Gender Inequalities in the Performance of Emotion Work in the Private Sphere', Conference Proceedings of the 1992 Cambridge Stratification Seminar: *Inequalities in Employment: Inequalities in Home Life* (Cambridge: Sociological Research Group).

Duncombe, J. and Marsden, D. (1993b), 'Love and Intimacy: The Gender Division of Emotion and Emotion Work (A Neglected Aspect of Sociological Discussion of Heterosexual Relationships)', *Sociology*, vol. 27: no. 2, May 1993, pp. 221–41.

Duncombe, J. and Marsden, D. (1995a), 'Theorising Intimacy: the Last Frontier of Gender Inequality', *Sociological Review*, vol. 43 (in press).

Duncombe, J. and Marsden, D. (1995b), 'Can Men Love? "Reading", "Staging" and "Resisting" the Romance', in Pearce, L. and Stacey, J. (eds), *Romance Revisited* (London: Lawrence & (Wishart).

Giddens, A. (1991), *Late Modernity and Self-Identity* (Polity Press).

Giddens, A. (1992), *The Transformation of Intimacy: Love, Sexuality and Eroticism in Modern Societies* (Oxford: Polity Press).

Gubrium, J. F. and Holstein, J. A. (1990), *What is Family?* (London: Mayfield).

Hochschild, A. R. (1983), *The Managed Heart: Commercialisation of Human Feeling* (London: University of California Press).

Hochschild, A. R. with Maching, A. (1990), *The Second Shift: Working Parents and the Revolution at Home* (London: Piarkus).

Ingham, M. (1984), *Men* (London: Century).

Kelly, L. (1992), 'Journeying in Reverse. Possibilities and Problems in Feminist Research on Sexual Violence', in Morris, A. (ed.), *Feminist Perspectives in Criminology* (Milton Keynes: Open University Press).

Laslett, B. and Rapoport, R. (1975), 'Collaborative Interviewing and Interactive Research', *Journal of Marriage and the Family*, vol. 37, pp. 968–77.

Larossa, R., Bennett, L. A. and Gelles, R. J. (1981), 'Ethical Dilemmas in Qualitative Family Research', *Journal of Marriage and the Family*, vol. 43.

Mansfield, P. and Collard, J. (1988), *The Beginning of the Rest of Your Life?* (London: Macmillan).

McKee, L. and O'Brien, M. (1983), 'Interviewing Men: Taking Gender Seriously', in Garmarnikow, E. *et al.* (eds), *The Public and the Private* (London: Heinemann).

Morgan, D. H. J. (1985), *The Family, Politics and Social Theory* (London: Routledge and Kegan Paul).

Morgan, D. H. J. (1990), 'Institution and Relationship within Marriage', paper presented to the I.S.A. World Congress in Madrid.

Morgan, D. (1990), *Focus Groups* (London: Sage).

Morris, L. D. (1990), *The Workings of the Household* (Oxford: Polity Press).

Murray, C. (1990), *The Emerging British Underclass* (London: IEA Health and Welfare Unit).

Oakley, A. (1981), 'Interviewing Women: a Contradiction in Terms', in Roberts, H. (ed.), *Doing Feminist Research* (London: Routledge & Kegan Paul).

Pahl, J. (1989), *Money and Marriage* (London: Macmillan).

Rubin, L. B. (1991), *Erotic Wars: What Happened to the Sexual Revolution* (New York: Harper Row).

Skolnick, A. (1983), *The Intimate Environment* (Boston, MA: Little, Brown).

Stacey, J. (1990), *Brave New Families* (New York: Basic Books).

Stanley, L. and Morgan,. D. H. J. (1993), 'Editorial Introduction', *Sociology*, vol. 27, no. 1, February, pp. 2–4.

Vaughan, D. (1987), *Uncoupling* (London: Methuen).

Voysey, M. (1975), *A Constant Burden: The Reconstitution of Family Life* (London: RKP).

Weiss, R. (1975), *Marital Separation* (New York: Basic Books).

Wise, S. (1987), 'A Framework for Discussing Ethical Issues in Feminist Research: a Review of the Literature', in Giffiths, V. *et al.* (eds), *Writing Feminist Biography 2: Using Life Histories*, Studies in Sexual Politics, Monograph, Manchester University Sociology Department.

Wright Mills, C. (1959), *The Sociological Imagination* (Oxford: Oxford University Press).

Young, M. and Willmott, P. (1973), *The Symmetrical Family* (Harmondsworth: Penguin).

9 Encouraging Voices: Towards More Creative Methods for Collecting Data on Gender and Household Labour[1]

ANDREA DOUCET

INTRODUCTION

For more than two decades, authors from many disciplinary perspectives have charted and documented the work and parenting lives of women and men in Europe and North America and have left an indisputable trail of evidence to confirm that, in spite of women's increasing labour market participation, women continue to take on most of the household's work.[2] Perhaps the most surprisingly consistent finding relates to the limited change that has occurred with regard to household *responsibility*: women continue to be the managers, planners, organisers and supervisors of housework and childcare-related activities in the home. Indeed, even in Sweden and Denmark with their very favourable and highly praised work-family policies (Melhuish and Moss, 1991), Scandinavian writers have recently pointed to the 'remarkable' persistence of gender divisions of labour in care-giving work (Leira, 1990) and to the fact that 'the responsibility for children still overwhelmingly lies with mothers' (Borchorst, 1990, p. 176).

In coming to such conclusions on this 'remarkable' persistence or the 'astounding stability' (Berk, 1985) in gendered household work and responsibilities, the authors who investigate these issues then devise categories to describe the views and practices of research respondents. Most studies have some typology of categories along the lines of 'traditional', 'transitional', 'egalitarian' (Hochschild, 1989) or 'traditional', 'traditional–rigid', 'traditional–flexible' and 'renegotiated' (Morris, 1985). Other authors deduce whether or not there is 'nearly equal sharing' or 'actual equal sharing' between women and men in relation to family work (Brannen and Moss, 1991, p. 180).

While it is understandable that authors must find ways to capture the complexity of such issues within descriptive and analytical categories and while it would seem that the well documented 'outstanding stability' of gendered household labour cannot be contested, I would argue, nevertheless, that what is required is a deeper analysis of issues of gender difference and gender equality within the household domain. In particular, it is important to attempt to understand these issues from the perspective of the people being researched. How do individual women and men experience this 'outstanding stability' of gendered household labour? Where do the views, ideas, and experiences of the research respondents fit into the development and use of categories such as, for example, 'traditional' and 'egalitarian'? How does it feel to be living within such categories? How would *they* describe their household division of labour? Would they use the word 'division'? Would their aim be 'actual equal sharing' and, if so, how would they propose to bring this about?

In an attempt to understand these and other questions, I argue that it is worth reconsidering the *methods* which have been used to collect and analyse data on the gendered division of household labour. We need to re-think and re-vision the ways in which we *encourage* and *listen* to the voices and views of the women and men in our research. In this regard, I would posit that there are *two* moves which might bring forth new evidence on gender divisions of household labour. The first move involves finding creative methods to encourage the participation of the researched during the data collection phase of research. A second move, would be to listen more attentively to the respondents during the data analysis phase.[3] This chapter will deal with the *first* move, that of encouraging greater participation and analysis by research respondents during the data collection stage. Drawing on my research with twenty-three British dual earner couples who are attempting to *share* in the work and responsibility for housework and childcare,[4] I argue that paying greater attention to encouraging and listening to the voices of the people we research may help to bring us towards a deeper understanding of *how* and *why* gender intersects with household life and parenting.

The organization of this chapter is as follows. Section I reviews *what* data have been collected in some of the current research on gender divisions of household labour. I shall highlight four weaknesses in this area and suggest an alternative definition of *what* data to collect on household work. Section II discusses the *how* of data collection in this subject area; here I will discuss two main weaknesses in how data has been collected on gender and household labour.[5] Section III of the paper describes a visual participatory technique which attempts to overcome some of the weaknesses in data collection methods described in the first two parts of the paper. This data collection technique which I developed for use in my interviews with couples (joint interviews with the women and man together) is entitled 'The Household Portrait'.[6]

I DATA COLLECTION: *WHAT* HOUSEHOLD WORK?

(i) Weaknesses in methods

Within the sociological and social psychological literature on the division of household labour and on parenting, there is a striking simplicity of categories employed to describe the work which goes on within households. In particular, it is worth highlighting four weaknesses.

First, there has been a tendency by many authors to simplify *childcare* tasks (Pahl, 1984; Morris, 1985; Jowell *et al.*, 1988; Brannen and Moss, 1991). In the British Social Attitudes study, for example, childcare tasks are limited to two items which include 'looking after children when they are sick' and 'teaching children discipline' (Jowell *et al.*, 1988, p. 197).

Second, there has also been a tendency to simplify *household work* tasks limiting them, in some cases, only to parenting tasks (Backett, 1982; Boulton, 1983; Ehrensaft, 1987; Kimball, 1988) while, in other cases, omitting general household maintenance and repair tasks (DIY) (Brannen and Moss, 1991).

Third, if the distinction is made at all between households with or without children, there is often no recognition made of the various stages and changing needs and demands of children as they grow up nor the fact that childcare tasks differ greatly depending upon the numbers and ages of children (Bird *et al.*, 1984; Pahl, 1984; Morris, 1985).

Finally, the housework contributions of other family members, such as older children and grandparents, have been neglected in the effort to focus only on women and men (but see Morrow, 1992; Solberg, 1988).

(ii) Defining household work

In light of the four methodological weaknesses mentioned above, we may not be obtaining an adequate picture of household life. If we wish to document the changes in gendered labour within the domestic sphere, then we need to have a more detailed portrait of the unique terrain of household life. In an attempt to enter this terrain, my research set out to explore a wide range of tasks and responsibilities within *seven* categories of household work, considering how these tasks and responsibilities changed as children grew older, and, in households with older children, how the children contributed as well.

The categories of tasks and responsibilities which I have explored include: (1) *housework*; (2) *caring work*;[7] (3) *'household service work'* (Sharma, 1986) and *'kin work'* (Di Leonardo, 1987);[8] (4) *DIY*; (5) *financial management*; (6) *household subsistence activities*;[9] and (7) *overall responsibility for housework and childcare*.[10]

A standard list of household tasks was drawn up with unique variations for some households, as household members had input into my definition of tasks and responsibilities. Thus, variations were found depending upon: the number and ages of children; household type and amount of DIY undertaken; household income and the ability to buy-in services; the contribution of older children to household work; as well as some households' own particular additions to the list of household work tasks. For example, one couple with a 2-year-old boy included: 'cutting Matthew's nails' as a child-care task; another couple included 'walking the dog'; while others reminded me to include caring tasks such as 'bed-time talks', 'confidences' and 'responding to children's emotional needs in a practical way'.

II DATA COLLECTION: HOW?

It may well be argued that researchers 'lack an adequate language for the work of everyday caring' (DeVault, 1991, p. 228). In a similar vein, it might be said that it is difficult for people living within households to conceptualise and articulate just how they run their households. If we stretch our imaginations for a moment and think about a household being run as though it were a workplace, then each household member might have a job description with a detailed list of tasks to do, a schedule to follow, and deadlines to meet. Household members might clock-in and clock-out of work, putting their feet up to relax and watch television after they had clocked out of work. Household meetings would be held to review problems with particular work tasks or with other household members, as well as for creative problem-solving, forward planning, and projections of future goals and aspirations. Team togetherness and team spirit might be encouraged or, alternatively, there might be an atmosphere of competition.

Let's come back from this imaginary scenario. Quite clearly, households do not run like this. Most households stand on a foundation which is built on the inter-locking structures of the ideological, socio-economic, cultural, psychological, emotional, historical and the 'symbolic' (Martin, 1984; Berk, 1985) which combine to create a sometimes inexplicable pattern for getting all the household work done. These largely inexplicable patterns might not be retrievable in response to interview or questionnaire questions as to *who does what*. Yet, most of the research carried out on household life revolves around the researcher asking who does what and the respondent replying. I would argue that the scope and degree of household work done by household members may be more difficult to obtain than is presumed to be the case within sociological research. Much of the information on how a household operates on a day-to-day basis is difficult to remember and conceptualise, much less to articulate.

A second related weakness in data collection methods within this subject area is the failure to elicit greater data analysis, at a preliminary level, by the research respondents[11]. It could well be that a simple question might encourage the respondent to think in a more analytical way, thus providing more detail on what are otherwise quite closed questions on household tasks. For example, in *Managing Mothers*, it appears that Brannen and Moss only asked their female respondents *who* took responsibility for a number of tasks. But they did not, for example, explore how each woman felt about the issue of household responsibility; for example, which parts of this responsibility did she enjoy and which parts did she not enjoy? This might have amounted to an insignificant addition to Brannen and Moss's research but, alternatively, it might have allowed them, as well as other researchers, to re-think what is meant by the concept of *responsibility* within household life. Whereas it seems to be assumed that household responsibility is a burden, asking respondents about it could possibly shed some light on this matter and further our understanding on this issue.[12]

If we wish to gain a deeper understanding of why there has been such a remarkable persistence of gendered household labour, then we should be more attentive to the issue of including research respondents' own analysis of these issues. It is important to hear what women and men feel and think about how life is organised within their own households. Which tasks do they like doing and which ones do they dislike? If they could change anything, what would they change? Which tasks are chores and which ones are not chores?[13] How and why has the division of labour changed over the years?

III 'THE HOUSEHOLD PORTRAIT'

In attempting to find methods which would encourage women and men to speak openly and analytically about issues of household life and parenting, I struggled with ways of eliciting information on the household division of labour. Throughout my pilot interviews, where I tried many variations on research questions within the format of semi-structured interview, I felt dissatisfied with the limited portraits of household life that were emerging. I began, therefore, to think that if I could somehow help people to visualise more clearly what their household division of labour looked like, then it would help them to speak about it. I felt that a *visual* technique would enable participants to speak more freely as it would help them to have a reference point from which to speak about household life. Moreover, a *participatory* technique would encourage a higher level of expression and analysis by the research respondents. Thus, I developed a visual participatory technique entitled the 'The Household Portrait'[14].

'The Household Portrait' technique for collecting data on the division of household labour allows both partners to reflect upon and discuss together how their household is run according to a broad range of tasks and responsibilities. The technique involves sorting through different sets of coloured papers which represent a broad range of colour coded household tasks and responsibilities according to the seven categories of household work described in Section I of this chapter. The couples then place these coloured slips of paper (with each colour corresponding to each of the seven categories of household work) in one of five columns on a large sheet of paper. The five columns represent the person who does that household task or takes on the responsibility for a selected range of tasks: (1) *Woman*; (2) *Woman with Man Helping*; (3) *Shared Equally*; (4) *Man with Woman Helping*; and (5) *Man*.[15]

Neither the technique itself nor the 'Portraits' that emerged are the central issues in this discussion. I did arrive at each household with my tape recorder, my seven envelopes filled with different coloured bits of paper, large sheets of paper with five columns, a glue stick, and a pen for adding in extra tasks which were unique to particular households. Nevertheless, the technique and its materials merely acted as a doorway into their household and into issues of parenting and household life. In a sense, the technique took me through the years of their lives and into the rooms of each household in ways that a more straightforward interview might not have done. Each couple took the technique into their hands, taking me along with them. Participants took great interest and pleasure in constructing their individual 'Portraits' and especially liked the way it was individualised in that their children's names were included on some of the little coloured pieces of paper (for example, 'putting Tommy to bed').

The data which emerges from 'The Household Portrait' technique is multi-dimensional and multi-layered: it includes noticing the way they had placed the papers (who led, who followed); how they spoke about the issues (where they laughed, where they were angry); the pauses and disruptions; the arguments; the shifting from difficult topics; their voices on tape and the resulting interview transcripts. In the end, however, the most important piece of data seems to be their actual voices on tape, what was said and how it was expressed, which were encouraged by the technique and its materials but which surpass the actual finished products, the 'Portraits', in their usefulness as raw data. Indeed, in some cases there are sharp contradictions between what is constructed in the 'Household Portrait' and what emerges through the discussion around it as well as through the individual interviews with the women and men. This relates to the fact that many of these issues which deal with the structural, ideological and emotional context of household life and parenting are deeply contradictory in and of themselves.

I shall outline some of the strengths of this visual participatory technique by drawing on my interviews with couples.

(i) *Reflection, debate, arguments*: ' . . . it's a conflict area. I don't know if you could define it . . . ' [Jeff]

'The Household Portrait' technique allowed both partners to reflect upon, discuss, debate, agree, or disagree on each partner's contribution to the running of their household. Sally and Jeff are speaking about the coloured piece of paper which denotes the task: '*making decisions about the children's behaviour*'. Sally puts it into the *Shared Equally* column, but then Jeff says that he doesn't agree with this. He mentions the example of trying to come to a decision on the children's sleeping patterns when they were infants. Sally felt they should hold on to the strategy of letting the children cry themselves to sleep whereas Jeff was much more inclined to want to attend to them in the middle of the night. Here are their words:

Sally: So, we do discuss that, don't we, rather than just, sort of – it's not me that's sort of...

Jeff: I'd say *you* tend to set the agenda for it.

Sally: Yeah.

Jeff: So that makes it better to go under 'Woman (Man Helps)'. [He moves the little coloured paper from 'Shared Equally' to 'Woman (Man Helps)']

Sally: Except it isn't really like that. I mean I think I'd like to say that . . .

Jeff: ...it's a conflict area. I don't know if you could define it . . .

Sally. I mean it's certainly not an area that I feel that I would want to control because I feel – even if it's somebody taking on more – that it should at least be *discussed* equally, or discussed thoroughly, you know between the two of us, so, you know, it's depending on how you perceive it, and not you're *doing* it more or you're actually *doing* it without discussion.

This discussion between Sally and Jeff underlines, among other things, the fact that they both have different views on the *definition* of the task *'making decisions about the children's behaviour'*. As Jeff says: '. . . it's a conflict area. I don't know if you could define it . . . '. For Sally, as long as the issue is *'discussed* equally, or discussed thoroughly', then it is a *shared* task. Speaking about it together allowed these differences to emerge.

(ii)   *Analysis*: 'the greatest bones of contention...' [Chris]

A second strength of 'The Household Portrait' was that it involved the participants in the analysis of the data at a preliminary level. I asked them what they were happy about and what they were unhappy about. If they could change anything, what would they change? What tasks did they like to do? Which did they loathe? How did they feel about having responsibility for certain tasks? How had the division of labour changed over the years and why?

Anna and Chris describe in some detail how their 'Household Portrait' has changed over the years. In thinking about their greatest areas of disagreement, Chris says, and Anna agrees: 'I think the greatest bones of contention have always been the cooking and the washing.' They speak about this for a while and then I ask Anna if she has always done the cooking and the washing. She replies:

Anna: Yes, and I think that's partly just to do with, you know, gender stereotyping and partly because we'd had very different experiences when we met. Although we were virtually the same age, whereas Chris had just been a student the whole time till we met, I had jobs and had my own flat and looked after myself in a way that [she turns to Chris] *you hadn't*. So that I think, in a way, you know, we just *arrived* together with different domestic experiences as well as being of opposite sexes with *all* that entailed as well. Our experiences of our early twenties tended to reinforce gender stereotyping.

Of course there were many other factors, as revealed throughout the joint interview and the individual interviews with Anna and Chris, which account for the fact that 'the greatest bones of contention have always been the cooking and the washing'. Anna's own words, both here and elsewhere in her interview transcripts, helped me towards a greater understanding of how she analysed issues surrounding gender and household life.

(iii) *Changes over the years*: 'And sometimes, even though I've known I've sort of wanted it to go more to the middle, I've *sort* of resisted it. And you've had to *push*.' [Mark]

One of the most appealing aspects of the technique is that it allowed the couple to enter into a discussion *together* of how they felt their household division of labour had changed over the years. The following dialogue demonstrates how Laura and Mark keep referring to their 'Household Portrait' as a reference point and in particular to the fact that during their twenty-five years of marriage they have, with some difficulty, kept trying to move household tasks and responsibilities to the middle column.

Mark: I think that, I mean, I think I quite *actively* not only supported you but *encouraged* you, in the very early days to find a sense of yourself. And then I have, I think *actively wanted* to share things as much as possible. There have certainly been times when, in a sense I've permitted or even arranged, perhaps forced if you like, the situation where *a lot* of the burdens of running of the household have been on your shoulders. And sometimes, even though I've known I've sort of wanted it to go more to the middle, I've *sort of* resisted it. And you've had to *push*. And I'm sure you *felt* that and I felt *guilty* about it even. But yes, yes it happened.

Laura: I mean I can see that I still *do* actually take responsibility for more things, but, um, the ones I take responsibility for I *actually*, you know, *enjoy* them and I'm quite happy with that. The things that I have felt *resentful* about or, you know, that it's not really fair, I find they're down the middle now, really.

(iv) *A view of household life*: 'It's quite interesting actually to see . . . ' [Anna]

In looking at their 'Household Portrait', many couples were interested, at times surprised, to see how it looked. One man, who was working nights and taking care of his sons full-time in the day, discovered that he was, in fact, not doing much housework. Looking at their 'Household Portrait', he comments: 'It has an awful ring to it when you confront it yourself.' Anna examines the 'Household Portrait' which she and Chris had done and she says:

Anna: It's quite interesting actually to see both what the pattern is *now* and to recognize how it's changed over the last ten years and over the past five years [since the children]. There's one set of you know, much more gradual shifts which began ten years ago and then some quite *dramatic* shifts which started *five* years ago. And really the most *positive* of these dramatic shifts is into the area of *shared* enterprise. Because we do *so* much that's actually shared.

(v)   *On gender differences*: 'And it *doesn't matter*, so we just let it fall as it happens.' [Elizabeth]

On the question of gender *difference*, Deborah Rhode has pointed out: 'The critical issue should not be difference, but the *difference difference makes*' (Rhode, 1989, p. 313; my emphasis). Yet this 'critical issue' has been dealt with only partially within the subject area of gender divisions of household labour.[16] On the one hand, the differences *within* household life have been held accountable for a wide range of impressively documented differences in the socio-economic positions of women and men *outside* of household life. In particular, it has been demonstrated how the weighting of the balance of household labour on the side of women has been very costly to many women. Many studies have pointed to how women's employment may suffer as it is mainly women who have had to make adjustments in their schedules in order to balance both paid and domestic work (Crouter, 1984; Berk, 1985; Pleck, 1985; Evetts, 1988; Hochschild, 1989; Brannen and Moss, 1991). Several studies have also pointed out that in dual earner households, it is the women who experience fatigue, anxiety, illness, role-strain, conflict and guilt in their decision to return to work and in their daily lives as parents and workers (Crouter, 1984; Thoits, 1987; Hochschild, 1989; Brannen and Moss, 1991). As described so well by Brannen and Moss, the fact that women continue to do most of the household work often leads to 'the potentially serious long-term consequences of subsequently leaving employment or leaving their full time job for another part-time one' wherein they often find themselves in a situation of 'occupational downgrading, with loss of earnings, pensions and other benefits'. They also mention how 'these actions affect future career prospects, pensions and long term household income' and they can also leave 'women (and their children) economically vulnerable to the future loss of their partner's financial support because of marital breakdown or for some other long-term reason' (Brannen and Moss, 1991, p. 253).

On the other hand, there is little attention paid to the daily, weekly, monthly, and yearly layers of difference which may move and change as children grow older and as women and men's experiences as mothers and fathers alter in relation to a wide range of indeterminate, constantly changing factors. These factors include, among others: expanding or narrowing opportunities at work (promotion, demotion, or redundancy); perceptions of their particular child or children's needs as related to the age of the child(ren), the personality and disposition of each child, availability and suitability of local childcare, and the birth of a second, third, or fourth baby; a change in the child(ren)'s childcare arrangements (the loss of a childminder or nanny); a child's transition into nursery or school; and personal incidents such as illness or the death of a significant loved one. In the main, gender difference is *problematised* within sociological literature on gender and household labour. In addition, there is little distinction between leisure and work so that there is a tendency to view all work which occurs in the home as part of the 'second shift' (Hochschild, 1989). In this sense, there is an implicit devaluation of what goes on *inside* the home so that this subject area is still informed by Oakley's findings two decades ago that housework is overwhelmingly isolating, monotonous and oppressive (Oakley, 1974).

There are two main points to be made on this issue of gender differences which emerge from the 'Household Portrait' technique. First, not all household tasks are 'chores'. The most obvious examples are childcare related activities which may be experienced much more as pleasures rather than as work (Oakley, 1974; Boulton, 1983). Yet, even on other routine household tasks, I was surprised at the range of differing attitudes about them expressed by women and men in my study. One man's hobby was 'ironing and listening to rock music'. Another man said, quite seriously: 'I love cleaning the toilet.' A woman who works long days told me: 'I love hanging out the laundry. But I'm not usually here to do it. So when I get the chance I do it.' Overall this may well point to the fact, as one woman pointed out, that 'there's a different feeling whether you're doing them under pressure or slowly'.

A second point on gender differences within household life which emerges from the 'Household Portrait' technique is that just as there are varied meanings attached to household work tasks, there are diverse definitions about what it means to *share* the household work or to be an *egalitarian* couple. Although all couples in my study identified themselves 'as attempting to share the work and responsibility for housework and childcare', the 'Household Portraits' represented a wide range of distinct patterns of sharing related to differing ideas on both the *meaning* and appropriate *structure* for sharing the household work. To give just one example, Elizabeth and Saxon, both in their mid-fifties, are well aware of the role played by their respective gendered upbringing and socialisation. Yet they are comfortable with doing different things in the household as long as there is an overall sense of sharing. They each feel that their household division of labour reflects their unique likes, dislikes, and relative competence in certain tasks. Their 'Household Portrait' reveals that he tends to do most of the DIY and she does most of the 'kin work'. They refer to their 'Household Portrait' as they speak:

Elizabeth: Just as *I've* pushed perhaps to do more of these [refers to *remembering birthdays and sending cards, buying Christmas presents* and so on] you've pushed to do more of that [refers to most *DIY*]. And, it *doesn't matter*, so we just let it fall as it happens. You know, if I'd felt very strongly about that, I would have pushed. If you'd felt about that very strongly *you* would have pushed. Just as you're, you're beginning to push . . . [laughs].

Saxon: Yes that's right, you're quite right. Those are your strengths and these are my strengths and we tend to do those things and they do *happen* to fall into relatively conventional role models as well.

Whereas it is true that Elizabeth and Saxon are, in his words, 'relatively conventional' in some aspects of their household division of labour, they also have a very 'unconventional' history as regards the sharing of household work. During their twenty-one years of marriage, they have both taken turns at doing flexi-time and part-time work and they each took time off from work to be at home both full-time and part-time with the children. Thus it would be difficult to classify this household as either 'traditional' or 'egalitarian' given that it is actually both of these. This may highlight the fact that interpreting data on the household division of labour only at the level of tasks and responsibilities may give us an incomplete, and indeed distorted, picture of just *how* and *why* women and men are changing within household life.

(vi) Not gender *equality*, but gender *differences*; not only differences but the *disadvantages* that follow from these differences

My study produced an enormously diverse range of 'Household Portraits' with varying personal biographies and structural and ideological explanations behind each 'Portrait' and its supporting interview transcripts. Yet, as I proceeded to analyse my data, it became increasingly difficult to discern just how to define or describe an 'egalitarian' couple (Hochschild, 1989) or an 'actual equal sharing' (Brannen and Moss, 1991, p. 180) between women and men in relation to family work. Indeed, one of the main findings of my research is that most of the couples in this study demonstrated considerable confusion and ambivalence over the issue of gender differences, both in terms of just what they were and where such differences should be permitted to prevail. Whereas equality in employment is more easily measured and tested against factors such as pay, promotions, and the relative positions of women and men, the issue of equality within the home is not so straightforward. Does it mean doing everything, even if that means that the women learn how to do plumbing and electrical chores for the first time whereas their male partner has been doing such tasks since he was a boy? Does it mean that men have to call up the baby-sitter as many times as the women do and go to the toddler groups or play group sessions where he might be the only man in the room? Moreover, does it mean that women and men have to share *everything* from the first day of their first child's life or that they may alternatively have periods where one parent does more than the other?

In my view, it remains difficult, if not impossible, to speak about *equality* within household life as measured by women and men's participation in, time spent doing, or taking responsibility for a broad range of household tasks. Gender differences existed for all couples in the present study. The scope and range of gender differences took on various configurations, but they nevertheless existed within all households, even those whom other authors might describe as fully 'egalitarian'. Thus, it would be more worthwhile to speak about gender *differences* and the *disadvantages* which follow from such differences (Rhode, 1989, 1990) rather than arguing for *equality* between women and men within household life. Although gender boundaries can and are crossed by women and men so that women are, for example, astrophysicists while men are primary caregivers, there is still a sense that boundaries *are* being crossed and these crossings may entail certain struggles, gains and losses which should be accorded greater attention rather than ignored.

CONCLUSION

In this chapter, I have argued that in light of the 'remarkable' persistence or 'outstanding stability' of gender divisions of household labour, it is important to re-consider whether or not we are getting a full picture of women and men's changing contributions to household labour and their own complex explanations which stand behind static or flexible gendered positioning within the household. If we wish to know *why* women continue to take on the responsibility for household life, then one way forward would be to find imaginative and creative methods to encourage and listen to the views and ideas of women and men as they speak about and untangle deeply knotted threads of thoughts, feelings, and experiences on the subject of gender differences within the fabric of their domestic lives. 'The Household Portrait' technique represents just one way forward in collecting data on these issues.

In summary, there are four concluding points to be made on the usefulness of a creative research technique, such as the 'Household Portrait', for gathering data on women and men's lives as parents and workers. First, this particular technique assisted the couples in my study to remember, conceptualise and articulate how they arranged and carried out the household work. It encouraged discussion, analysis, debate, agreement and disagreement over how each household's particular division of labour had changed over the years and women and men's own views as to *why* these changes did or did not occur. Second, 'The Household Portrait' technique may have instilled a certain amount of trust in the couples I interviewed since they had a sense of the sort of picture that I left with. Rather than simply walking away with all their words on a tape recorder for me to analyse on my own, I left with a 'Household Portrait' that they had constructed together, discussed and, to some extent, analysed with me. Third, it encouraged a wide ranging discussion on a number of dimensions of *difference* within household life. There were differences in how individual women and men defined household tasks as chores, hobbies or leisure activities as well as differences in how certain tasks were defined (for example, 'making decisions about the children's behaviour'). Finally, a critical theoretical point has emerged from the utilisation of this data collection technique in that it uncovered the complex layers of gender *differences* which may exist within household life, the diverse definitions about what it means to *share* household work, and the difficulty with defining and describing *equality* between women and men within the domestic domain.

Notes

1. I should like to thank Bob Blackburn, Karen D. Hughes, Ginny Morrow and Natasha Mauthner for their helpful comments on an earlier draft of this paper.

2. Since the 1970s, academic studies of gender divisions of labour within the household have collected basically three major types of data: (i) *time-budgets* (Meissner *et al.*, 1975; Gershuny *et al.*, 1986); (ii) qualitative or quantitative data on the distribution of household *tasks* (Pahl, 1984; Jowell *et al.*, 1988); and (iii) data which also includes the issue of *responsibility* for these same household tasks (Morris, 1985; Hochschild, 1989; Brannen and Moss, 1991). Some research has collected data on both time and tasks (Berk, 1985) or all three types of data: time, tasks, and responsibility (Brannen and Moss, 1991; Morris, 1985).

3. I am very grateful to Carol Gilligan for her insights on staying attentive to 'voice' and distinguishing between the various voices within research projects (the researcher, the respondents, and the existing literature on the topic in question). Her recent book, *Meeting at the Crossroads* (Brown and Gilligan, 1992), particularly Chapter Two, provides an excellent guide to in-depth data *analysis* which listens attentively to the voices of the researched. For an example of how this method was used in listening to women's experiences of postnatal depression, see Mauthner, (1994).

4. See Doucet (1995).

5. I wish to comment at this point that my critique is not of the authors' entire work in question, most of which is very admirable, but rather about some of the data collection methods which were utilised for obtaining data on gender divisions of household labour.

6. An example of a 'Household Portrait' is included in Appendix A.1.

7. In my study, caring work includes only childcare as none of my households had elder care responsibilities. I also distinguished between 'caring for' ('tending') and 'caring about' (the more emotional or expressive aspects of caring about other household members) (Graham, 1983).

8. 'Household service work' includes the work of maintaining contact and relationships with social, community and extended family networks; in a similar vein, 'kin work', refers to 'the conception, maintenance and ritual celebration of cross-household ties . . . ' (Di Leonardo, 1987, pp. 442–3).

9. This category overlaps with DIY to some extent and reflects what Ray Pahl (1984) refers to as the sphere of 'self-provisioning' which is the production and consumption of goods and services undertaken by household members for themselves. For some households, these are 'hobbies'.

10. For a typical detailed list of the household tasks in each of the seven categories, please refer to 'The Household Portrait' in Appendix A.1.

11. Such issues are, however, considered within 'cooperative enquiry' and more collaborative and experiential research such as that found in *Human Enquiry: A Sourcebook of New Paradigm Research* (Reason and Rowan, 1981). It remains surprising how so few of these ideas have spilled over into sociological research on gender divisions of household labour.

12. This underpins a deeper theoretical weakness on the issues of *care* and *responsibility* in the subject area of gender divisions of household labour and the failure to distinguish between a 'feminine' and a 'feminist' approach to caring. As described by Tronto: 'The *feminine* approach to caring carries the burden of accepting traditional gender divisions in a society that devalues what women do. . . . A *feminist* approach to caring, in contrast, needs to begin by broadening our understanding of what caring for others means,

both in terms of the moral questions it raises and in terms of the need to re-structure broader social and political institutions if caring for others is to be made a more central part of the everyday lives of everyone in society' ('Tronto, 1989, pp. 184–9; see also Tronto, 1993). Finch and Mason (1993) is an excellent example of combining rich empirical data with a sophisticated understanding of the issues of care and responsibility in the context of family and kin relationships.

13. Some researchers get at this issue of the respondents' feelings about the particular tasks through detailed diaries (see Berk, 1985). It remains the case, however, that this sort of analysis seldom enters into the interview situation.

14. The process of developing the technique was informed by principles from non-formal participatory education and my experience in creative non-formal education work with UNICEF and the United Nations Development Programme in Central and South America. The basic principles of this approach are summed up in Srinivasan (1977, 1990).

15. See Appendix A.1.

16. See Doucet (in press) for a theoretical discussion of gender equality and gender difference as applied to the subject area of gender divisions of household labour.

References

Backett, K. C. (1982), *Mothers and Fathers: A Study of the Development and Negotiation of Parental Behaviour* (London and Basingstoke: Macmillan).

Berk, S. F. (1985), *The Gender Factory: The Apportionment of Work in American Households* (New York: Plenum).

Bird, G. W., Bird, G. A. and Scruggs, M. (1984), 'Determinants of Family Task Sharing: A Study of Husbands and Wives', *Journal of Marriage and the Family*, May 1984: pp. 345–55.

Borchorst, A. (1990), 'Political Motherhood and Childcare Policies: A Comparative Approach to Britain and Scandinavia', in Ungerson, C. (ed.), *Gender and Caring: Work and Welfare in Britain and Scandinavia* (London: Harvester Wheatsheaf).

Boulton, M. G. (1983), *On Being A Mother* (London: Tavistock).

Brannen, J. and Moss, P. (1991), *Managing Mothers: Dual Earner Households After Maternity Leave* (London: Unwin Hyman).

Brown, L. M. and Gilligan, C. (1992), *Meeting at the Crossroads: Women's Psychology and Girl's Development* (Cambridge, MA: Harvard University Press).

Crouter, A. (1984), 'Spillover from Family to Work: the Neglected Side of the Work–Family Interface', *Human Relations*, vol. 37, pp. 425–42.

DeVault, M. (1991), *Feeding the Family: The Social Organization of Caring as Gendered Work* (Chicago, IL: University of Chicago Press).

Di Leonardo, M. (1987), 'The Female World of Cards and Holidays: Women, Families, and the World of Kinship', *Signs*, 12: pp. 440–53.

Doucet, A. (1992), 'What Difference does Difference Make? Towards an Understanding of Gender Equality and Difference in the Household Division of

Labour', in Dunne, G. A., Blackburn, R. M. and Jarman, J. (eds), *Inequalities in Employment, Inequalities in Home-Life: Conference Proceedings for the 20th Cambridge Social Stratification Seminar* (Cambridge: Sociological Research Group, Faculty of Social and Political Sciences, University of Cambridge).

Doucet, A. (1995), 'Gender Differences, Gender Equality and Care: Towards Understanding Gendered Labour in British Dual Earner Households', unpublished doctoral dissertation, Faculty of Social and Political Sciences, University of Cambridge.

Doucet, A. (1995), 'Gender Differences, Gender Equality and Gender Differences within Household Work and Parenting', *Women's Studies International Forum*, vol. 18.

Ehrensaft, D. (1987), *Parenting Together: Men and Women Sharing the Care of their Children* (London: Collier Macmillan).

Evetts, J. (1988), 'Managing Childcare and Work Responsibilities: The Strategies of Married Women: Primary and Infant Teachers', *The Sociological Review*, vol. 36, no. 3, pp. 503–31.

Finch, J. and Mason, J. (1993), *Negotiating Family Responsibilities* (London: Routledge).

Gershuny, J. I., Miles, I., Jones, S., Mullins, C., Thomas, G. and Wyatt, S. M. E. (1986), 'Preliminary Analysis of the 1983/4 ESRC Time-Budget Data', *Quarterly Journal of Social Affairs*, vol. 2, pp. 13–39.

Graham, H. (1983), 'Caring: A Labour of Love,' in Finch, J. and Groves, D. (eds) *A Labour of Love: Women, Work and Caring* (London: Routledge and Kegan Paul).

Hochschild, A. (1989), *The Second Shift* (New York: Avon Books).

Jowell, R., Witherspoon, S. and Brook, L. (eds) (1988), *British Social Attitudes: The Fifth Report* (Hants: Gower).

Kimball, G. (1988), *50/50 Parenting: Sharing Family Rewards and Responsibilities* (Lexington, MA: Lexington Books).

Leira, A. (1990), 'Coping with Care: Mothers in a Welfare State', in Ungerson, C. (ed.), *Gender and Caring: Work and Welfare in Britain and Scandinavia* (London: Harvester Wheatsheaf).

Martin, B. (1984), '"Mother Wouldn't Like it!" Housework as Magic', *Theory, Culture and Society*, 2: pp. 19–36.

Mauthner, N. (1994), 'Postnatal Depression: A Relational Perspective', unpublished doctoral dissertation, Faculty of Social and Political Sciences, University of Cambridge.

Meissner, M., Humphreys, S. M., Meis, M. and Scheu, W.J. (1975), 'No Exit For Wives: Sexual Division of Labour and the Cumulation of Household Demands', *Canadian Review of Sociology and Anthropology*, vol. 12, no. 4, pp. 424–39.

Melhuish, E. C. and Moss, P. (eds) (1991), *Day Care for Young Children: International Perspectives* (London: Routledge & Kegan Paul).

Morris, L. (1985), 'Renegotiation of the Domestic Division of Labour' in Roberts, B. *et al.* (eds), *New Approaches to Economic Life* (Manchester: Manchester University Press).

Morrow, V. (1992), 'Family Values: Accounting for Children's Contribution to the Domestic Economy', *Working Paper Series*, Working Paper No. 10 (Cambridge: Sociological Research Group, Faculty of Social and Political Sciences, University of Cambridge).

Oakley, A. (1974), *Housewife* (London: Allen Lane).

Pahl, R. E. (1984), *Divisions of Labour* (Oxford: Basil Blackwell).

Pleck, J. H. (1985), *Working Wives, Working Husbands* (Beverly Hills, CA: Sage).

Reason, P. and Rowan, J. (eds) (1981), *Human Inquiry: A Sourcebook for New Paradigm Research* (Chichester: John Wiley).

Rhode, D. L. (1989), *Justice and Gender: Sex Discrimination and the Law* (London: Harvard University Press).

Rhode, D. L. (ed.) (1990), *Theoretical Perspectives on Sexual Difference* (London: Yale University Press).

Sharma, U. (1986), *Women's Work: Class and the Urban Household: A Study of Shimla, North India* (London: Tavistock).

Solberg, A. (1988), 'The Everyday Life of Norwegian Children', paper presented to the Third International Workshop, The Ethnography of Childhood, Cambridge, 3–6 July, 1988.

Srinivasan, L. (1977), *Perspectives on Non-formal Adult Learning* (Boston, MA.: World Education).

Srinivasan, L. (1990), *Tools for Community Participation: A Manual for Training Trainers in Participatory Techniques* (New York: PROWWESS/United Nations Development Programme).

Thoits, P. A. (1987), 'Negotiating Roles', in Crosby, F. J. (ed.), *Spouse, Parent, Worker: On Gender and Multiple Roles* (New Haven CT: Yale University Press).

Thompson, L. and Walker, A. J. (1989), 'Gender in Families: Women and Men in Marriage, Work, and Parenthood', *Journal of Marriage and the Family*, vol. 51, pp. 845–71.

Tronto, J. (1989), 'Women and Caring: What Can Feminists Learn about Morality from Caring?', in Jaggar, A. M. and Bordo, S. R.(eds), *Gender/Body/Knowledge: Feminist Reconstructions of Being and Knowing* (New Brunswick: Rutgers University Press).

Tronto, J. (1993), *Moral Boundaries: A Political Argument for an Ethic of Care* (New York: Routledge).

Appendix A.1 'The Household Portrait'–An Example from 'Laura' and 'Mark'

Woman	Woman (Man Helps)	Shared Equally	Man (Woman Helps)	Man
Watering plants	Tidying up	Buying of minor household (kitchen items)	Cleaning cooker	Cleaning bathroom/WC
Laundry – doing it		Washing up		Cooking evening meal (weekends)
Garden: flowers		Laundry – putting it away		
Changing beds		Making breakfast		Shopping
Main listener/comforter for Anne and Jessica's concerns/problems		Cooking evening meal (weekends)		When Anne, Jessica Russell and Joe were little: physical play/sports
After-school care when children were younger		Main listener/comforter for Russell and Joe's concerns/problems		
	Arranged babysitting when children were little	Car maintenance	Home improvement	Car maintenance
Organises childcare arrangements (early years)	When Anne, Jessica Russell and Joe were little: creative play	Bed-time talks		Home improvement
Bought (buy) children's clothes			Bicycle maintenance	Bicycle maintenance
		Driving children to activities		Minor repairs; plumbing, electrical
When Anne, Jessica Russell and Joe were little took them to doctor/dentist		Prepared children's room(s) (before or when they were babies . . .)		
		Helping with homework		Household bills
Taking photos	Organised birthday parties			Overall budgeting and financial management

Appendix A.1 Continued'

Woman	Woman (Man Helps)	Shared Equally	Man (Woman Helps)	Man
Making photo albums	Remembering birthdays and sending cards	Sending Christmas cards	Overall budgeting	
Buying Christmas presents				
	Cooking for guests			
Knitting	Decorating house	Family contacts (letters / phone calls)	Making jams	
	Had the responsibility for childcare in pre-school years	Organising family outings / activities		
	Had the responsibility for childcare during early school years	Organising entertaining (setting it up)		
	Deciding what needs doing for housework	Attending school activities		
		Parent–teacher evenings		
		Buying major household appliances		
		Repairing clothes		
		Making decisions about children's behaviour		
		Planning meals		
		Has the responsibility (now) for ensuring that all is going well with the children		

10 Researching Value-loaded Issues: The Management of Food in Households

KATE PURCELL

INTRODUCTION

Over the past twenty-five years, economic growth in most Western industrialised countries has been associated with a rise in the labour force participation of women. The increased involvement of women in paid work has been reflected in the growing share of gross domestic product attributable to households and the rising demand for domestic and labour-saving consumer goods and services. However, the gains from rising prosperity (and the costs of recessionary fluctuations) have been unequally distributed throughout the population, with increasing polarisation between rich and poor and, in the workforce, between dual-earner and unemployed households. Married women's employment has long been recognised as lifting a significant proportion of low-income households above the poverty line (Diamond, 1980), whereas at more affluent levels, dual incomes substantially reinforce other advantages (Pahl, 1984; Morris with Ruane, 1989).

In some households, women make a direct contribution to the formal economy via part-time employment, often in low-status, low paid jobs, while taking primary responsibility for running the home and parenting; in others, women combine domestic responsibilities with full-time employment; and in a small and declining proportion of households, women are full-time homemakers and parents for at least part of the family life-cycle. Individual and household decisions about domestic divisions of labour and participation in paid work reflect the demand for labour and availability of childcare and other forms of support (such as transport) at different times and in different localities, as well as internal work preferences (Ballard, 1984; Grieco, 1987), but there has been a clear convergence of male and female lifetime employment patterns in recent decades, with women taking shorter breaks from employment at the family-building stage of the life-cycle.

In the public sphere, women's political and legal emancipation, reinforced by equal opportunities legislation and demographic trends, have led to substantial movement towards sex equality in employment opportunities;

which suggests increasing tension between the private and the public spheres. Women's labour and time are being sought by employers. Parallel to the accelerating post-war increase in the employment of married women, substantial growth has been experienced by those industries which provide products and services traditionally produced by women in the home; notably the food processing, distribution and catering industries. Growth in employment in these industries has been particularly significant over the last two decades and, particularly in catering, is projected to continue (Hotel and Catering Industry Training Company (HCTC), 1992, 1994). These are industries in which women, particularly married women in part-time employment, are employed in large numbers (Walsh, 1991; Purcell, 1993; Scott, 1994b; Employment Department Labour Force Surveys, various). Is it the case, as Novarra (1982) has suggested, that such patterns largely represent the transfer of women's labour from the private to the public spheres, where a substantial proportion of women fulfil much the same functions collectively for the wider community as women produced for individual households in the past? Conversely, do they indicate more radical change in the divisions of work, employment and leisure among households, between the private and the public, and between women and men?

HOUSEHOLD WORK STRATEGIES AND WOMEN'S EMPLOYMENT

Households are generally regarded as units of consumption but they are also units of production and social reproduction. As such, they are complex organisations with attendant maintenance work and indeed, for most people some of the time and for some people all of the time they are also workplaces. Allocation of domestic labour, management responsibilities, childcare and discretionary time within households is asymmetrically distributed in most cultures, with women generally being allocated more responsibilities and less rights than men; a distribution which has become gradually less extreme throughout the twentieth century in most Western industrialised countries, but which remains far from equal. Research on dual income households (Pahl, 1984; Hertz, 1986; Hochschild, 1989; Cook, 1992) suggests that women's participation in paid employment tends to lead, within households, to redefinitions and re-evaluations as to which activities are mandatory and which discretionary, and to some degree of re-allocation of roles and responsibilities between partners.

Time-budget evidence suggests that the distribution of total household labour between women and men has become less asymmetrical as married women have increasingly entered the labour market (Pleck, 1985, Gershuny, 1992); men with wives who have full-time paid employment are most likely to make a substantial contribution to unpaid work in the home (Kiernan, 1993). The most recent UK contribution to the debate (Gershuny *et al.*, 1994) argues that a process of 'lagged adaptation' – defined as an 'extended process of household negotiation (and perhaps reconstitution), extending over a period of many years, and indeed across generations' – leads to gradual change in the sexual division of labour where practice changes more slowly than ideology. The evidence from all the studies is unequivocal, however, that women continue to bear the main burden of household responsibilities in most households; they are the primary homemakers and parents in most cases, although they receive more practical support from their partners than previous generations of wives and mothers. Evidence of increased male participation in the private sphere suggests that such increased participation is incremental rather than substantial. Research on household divisions of labour in Greater Manchester concluded that the overall male contribution to most household tasks previously seen as 'women's work' appears to be relatively inelastic (Warde and Hetherington, 1993, p. 33) with exceptions deriving from 'relatively haphazard and probably circumstantial pressures' (p. 43). But what are the pressures and particular circumstances which are correlated with adherence to tradition and divergence from convention?

CONSUMER TRENDS AND THE MANAGEMENT OF FOOD IN HOUSEHOLDS

It is well established that household consumption patterns vary according to size, income, life-cycle stage and locality. It is also clear that expenditure on leisure goods and services is positively correlated with household income level (Central Statistical Office, 1993, etc.). Research suggests that the extent to which households engage in self-provisioning (Gershuny, 1985) is related to earned income and social class, and to whether, in two-adult households, one, both or neither partners are in paid employment (Pahl, 1984; Morris, 1989). Gofton (1989, p. 25) discusses how six trends in contemporary Western societies are identified by most commentators on food trends to have a significant influence on patterns of consumption: growing concern with health, home-centred living, redefinition of social roles within the household, the rise of dual-earner households, increasing

available time for home and leisure pursuits and a new emphasis on indi-
vidualism, hedonism and elitism. The relationship between these trends
and household food management is reflexive, as Gofton recognises, going
on to cite Mary Douglas's work on household food systems as 'a coded
expression of underlying relations between members, individual responsibilities and rights, conventions concerning the proper uses of resources
and so on' (Gofton, 1989, p. 26): but which variables determine the symbolic vocabulary (and diet) of which families – and why?

HOUSEHOLD DIVISIONS OF LABOUR ANALYSIS: THE MISSING CORE

Most studies of women in employment or household divisions of labour
have looked at the extent to which dual job and career families rely on
paid or unpaid help for childcare, house cleaning and gardening,
(Rapoport and Rapoport, 1976; Hertz, 1986; Hochschild, 1989; Brannen
and Moss, 1990). Time budget research has investigated the extent to
which gender divisions of labour in households are related to women's
economic activity and gender ideologies (Szalai *et al.*, 1972; Gershuny,
1985, 1992; Pleck, 1985; Kiernan, 1993) and indeed, recent work exploring the Social Change and Economic Life Initiative (SCELI) time budget
diaries throws considerable light on domestic divisions of labour in the
1980s (Gershuny, 1992; Anderson *et al.*, 1994). But none of these studies
engages at a detailed level either the extent to which household labour is
substituted for by work done by others or with the *management* of the
household. How far is the disjunction between the growth in women's
economic activity and limited growth in men's domestic participation
rates (Calasani and Bailey, 1991; Warde and Hetherington, 1993) accommodated by commercially-produced goods and services, or how far are
movements towards greater equality in domestic divisions of labour lubri-
cated by such supplementary sources?

   In addition, there is a strange lacuna in the household divisions of
labour studies when it comes to food management. All the studies include
the statutory 'who normally shops?' and 'who normally cooks?' questions,
but with the honourable exceptions of Warde *et al.* (1991, 1993) and, to a
lesser extent, Pahl (1984) the realisation that food planning and preparation are absolutely central to the identity and maintenance of households
appears to have eluded all but the sociologists of food (Murcott, 1983,
1988, Charles and Kerr, 1988) and anthropologists (Levi Strauss, 1969,

Goody, 1982, Douglas, 1984). Analyses have been made of household financial management (Pahl, 1984, 1990; Pahl and Vogler, 1993; Vogler, 1994), but there appears to have been no substantial investigation of the relationship between the economic activity levels of households, their internal divisions of labour in terms of both paid and unpaid work and the extent to which they take decisions to 'buy in' and 'subcontract' household services in order to substitute for their own domestic labour in the area of *food management*. Mason (1993, p. 154) has pointed out, in a review of the only recent (American) study which directly engages with these issues (Devault, 1991) that provisioning households 'involves not only shopping, but a good deal of mental labour in, for example, menu planning, improvising and re-arranging menu and shopping plans on the spot in response to price variations, and so on' and that producing a meal 'involves understanding the needs of others, juggling dietary requirements and individual preferences, attempting to synchronise the timetables of family members, and orchestrating social relations during the meal itself – in fact, management, craft, relatively unskilled work and emotional work' (Hochschild, 1989). The centrality of food management to home-making is neatly illustrated by the fact that, during wartime, government and local authority restaurants, like nurseries, were set up to facilitate women's employment participation (Land, 1978; Summerfield, 1984, pp. 99–104 *passim*). Indeed, households have been usefully defined as 'people who eat from the same pot'.

THE SOCIOLOGY OF HOUSEHOLD MEALS

Studies which have been centrally concerned with the sociology of food have tended to take a specialist focus (for example, Mennell, 1982, 1983, 1988; Charles and Kerr, 1988; Finkelstein, 1989; Gofton, 1989; Warde, 1991; Mennell *et al.*, 1992) rather than undertaking detailed examination of the relationship between the management of food and household work strategies in the private sphere, and between household food management and food production, processing, marketing and consumption in the public sphere. National statistical databases provide some evidence of changing patterns of consumption of fairly broadly-defined categories of foods and the incidence of eating out (Central Statistical Office (CSO) *Family Expenditure Survey* (1994), and *National Food Survey*, Mintel (1993) etc.), but little insight into qualitative shifts among types of product or the rationale which underlies consumer choice. For example, it is clear that demand for basic foods such as red meat and milk has fallen, but trends in consumption of prepared and processed foods containing these raw materials are considerably less well-documented (Daly and Beharrel, 1988) and the relationship between basic and processed food in household diets has received limited attention, either with regard to the nutritional or time-management implications. Warde (1991) argued that nutrition, tradition and the desire for novelty all contribute towards food choices and household food management, but concluded that no trend appeared to be preeminent; although if anything, close scrutiny of the Manchester data suggests that tradition may be the most powerful influence (Warde, 1991). Market research data (Mintel, 1993, etc,) gives some indication of eating out patterns, focusing on eating out largely as an evening leisure-centred activity, but relationships between eating out as a component of household food management; that is, as an alternative to or substitute for food preparation and consumption in the home; has not been explored.

THE OXFORD STUDY

In order to explore some of these linkages, a survey of women between the ages of 25 and 54 (mainly resident in Oxford) was carried out in the summer of 1991 (Purcell, 1991, 1993). These age groups were targeted on the basis that they cover the stages of the family life-cycle at which women have traditionally been assumed to have a choice of whether to seek full or part-time employment or specialise within the household on unpaid homemaking work (Becker, 1985; Owen, 1987). The survey respondents were not randomly selected, but were representative of the wider population from which they were drawn in terms of identifiable socio-economic and demographic variables. They were required to fill in a self-completion questionnaire containing *factual* questions about domestic divisions of labour, shopping, food preparation, cooking, eating and dining out, and *attitudinal* questions about food, food preparation, consumer preferences and healthy eating.

The focus of the study was on exploring the incidence and extent to which different types of households substitute and supplement domestic labour with 'bought in' household-based and catering industry services, thus contributing to the growth of those sectors of the economy which provide low-status, low-paid work for women. In general, the survey showed that households with dual-earner partners claim to use ready-prepared food products and consume services provided by the hotel, catering and leisure industries more frequently than 'breadwinner' households. But how is consumption of such services and products related to strategic and contingent differences among households in their access to and management of the finite resource of *time*? Patterns of consumption are clearly constrained or facilitated by the availability of time and money, but when is the trade-off between time and money a *cause* of household divisions of labour and when is it an *effect*? In general, do dual-earner families reluctantly and guiltily buy convenience foods or eat out *because* neither partner has time or energy to cook after a hard day's paid work, or do members of households make individual or collective decisions to maximise their earning power *in order to be able to* purchase such services? Which households use these services, under what circumstances? How far do members of households individually and collectively make strategic decisions about their use of time?

PAID WORK AND HOUSEHOLD FOOD MANAGEMENT: 'CONTRACTING OUT', 'BUYING IN' AND DIY LABOUR

American research suggests that households where wives have paid work eat out more often than non-employed wives' households and such consumption is clearly related to the desire to save time on provisioning and food preparation, but such wives do not use convenience or 'easier to prepare' foods more frequently (Darian and Tucci, 1992). It is suggested that possibly employed women 'compensate' for the higher eating-out incidence by preparing more labour-intensive food when they *do* cook, in acquiescence to traditional female gender-role expectations; reminiscent of findings on the significance of 'the proper meal' in women's identity as 'good' wives and mothers (Murcott, 1983; Charles and Kerr, 1988) and the rationalisation of 'quality time' referred to by parents in full-time employment in response to questions about childcare. How does women's paid work and the consequent increased commodification of time (Thompson, 1967) in households lead to different uses of time and divisions of labour between partners, between men and women, and between household members of all ages? Reconsideration of how time is allocated in the relationship between work (in all its guises) and leisure has been identified as the key to greater equality of opportunity between the sexes (Hewitt, 1993).

Given the evidence from dual career household studies that women generally do most domestic work whether or not they have employment, it is certainly worth investigating how the household food management of women in part-time employment compares with that of full-time employees and non-employed women and worth exploring the Oxford survey data further, with particular reference to the relationships between attitudinal and factual responses. The findings which follow derive from the 'Eating To Live' survey, selecting out only those 227 women from two-adult households. The Oxford survey suggests interesting hypotheses, as will be discussed below, but (being based on self-completion questionnaire) could not explore contingent relationships at the level of decision-making. For example, responses to questions such as 'Who normally does the food shopping in your household?' show interesting and intuitively persuasive patterns: 46 per cent of the women in full-time employment said that they did *most or all* the household food shopping, compared to 77 per cent of part-time employees and 90 per cent of women not seeking employment – which looks like a satisfying and significant linear correlation between economic activity and gendered shopping practices in households, reinforcing Kiernan's (1993) findings from the *British Social Attitudes* Survey, that part-timers' responses were skewed towards those of full-time homemakers. But we do not know whether part-timers' responses and practices reflect hours worked (and consequently, availability of time) or work status (and consequently, how much of their identity is invested in their respective home-making and occupational roles).

INSIGHTS FROM THE OXFORD SURVEY FINDINGS

It is evident from the findings of the survey that food preparation is a clearer discriminator than food purchasing of gender role relationships in households. When we compare responses on who normally prepares meals, those of part-time employed women generally appear to be closer to non-employed women than to their full-time employed equivalents, as Table 10.1 reveals.

It is clearly the case that part-time employment indicates acceptance of a larger share of domestic work in the domestic division of labour, which exhibits a greater practical if not ideological commitment to the traditional 'female' conjugal role. But decisions about whether to take full or part-time paid work may have more to do with domestic constraints than 'choice' (Dex, 1987) and ideology is apparently more egalitarian than practice: when the question 'Who prepared the evening meal yesterday?' was asked, the respective figures for 'Female did it' were 67 per cent for full-time employees, 83 per cent of part-timers and 96 per cent for non-

Table 10.1   *The relationship between female economic activity and who prepares the food*

Who prepares the food?	Female economic activity (%)		
	Full-time	Part-time	Not seeking employment
Female does all or most	58	90	96
Partners share	23	6	0
Male does all or most	12	1	4
Other	7	2	0

n = 227

employed women – which reflects a significant disjunction between 'normal' and 'yesterday' for full-time employed women and the first clue that we are dealing with an emotive and politically-sensitive area of investigation. Vogler (1994, p. 60) suggests that such contradictions may reflect the gap between normative conceptual models (what it is believed 'ought to' happen) and practice (what does happen). Both Hochschild (1989) and Kiernan (1992) have discussed the gap between the ideology of sharing and *actual* household divisions of labour and both Warde and Hetherington's and my own data indicate discrepancies between answers to 'who normally does .' and 'who *last* did ...' questions. As far as domestic labour is concerned men appear to 'normally' carry out tasks more often than they did last week, or yesterday, or during the period when a time-budget diary was kept.

EATING AT HOME

'Preparing the evening meal' is a very simple way of describing an extremely wide-ranging set of activities which encapsulate opening a tin or package at one end of a long continuum which extends to gourmet food production involving lengthy and highly-skilled culinary activity. It is not possible from the available data to explore whether there were systematic qualitative differences in the food prepared by male and female partners. It could be hypothesised that women may be more effectively socialised and equipped with greater tacit skills and/or be likely to have greater emotional investment in food preparation or, conversely, that men who *do* cook are perhaps more likely to be self-selected culinary enthusiasts.

The findings of the survey do investigate the reported frequency of convenience food use; which is again interesting in relation to female economic activity. The notion of 'convenience food' is another complex 'umbrella term' which encompasses a very wide and diverse range of food products, but it was defined in the survey questionnaire as *'pre-packed foods where the preparation and processing are largely done for the consumer prior to purchase'* to encourage respondents to consider it in its broader sense rather than the commonly used narrowly stereotypical meaning, pejorative with connotations about nutritional value. Charles and Kerr (1988, pp. 130–4) discuss the guilt expressed by their respondents about using 'convenience foods' – giving examples which clearly indicated a narrow definition of the concept. But although convenience foods increasingly include prepared natural and unprocessed foods (such as pre-packed washed and sliced fresh salads and vegetables) as well as tinned foods and microwave meals, it is likely that, despite the definition given, the term will have been differently interpreted by different respondents; and it is likely that there are systematic differences between socio-economic categories. Of women in professional and managerial classes included in the survey, 36 per cent said their households used convenience foods as defined, compared to only 24 per cent of semi-professionals and self-employed respondents and 40 per cent of routine white collar and manual employees: but are they talking about the same things? The one clear finding, given documented consumer trends, is that there is likely to have been a general tendency to underestimate or omit consideration of a wide range of convenience foods (CSO, 1994).

Table 10.2 would appear to suggest that dual-employment partners are significantly greater users of convenience foods, or at least significantly more likely to feel able to say that they make use of such products. This contrasts with Darian and Tucci's (1992) finding, cited earlier, that 'working wife' households appeared not to consume more convenience foods than others. The claimed lower propensity to use such foods of non-employed women in the Oxford survey may reflect less need to economise on time in food preparation, or a greater commitment to food preparation in the home, or greater association of guilt with 'shop bought' alternatives to home cooking (as found in previous studies; for example, Murcott, 1983); or simply, cognitive

Table 10.2 *The relationship between female economic activity and frequency of convenience food use*

Frequency of use of convenience food	Female economic activity (%)		
	Full-time	Part-time	Not seeking employment
A lot or fairly often	43	32	19
Occasionally	39	35	54
Rarely or never	18	33	27
n = 227			

dissonance which leads women who are *ipso facto* homemakers to minimise such commercial complements to their own work effort.

Table 10.3, which follows, reports the distribution of precoded responses to the question *'What are your feelings about food products such as frozen lasagne or stew?'*. These suggest that women overwhelmingly see convenience foods as, if anything, complements rather than alternatives to food prepared in the home, but do reinforce the picture that women in full-time employment are most likely to regard such food positively and least likely to associate their use with failure on their own part.

The above question referred to one type of convenience food, which symbolises the kind of product that the term is popularly understood to represent. Consequently, it is interesting to compare the reported household menus for the evening meal on the day prior to questionnaire completion, which were *post facto* coded, rather simply and unscientifically, according to the basic established nutritional guidelines and taking account of the time spent preparing the meal, into three categories: processed convenience food; 'healthy menu' freshly-prepared food served with fresh vegetables or salads; and 'other home-made'. For example, 'grilled salmon steaks, green salad, wok-fried Chinese vegetables, fresh fruit' was classified as 'healthy', 'spaghetti bolognese and salad (Ready Made Meal, Lean Cuisine)' as 'processed convenience' and 'toad in the hole, fried potatoes, peas and gravy; as 'other home made'.

Table 10.3   *The relationship between female economic activity and feelings about using prepared food products*

Feelings about pre-prepared food	Female economic activity (%)		
	Full-time	*Part-time*	*Not seeking employment*
Great	3	1	0
Useful but not everyday	43	31	35
Guilty – I think I should be providing 'home made food'	8	11	12
Don't use them	43	51	54
Other	2	5	0

$n = 227$

On the whole, the respondents cited such overwhelmingly healthy, well-balanced, labour-intensive meals that it is hard to escape the conclusion that there may be a tendency to present 'correct' answers. Only 10 per cent reported eating food which was unequivocally processed convenience food (which, as the example above shows, was most often far from an unhealthy option) and well over half described balanced healthy meals based on fresh ingredients, as Table 10.4 shows.

I am inclined to suspect that the responses reflect a desire to present, even in an anonymous survey, a public face of 'household best practice' uncontaminated by routine compromise, reflecting women's anxieties about their nurturing role.

Non-employed women appear to have been most likely to use processed food and least likely to conform to the 'healthy eating' category, but does this reflect lesser economic power, lesser concern with healthy eating, more time to cook traditional relatively rich, labour-intensive foods or simply, less guilt and lower awareness of the 'politically correct' response? Their reasons for using convenience foods may throw some light on this. Table 10.5 suggests that full-time employees are more inclined to use convenience foods to save time ran their part-time employed or non-employed sisters.

Table 10.4   *The relationship between female economic activity and menu of last evening meal*

Menu of last evening meal	Female economic activity (%)		
	Full-time	*Part-time*	*Not seeking employment*
Processed convenience food	9	4	12
'Healthy' fresh food and fresh veg/salad	58	63	42
Home-prepared food (other)	31	33	46

n = 227

Table 10.5   *The relationship between female economic activity and reasons for using convenience foods*

Reasons for using convenience foods	Female economic activity (%)		
	Full-time	*Part-time*	*Not seeking employment*
To save time	80	74	62
To save effort	44	33	58
They are economical	3	2	12
For flexible mealtimes	27	23	15
Health and hygiene	2	1	0
Other	10	9	15
None of these	5	5	0

n = 227

N.B.   multiple-response question.

Those not seeking employment were considerably more likely to cite economy as a reason for using convenience foods, which does suggest that they are considering baked beans rather than individually-packaged gourmet cook–chill meals. Full-time employees were, surprisingly, least likely to claim to use convenience foods to *save effort* but they reported that they most often used such products in order *to allow for flexible meal times*. The response to the survey showed a significantly greater propensity for the breadwinner/homemaker households to maintain formal sit-down family mealtimes, with two full-time earner households least likely to do so, as will be discussed below. This might seem to provide evidence that 'grazing' is more prevalent in households in which the female is employed full-time, but it is also, perhaps predominantly, a reflection of family life-cycle stage: the non-employed women were most likely to have dependent children in the pre- or primary-school age groups. This age/stage bias probably also accounts for the similarities and differences between full-time, part-time and non-employed respondents in takeaway food purchasing, with full-time employed women most likely to report frequent purchase, but with the greatest differences in reasons for use. Seventy per cent of the full-timers cited 'work-related' reasons (to save time, effort, or because they were 'too tired to cook') rather than 'intrinsic' reasons ('as a treat' or 'to enjoy food not normally cooked at home') compared to 58 per cent of part-timers and 57 per cent of non-employees.

EATING OUT

Women in full-time employment reported eating out more frequently than part-timers who, in turn, reported more frequent eating out than full-time homemakers (see Table 10.6).

This pattern could reflect differences in affluence, access to and involvement in social networks or again, life cycle stage. The same pattern of response was apparent in questions about the most recent date of weekend and mid-week eating out, with a greater polarisation between full-time and non-employed eating out at the weekend than at mid-week. This could reflect greater affluence leading to more frequent 'leisure eating' or it could reflect Friday night as the point at which depleted energy levels lead to subcontracting of domestic labour. Perhaps, again, the reasons given will shed some further light on this (see Table 10.7).

As indicated in previous responses, women in employment eat out more frequently and it appears that they do so, more than non-employed

Table 10.6   *The relationship between female economic activity and frequency of eating out*

Frequency of eating out	Female economic activity (%)		
	Full-time	*Part-time*	*Not seeking employment*
At least once a fortnight	21	13	4
At least once a month	23	21	19
At least once a quarter	35	35	31
At least once every 6 months	13	20	27
Less than every 6 months or never	9	10	19

n = 227

Table 10.7   *The relationship between female economic activity and reasons for eating out in the last four weeks*

Reasons for eating out in the last four weeks	Female economic activity (%)		
	Full-time	*Part-time*	*Not seeking employment*
As a treat	44	40	19
To enjoy food not normally cooked at home	10	12	0
To save time	7	4	4
To save effort	10	12	8
Too tired to cook	9	5	4
No food at home	2	1	0
As a social activity	34	40	27
Other	12	7	19

n = 227

N.B.   multiple-response question.

Table 10.8   *The relationship between female economic activity and feelings about cooking*

Feelings about cooking	Female economic activity (%)		
	Full-time	Part-time	Not seeking employment
Really enjoy it	25	27	46
Enjoy it but don't have the time	61	43	42
Enjoy doing special meals	50	38	54
Dislike everyday cooking	23	26	23
Don't like cooking at all	5	5	0
Other	3	6	8

n = 227

N.B.   Multiple-response question.

women, for both leisure and work-related reasons, which could lend potential support to any and all of the hypotheses postulated above.

ATTITUDES TO FOOD PREPARATION

The survey covered an ambitious range of questions on food management and attitudes to food, but my interest in this paper is in exploring the relationship between the respondents' employment status and management of the *work* involved in household food management. It is, nevertheless, incumbent upon us to consider whether attitudes towards the traditional (though not inevitable) central component of household food production – cooking – might be casually related to labour market decisions. That is, those women who accept the homemaker role might do so because they enjoy the unpaid work involved, whereas those who engage in paid work may be avoiding work that they would rather find ways of sharing or subcontracting. A question about respondents' feelings about cooking was included in the survey and the results are reported in Table 10.8.

Table 10.9 *The relationship between female economic activity and frequency of members of household sitting down at table to have a meal together*

'Sit down meal' frequency	Female economic activity (%)		
	Full-time	Part-time	Not seeking employment
Once a day or more	28	34	46
Most days	29	29	39
Two or three times each week	25	22	15
Once a week	8	10	0
Less often	4	4	0
Other	5	1	0

$n = 227$

This does not reveal any simple relationship between attitudes to cooking and economic activity. The clearest finding is that very few women claimed that they did not enjoy cooking at all, although around a quarter of all subsamples disliked everyday cooking. Thus, it appears that most of the women derived satisfaction from cooking some of the time: the full-time homemakers most positive and the full-time employees most likely to claim time as a constraint. But does this reflect varied versions of *post facto* rationalisation or cognitive dissonance?

Everyday cooking and household food management can be argued to be a more important component of the role-set of non-employed women, so that it is perhaps not surprising that such women are most likely to say that they enjoy cooking, but more surprising that they are as likely as members of the other subsamples to dislike everyday cooking. One of the most significant differences among full-time, part-time and non-employed women was the reported incidence of 'family meals' in the households (see Table 10.9).

As I have already argued, life-cycle stage is clearly a variable here, but the net effect is that the family meal is more often a routine and central component of daily life in the non-employed women's households than in others. This might mean, of course, that 'everyday cooking' is indeed more onerous in such households than in others and, when subsamples respond to the concept of 'everyday cooking', they are envisaging different orders of activity. Whether this reflects life-cycle stage, ideological commitment to 'family meals' or a structuring deriving directly from the professional specialism of homemaking – the building in of routines and structures to punctuate the working day and to recognise and affirm the contribution of the homemaker/food preparer – requires further investigation.

Clearly, these are small and possibly unrepresentative subgroups of women, at least some of whose work or non-work decisions are most certainly prescribed or constrained by socio-economic circumstances. It is consequently very useful to have access to time budget diary data that was collected from a large sample in six local labour markets in Britain in 1987–8, as part of the *Social Change and Economic Life* (SCELI) initiative (Gallie, 1994b), because this, collected primarily to enable investigation of household divisions of labour and the relationship between paid work and household activities and interdependencies, gives insight into household food management which is not directly contaminated by having the spotlight on food issues, as the studies previously cited. It would be naive to assume that time budget diaries give completely accurate records of time use but they, none the less, remain the best alternative to observation in providing evidence about social action, particularly if the activities investigated are an incidental rather than focal aspect of the exercise. Thus, to ask respondents to keep a diary of 'food and drink consumed by everyone in the household' over a two-week period (as by Charles and Kerr, 1988, p. 7) yields useful data, but there is the suspicion that behaviour and food choices might be modified by an awareness of the need to fill in the diary, as responses to my 'What did you have for your evening meal last night?' question. On the other hand, where respondents were asked simply to record all activities throughout the day in a given period (as in the *Social Change and Economic Life Initiative* Household Diaries), there is less likelihood that behaviour (or response) would have been biased in a particular direction, although this less focused data inevitably lack some of the detail of a specific study of food management.

There was, ironically, little data on food management collected in the SCELI questionnaires, but the time-budget diaries provide a wealth of information about a sufficient number of households in six localities to enable a useful exploratory analysis, related to questions in the household survey about household characteristics, economic activity and attitudes towards gender roles. Horrell's (1994, p. 208) analysis of the time budget data according to work status shows similar relativities among non-working, part-time and full-time employees so far as meal preparation is concerned, but most of her (and Gershuny *et al.*'s. 1994) analysis of the

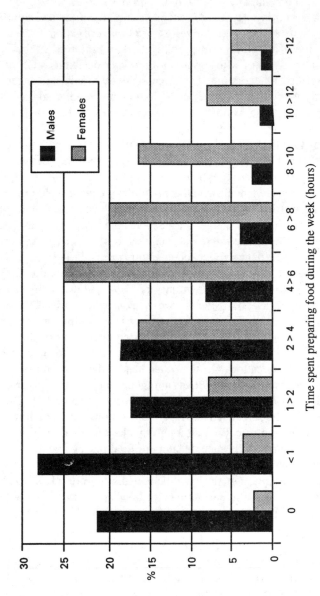

Figure 10.1 *The relationship between sex of respondent and time spent preparing food*

data so far, has tended largely to subsume 'meal preparation' within 'routine domestic work'. It is worth looking at the simple relationship between sex of respondent and time spent on meal preparation (Figure 10.1), because it is so elegantly asymmetrical, statistically significant and similar to the comparable Oxford survey findings.

The distribution of full, part-time and non-employed women varies systematically as in the Oxford study's subjective responses. Further examination reveals that there is a correlation between women's age and the time recorded preparing meals, with the time spent progressively greater, on average, the older the cohort. This lends support to Gershuny *et al.*'s 'lagged adaptation' thesis, discussed earlier (p. 178). Surprisingly, there appears to be no correlation between either number or age of children and time spent preparing meals, but an interesting relationship between employment status and hours preparing meals, as Figure 10.2 reveals: the profile of women in part-time employment resembles that of full-time home-makers rather than full-time employees.

The diary findings endorse the Oxford study findings both that women, whatever their economic activity, most often do most of the food preparation in most households, and that there is an inverse relationship, on average, between women's participation in employment and household food preparation. Careful comparison of the SCELI survey attitudinal data

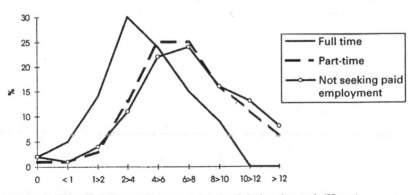

Time spent by women preparing food during the week (Hours)

Figure 10.2   *Female employment status by time spent on food preparation*

and time budget diary data (Gershuny *et al.*, 1994, *ibid.*) suggested that the time budget data provided substantially more consistent and reliable data, but concluded that survey data was sufficiently indicative of reported practice to be regarded as an acceptable, if impressionistic, proxy, for the sorts of 'how often and for how long?' questions that are most often addressed. The fact that the food management findings from the diaries, as far as they go, reinforce the Oxford survey findings, lends confidence to the representativeness and validity of the latter.

'WOMEN'S ROLE' IN HOUSEHOLD DIVISIONS OF LABOUR: THE REFLECTION OF IDEOLOGY IN PRACTICE

The systematically different clustering of responses among the three sub-groups of full-time, part-time and non-employed women, although complex, allows for the possibility that we may be exposing different ideological models as well as different behaviour patterns, where respondents have different views of 'natural' gender roles and 'correct' family dining and nutritional procedure which may, as well as being reflected in different practices, be predisposed to give 'politically-correct' images of household divisions of labour according to their models of 'normal' and/or desirable household divisions of labour. Detailed research (Hakim, 1991; Scott, 1994a) increasingly suggests that the female labour force may polarise into women for whom their occupation is, and remains, a central life interest and aspect of their identity (normally full-time employees with relatively continuous labour market participation) and women who have substantially adapted their labour market activity to fit family-building, to which they regard it as subordinate (normally women whose employment is discontinuous and/or part-time for a substantial part of their adult lives): what Hakim has controversially characterised as 'self made women and grateful slaves' (Hakim, 1991). It is certainly clear that women's decisions to take family-related career breaks frequently leads to downward occupational mobility and reinforces the likelihood that they will gravitate towards jobs which are less inherently likely to provide the scope to be central life interests (Dex, 1987; Joshi, 1987; Elias, 1994; Scott and Burchell, 1994). Although the contribution of even the least skilled and lowest-paid work to self-esteem has often been underestimated, it is, none the less, well established by classic sociological studies that employees in intrinsically impoverished jobs are least likely to regard work as the core focus of life (Dubin, 1956; Goldthrope and Lockwood, 1968). Most (although not all) part-time employment tends to be relatively low-level in terms of skills, status and reward, and recent research suggests that part-time employees tend to underestimate the skills required and exercised in their jobs (Gallie, 1994). Do many women, as Hakim suggests, opt for part-time work because they have chosen to give priority to their family roles? Or do women in part-time employment, having had their human capital potential eroded by the constraints of parenthood, and/or finding themselves in jobs with few intrinsic satisfactions, displace their energies and identity sources from employment to family roles, where there is generally more scope for gratification? Can the reported household food management patterns discussed in this paper throw light on this debate?

CONCLUSIONS

The Oxford survey results indicated a complex but clear relationship between household food consumption patterns and women's economic activity, related to but not dependent upon occupation, income and life-cycle stage. To summarise somewhat simplistically: households with two full-time employed adults were more likely to use convenience foods regularly, to eat out and consume takeaway food relatively frequently, and (as discussed in previous publications: Purcell, 1991, 1993) to share shopping and food preparation tasks more than in other two-adult partnerships and to involve children in these activities. As in most studies of household divisions of domestic labour, the findings indicated that the overwhelming majority of women, even of those in full-time employment, appear to do most food management work in the households represented in the survey.

One of the key preoccupations underlying this analysis has been the relationship between the extent of women's economic activity and their household management of food. Tentatively, I would like to argue that careful consideration of responses to the factual and attitudinal question does move the argument on, although it highlights the need for further research. Women who are in part-time employment appear, on the whole, to be more like full-time home-makers in their reported propensities to *do* food-management-related work but, paradoxically, are often more like full-time employed women in their attitudinal responses. This might suggest that giving priority to family responsibilities is more often a response to part-time work than a normative determinant of the decision to work part-time; but the clustering of responses is by no means unambiguous.

These findings thus raise as many questions as they answer and indicate the need for more detail about underlying decisions and context, which requires the collection of further qualitative data. Similarly, the SCELI diaries reveal time spent in shopping, food preparation and eating by different members of households, and the incidence of eating out, but they have nothing to say about menu planning, the basis of decisions about when, where and what to eat: the food *management* component and its relation to the *quality* of consumption.

Quality (nutritional and culinary) has emerged in previous studies as the most emotive aspect of food management, deriving from precepts of a traditional, patriarchal model of gender divisions (e.g. Delphy, 1979), women's emotional involvement in food as an expression of their love and caring responsibilities to partners and children (e.g. Murcott, 1983), women's professional investment in culinary expertise as a cornerstone of the wife/mother role (e.g. Charles and Kerr, 1988) and finally, women's concern with healthy eating and the well-documented high incidence of women having an ambivalent orientation to food (Orbach, 1981; Chernin, 1983).

This illustrates the paradox that, while the traditional tacit cooking skills passed down from mother to daughter are undoubtedly being lost (see Warde and Hetherington (1991) on the low incidence of jam and bread-making among their respondents and, in the Charles and Kerr (1988) study, references by the women to their own mothers' 'lovely' cooking compared to their own), women almost certainly know more about food values and nutrition than in previous generations. 'Food scares' about the health implications of food additives and farming methods have raised public consciousness about the importance of healthy eating. It is plausible that this leads to greater anxiety in attitudes to food and to household food management, particularly on the part of women who accept the cultural mandate that they are responsible for their family's nutrition.

Related to growing *concern about* food is *interest in* food. Throughout the 1980s, characterised by postmodernist concern with design and presentation over substance in virtually all areas of consumption, food became increasingly an expression of conspicuous consumption of 'distinction' (Bourdieu, 1984) for the more affluent strata of society. It is a further paradox that households buy in more prepared foods from the food and catering industries and eat out more than ever before (CSO, 1994; Caterer and Hotelkeeper, 1994), while interest in cooking correspondingly appears greater than ever, if sales of cookery books (Norman, 1991) and TV programmes devoted to food and cooking are anything to go by (six programmes exclusively concerned with food and cooking in the week beginning 24 March 1993, quite apart from features within other 'magazine' programmes).

I conclude that food practices are the last great taboo in our 'destructive *gemeinschaften*' culture given its increasingly normative subtext and women's emotional and moral investment in 'doing it right', referred to above. The picture is further complicated by the anomie which the majority of women currently experience when faced with the lack of a clear normative blueprint for the female adult gender role in the face of women's economic activity 'choices' (Rose, 1991). What all the findings discussed in this chapter indicate is a need, where questions of value are concerned, to develop sensitive qualitative research to explore the subjective experiences and explanations which underlie household and individual decisions: whether the decision is to order a Chinese takeaway or apply for a part-time job.

Acknowledgements

Tom Anstey, Senior IT Technician in the School of Hotel and Catering Management of Oxford Brookes University, was enormously helpful at the data entry and preliminary analysis stages of the Oxford Survey. Christopher Bates, Research Assistant, contributed to the analysis of both data sets. I am grateful to them both for their contribution.

References

Anderson, M., Bechhofer, F. and Gershuny, J. (1994), *The Social and Political Economy of the Household* (Oxford: Oxford University Press).
Ballard, B. (1984), 'Part-time Employees', *Employment Gazette*, vol. 92, September, pp. 400–16 (London: Department of Employment).
Becker, G. (1985), 'Human Capital, Effort, and the Sexual Division of Labour', *Journal of Labour Economics*, vol. 3, pp. 33–58.
Bourdieu, P. (1986), *Distinction: A Social Critique of the Judgement of Taste* (London: Routledge & Kegan Paul).
Brannen, J. and Moss, P. (1990), 'Managing Mothers', *Dual-Earner Households after Maternity Leave* (London: Unwin Hyman).
Calasanti, T. and Bailey, C. (1991), 'Gender Inequality and the Division of Household Labour in the United States and Sweden: A Socialist–Feminist Approach', *Social Problems*, vol. 38, pp. 34–53.
Caterer and Hotelkeeper (1994), 'Industry Trends', issue of 22 September, p. 18.
Central Statistical Office (1993), *Social Trends* (London: HMSO).
Central Statistical Office (1994), *Family Expenditure Survey: A Report for 1993 Giving the Results for the United Kingdom* (London: HMSO).
Charles, N. and Kerr, M. (1988), *Women, Food and Families* (Manchester: Manchester University Press).

Chernin, K. (1983), *Womanize: The Tyranny of Slenderness* (London: Women's Press).

Cook, A. (1992), 'Can Work Requirements Accommodate to the Needs of Dual-earner Families', in Lewis, S., Izraeli, D. and Hootsman, H. (eds), *Dual Earner Families: International Perspectives* (London: Sage).

Daly, L. and Beharrel, B. (1988), 'Health, Diet and the Marketing of Food and Drink: Some Theoretical Problems', *British Food Journal*, vol. 90, no. 1, p. 5.

Darian, J. and Tucci, L. (1992), 'Convenience Orientated Food Expenditures of Working-wife Families: Implications for Convenience Food Manufacturers', *Journal of Food Products Marketing*, vol. 1, no. 1, pp. 25–36.

Dex, S. (1987), *Women's Occupational Mobility* (London: Macmillan).

Diamond, Lord (1980), *Royal Commission on the Distribution of Income and Wealth Report* (London: HMSO).

Devault, M. L. (1991), *Feeding the Family: The Social Organisation of Caring as Gendered Work* (London: Chicago University Press).

Douglas, M. (1984), *Food in the Social Order: Studies of Food and Festivities in Three American Communities* (New York: Russell Sage Foundation).

Dubin, R. (1956), 'Industrial Workers' Worlds: A Study of the "Central Life Interest" of Industrial Workers', *Social Problems*, no. 3, 131–42.

Elias, P. (1994), 'Occupational Change in a Working-Life Perspective: Internal and External Views', in *Skill and Occupational Change*, ed. R. Penn, M. Rose and J. Rubery (Oxford: Oxford University Press).

Employment Department (1992), 'Results of the 1991 Labour Force Survey', *Employment Gazette*, April (London: HMSO).

Finklestein, J. (1989), *Dining Out: A Sociology of Modern Manners* (Cambridge: Polity Press).

Gallie, D. (1994a), 'Patterns of Skill Change: Upskilling, Deskilling or Polarisation?' in R. Penn *et al.*, *Skill and Occupational Change* (Oxford: Oxford University).

Gallie, D. (1994b), 'Methodological Appendix: the Social Change and Economic Life Initiative', in M. Anderson, F. Bechhofer and J. Gershuny (eds), *The Social and Political Economy of the Household* (Oxford: Oxford University Press).

Gershuny, J. (1985), 'Economic Development and Change in the Mode of Production of Services', in N. Redclift and E. Mignione, *Beyond Employment: Household, Gender and Subsistence*, (Oxford: Blackwell).

Gershuny, J. (1992), 'Change in the Domestic Division of Labour in the UK, 1975–87: Dependent Labour versus Adaptive Partnership', in N. Abercrombie and A. Warde (eds), *Social Change in Contemporary Britain* (Cambridge: Polity Press).

Gershuny, J., Godwin, M. and S. Jones (1994), 'The Domestic Labour Revolution: a Process of Lagged Adaptation', in M. Anderson, F. Bechhofer and J. Gershuny (eds), *The Social and Political Economy of the Household* (Oxford: Oxford University Press).

Gofton, L. (1989), 'Sociology and Food Consumption', in *British Food Journal*, vol. 91, no. 1, pp. 25–31.

Goldthrope, J. H., Lockwood, D., Bechhofer, F. and J. Platt (1968), *The Affluent Worker: Industrial Attitudes and Behaviour* (Cambridge: Cambridge University Press).

Goody, J. (1982), *Cooking, Cuisine and Class* (Cambridge: Cambridge University Press).

Grieco, M. (1987), *Keeping it in the Family: Social Networks and Employment Change* (London: Tavistock).

Hakim, C. (1991), 'Grateful Slaves and Self-made Women: Fact and Fantasy in Women's Work Orientations', *European Sociological Review*, vol. 7, no. 2, pp. 101–21.

Hertz, R. (1986), *More Equal Than Others: Women and Men in Dual-Career Marriages* (Berkeley and Los Angeles: University of California Press).

Hewitt, P. (1993), *About Time* (London: Rivers Oram Press).

Hochschild, A. (1983), *The Managed Heart* (Berkeley and Los Angeles: University of California Press).

Hochschild, A. with A. Machurg, (1989), *The Second Shift: Working Parents and the Revolution at Home* (London: Paitkus).

Horrell, S. (1994), 'Household Time Allocation and Women's Labour Force Participation', in M. Anderson, F. Bechhofer and J. Gershuny (eds), *The Social and Political Economy of the Household* (Oxford: Oxford University Press).

Hotel and Catering Training Company (HCTC) (1992), *Meeting Competence Needs in the Hotel and Catering Industry: Now and in the Future* (London: HCTC).

Hotel and Catering Industry Training Company (HCTC) (1994), *Catering and Hospitality Industry – Key Facts and Figures* (London: HCTC).

Joshi, H. (1987), 'The Cost of Caring', in Glendinning, C. and Millar, J. (eds), *Women and Poverty in Britain* (Brighton: Wheatsheaf).

Kiernan, K. (1993), 'Men and Women at Work and at Home', in *British Social Attitudes*, ed. R. Jowell, L. Brook and L. Dowds (London: HMSO).

Land, H. (1978) 'Who Cares for the Family?', *Journal of Social Policy*, vol. 7, no. 3, pp. 257–84.

Levi-Strauss, C. (1969), *The Raw and the Cooked* (London: Jonathan Cape).

Mason, J. (1993) 'Review of M. Devault, *Feeding the Family: The Social Organisation of Caring as Gendered Work*, London: Chicago University Press', *Work, Employment and Society*, vol. 7, no. 1, pp. 154–5.

Mennell, S., Murcott, A. and Van Otterloo, A. M. (1992), *The Sociology of Food, Eating, Diet and Culture* (London: Sage).

Mintel (1993) *The British Consumer: Patterns of Income and Expenditure* (London: Mintel).

Morris, L. (1989), 'Household Strategies – The Case of Married Couples', *Work, Employment and Society*, vol. 3, no. 4, pp. 447–64.

Morris, L. with Ruane, S. (1989), *Household Finance, Management and Labour* (Aldershot: Gower).

Murcott, A. (1982), 'On the Social Significance of the "Cooked Dinner" in South Wales', in *Social Science Information*, vol. 21, nos 4/5, pp. 667–95.

Murcott, A. (1983), *The Sociology of Food and Eating* (Aldershot: Gower).

Murcott, A. (1988), 'Sociological and Social Anthropological Approaches to Food and Eating', *World Review of Nutrition and Diet*, vol. 55, pp. 1–40.

Norman, J. (1991), 'Cooking by the Book: the Influence of Cookery Books on Eating Habits in Britain', *Proceedings of the British Association for the Advancement of Science Annual Conference 1991*, Plymouth, 26 August.

Novarra, V. (1982), *Women's Work, Men's Work: The Ambivalence of Equality* (London: Marion Boyars).

Orbach, S. (1981), *Fat is a Feminist Issue* (London: Hamlyn).

Owen, S. (1987), Household Production and Economic Efficiency: Arguments for and against Domestic Specialisation', *Work Employment and Society*, vol. 1, no. 2, pp. 157–78.

Pahl, J. (1984), 'The Allocation of Money and the Structuring of Inequality within Marriage', *Sociological Review*, vol. 31, no. 2, pp. 237–62.

Pahl, J. (1989), *Money and Marriage* (London: Macmillan).

Pahl, J. and Vogler, C. (1993), 'Social and Economic Change and the Organisation of Money within Marriage', *Work Employment and Society*, vol. 7, no. 1, pp. 71 -95.

Pahl, R. E. (1984), *Divisions of Labour* (Oxford: Blackwell).

Parsons, T. (1955), *Family, Socialisation and Interaction* (Glencoe: The Free Press).

Pleck, J. (1985), *Working Wives/Working Husbands* (Beverly Hills, CA: Sage).

Purcell, K. (1991), 'Eating to Live or Living to Eat? Time, Work and the Quality of Life', *Proceedings of the Annual Conference of the British Association for the Advancement of Science*, Plymouth, 25–30 August.

Purcell, K. (1992), 'Women's Employment and the Management of Food in Households', in *Food and Beverage Europe* (London: Sterling Publications) pp. 145–8.

Purcell, K. (1993), 'Equal opportunities in the Hospitality Industry: Custom and Credentials', *International Journal of Hospitality Management*, vol. 12, no. 2, pp. 127–40.

Rappoport, R. N. and Rappoport, R. (1976), *Dual Career Families Revisited* (Oxford: Martin Robertson).

Rose, M. (1991), 'The Work Ethic: Women, Skill and the Ancient Curse', Presidential Paper for Section N (Sociology), British Association for the Advancement of Science Annual Conference, Plymouth, August.

Scott, A. MacEwan (1994a), *Gender Segregation in British Labour Markets* (Oxford: Oxford University Press).

Scott, A. MacEwan (1994b), 'Gender Segregation in the Retail Industry' in Scott (1994a) op. cit.

Scott, A. and Burchell, B. (1994), '"And Never the Twain Shall Meet?" Gender Segregation and Work Histories' in Scott, (1994a), op. cit.

Summerfield, P. (1984) *Women Workers in the Second World War* (London: Routledge).

Szalai, A. (1972), *The Use of Time* (The Hague: Mouton).

Thompson, E. P. (1967), 'Time, Work and Industrial Capitalism' *Past and Present*, vol. 37, pp. 56–97.

Vogler, C. (1994), 'Segregation, Sexism and Labour Supply', in Scott (1994a), op. cit.

Walsh, T. (1990), '"Flexible" Employment in the Retail and Hotel Trades' in A. Pollert (ed.), *Farewell to Flexibility?* (Oxford: Blackwell).

Warde, A. (1991), 'Guacamole, Stotty Cake and Thick Double Cream', *Paper given at the British Association for the Advancement of Science Annual Conference*, Section N (Sociology), Plymouth, 25–30 August.

Warde, A. and Hetherington, K. (1993), 'A Changing Domestic Division of Labour?: Issues of Measurement and Interpretation', *Work, Employment and Society*, vol. 7, no. 1, pp. 23–45).

11 Researching Domestic Violence: The North London Domestic Violence Survey*

JAYNE MOONEY

The North London Domestic Violence Survey was developed in response to the need for better information on the extent of domestic violence in the general population. For as Smith (1989) has pointed out in her wide ranging review of the literature, such data are necessary if we are to begin to argue for the quantity and range of resources necessary to combat the problem of domestic violence.

In Great Britain there are three major sources of data as to the extent of domestic violence: cases known to the agencies, survey material available from national and local victimisation surveys, and the work of feminist researchers. Cases known to agencies such as the police or refuges point to a widespread problem, but suffer from the obvious limitations of merely representing the 'tip of the iceberg' and indeed reflecting more the limited availability of agency resources rather than the overall extent of the problem.

National and local surveys have generated a series of figures for the general population. Yet their figures are frequently recognised by the researchers themselves as under-representative and there are grave doubts as to whether mass surveys of the whole gamut of crime have the sensitivity to pick up all but a fraction of the actual incidence of domestic violence (Walklate, 1989). For instance the 1988 British Crime Survey indicates an incidence rate against women of 4 per cent (Mayhew *et al.*, 1989); the Merseyside Crime Survey, 3 per cent (Kinsey, 1985); the First Islington Crime Survey, 8 per cent (Jones *et al.*, 1986). Feminist research, in contrast, although limited by lack of funding has pointed to much higher figures–for example, the pioneering work of Hanmer and Saunders (1984) and Hall (1985). They have also been aware of the profound methodological

*The study was commissioned by Islington Council. Financing was provided by the Department of the Environment's Partnership Scheme and Middlesex University, PCFC funding.

inadequacies of conventional surveys, for example, in the area of definition, the problem of what actually constitutes domestic violence; the use of self-complete questionnaires, as in the Manchester Women and Violence Survey (Bains, 1987); the need for sensitive interviewing techniques and the problems of creating adequate crosstabulations within various sub-groups of the population. This survey has attempted to bring together these feminist insights and to couple this work with a random survey large enough to make cross tabulations by age, class and ethnicity. It is the largest survey, so far, to be conducted on domestic violence in Great Britain.

DEFINING DOMESTIC VIOLENCE

In researching domestic violence, the first issue that needs to be confronted is that of definition. There has been a lack of consistency between researchers, policy makers, members of the public and so on, over the relationships and types of behaviour that should be included under the rubric of 'domestic violence', and considerable debate over whether the term should be used at all (see, for example, Bograd, 1988; Smith, 1989; DeKeseredy and Hinch, 1991).

With respect to relationships, 'domestic' can quite clearly be referring to violence that occurs in the context of marriage or co-habitation between heterosexual partners, between siblings, between parent and child, and in gay and lesbian relationships. It can, in addition, be used to cover pre-domestic relationships, for example, dating relationships, and post-domestic relationships as in the case of ex-partners who are no longer living together. Domestic violence has been the term most favoured in policy-making areas because it is seen as covering all domestic relationships (Smith, 1989). Many commentators have, however, argued for more specific terminology for – although domestic violence may be useful as a contrast to 'stranger violence', serving to highlight the fact that a large amount of violence occurs in domestic relationships – its generality is not helpful with regard to theoretical or policy concerns. For it is necessary to identify the specific relationships involved, as each type may involve different factors and have different needs which will have to be matched by specific policies. More importantly, as feminist researchers have pointed out, domestic violence is a gender-neutral term and as such fails to clarify who is the victim and who is the perpetrator, masking the fact that, in heterosexual relationships, women are most frequently subjected to violence *by men*. It is for this reason that various researchers have preferred to use terms such as 'wife battering', 'wife abuse' or 'woman abuse' in order to emphasise against whom the violence is directed (Bograd, 1988; DeKeseredy and Hinch, 1991). Edwards (1989) and Walklate (1992a, b) have in their work enclosed 'domestic' in inverted commas to acknowledge its problematic character, particularly in the light of the controversial research of the Family Research Laboratory of the University of New Hampshire, USA, which denies the gender dimensions to this subject (Straus *et al.*, 1981; Straus and Gelles, 1986, 1988).[1]

In this project the gendered nature of much domestic violence is emphasised and we have tried to be as specific as possible in clarifying the relationships involved. The term 'domestic violence' has been retained for convenience purposes only as information has been collected on violence in a wide range of relationships including parent and child, between siblings and against women in dating relationships. The focus in the main has, however, been on violence perpetrated on women by husbands or boyfriends, including ex-husbands and ex-boyfriends.

The second problem of definition relates to 'violence': what is it that constitutes violence? This has two levels: how the different researchers define violence and the various definitions that women themselves make. It is abundantly clear that different rates of domestic violence will be calculated depending on the yardstick the researcher uses. Is a shove, for example, domestic violence or not? What is the status of threats of violence or mental cruelty? Some researchers have preferred to confine their attention mainly to physical behaviour. Bograd, for example, in *Feminist Perspectives on Wife Abuse* states that:

> Wife abuse is defined in this volume as the use of *physical force* by a man against his intimate cohabiting partner. . . . Violence may qualitatively change the nature of intimate relationships, even if they were characterised previously by the presence of severe psychological abuse. Violence threatens the physical safety and bodily integrity of the woman, and intensifies and changes the meanings of threats and humiliation. (1988, p. 12; my emphasis)

Gelles and Cornell[2] – although presenting a different theoretical position to Bograd – likewise, restrict their definition arguing that, 'from a practical point of view, lumping all forms of malevolence and harm-doing together may muddy the waters so much that it might be impossible to determine what causes abuse' (1985, pp. 23–4). The implication is that physical violence is worse than psychological abuse/ mental cruelty. Walker (1979) has, however, reported in her study that most of the women described verbal humiliation as their worst experience of battering, irrespective of whether physical violence had been used. *The North London Domestic Violence Survey* starts from the premise that mental cruelty, threats, sexual abuse, physical violence and any other form of controlling behaviour used against a woman by her husband or boyfriend are all domestic violence, serious and merit individual investigation; this has been reflected in the questions asked. It is made clear throughout exactly what definition is being used with respect to the various categories of domestic violence and the different rates which result from any given definition.

Furthermore, respondents themselves will vary, like the researcher, in defining what constitutes 'real' violence (see Kelly, 1988). Some respondents will define a push or shove as physical violence, whereas, others will not. The values held by the respondent are likely to be affected by their gender, age, ethnicity, class and education. For this reason the very first question in the self-complete questionnaire (Stage 2 of the research) establishes women's definitions of violence, and subsequent questions are based on separating out the incidence of the various forms of domestic violence. Qualitative interviews have, in addition, been incorporated into the project to examine in more depth how women define their experiences.

THE METHOD USED TO RESEARCH DOMESTIC VIOLENCE

The method used in the survey was essentially a variation of the victimisation survey, adapted to try to deal with the specific problems involved in researching domestic violence, for example, those of definition and fear of reprisals (that is, the perpetrator may be near to the interview situation), embarrassment and so on. Before commencing this project, two pilot studies were conducted in 1990 and 1991 at separate locations involving a sample of eighty women. The purpose of the pilots was to test the use of supplementary self-complete questionnaires (see Stage 2, below). This resulted in revisions to the questionnaire and field work strategies.

The North London Domestic Violence Survey has been in three stages but before the first stage could commence, a sample had to be constructed, an interviewing team selected and a questionnaire designed.

In order to construct the sample, the Post Office Address File was employed as the sampling frame. This is considered to be superior to the Register of Electors, which has often been used as the sampling frame for victimisation surveys, as it is updated every 3 months and does not suffer from the under-representation of minority groups. It has been established that the Register of Electors excludes about 4 per cent of private households, in particular those with young people, the unemployed, ethnic minorities and those in rented accommodation (Todd and Butcher, 1982). Poll tax evaders are also unlikely to be on the Register of Electors.

From the Post Office Address File 50 per cent of all households in the survey area were selected. At each household an alternate male/female respondent, aged 16 years or over, was identified for interview. To ensure a random selection within the household a Kish grid was used (Kish, 1965).

Given the sensitive nature of this research, great care was taken over the selection of the interviewing team. All were chosen for their understanding of and active concern about the problem of domestic violence. The majority of the interviewers were highly experienced, having worked on previous surveys. Six interviewers were recruited from the minority groups represented in the study area, of these five could speak some of the relevant community languages. All received intensive training and information on the help available to those experiencing domestic violence. They were monitored in the field by a fieldwork supervisor with counselling and social work experience.

A major feature of the interviewing brief was to interview respondents on their own. This was to try to ensure that the respondent did not feel inhibited, and that neither their safety nor that of the interviewer was compromised in any way. All respondents received Help-Line cards which featured the telephone numbers of a wide range of agencies. Our intention was to avoid the 'interview and run' style that has characterised many surveys: we wanted to ensure, should the need arise, that support was available (see Radford, 1987).

The questionnaires employed were carefully formulated, particularly in the light of the difficulties involved in defining and measuring violence. We tried to be as specific as possible in clarifying the relationships involved and used subjective and objective indices of violence. With respect to measurement, data has been collected on prevalence (the number who have experienced violence at some time in their lives and in the last 12 months) and on the number of incidents of domestic violence that have occurred in the last 12 months. The latter has enabled us to generate a rate that is comparable to police figures.

Stage 1

This stage of the survey was conducted along the lines of the traditional victimisation survey method. An interviewer-administered questionnaire was used and included questions on avoidance behaviour, victimisation and policing. The questionnaire was constructed so that the more general questions relating to crime were asked first, thus providing a useful lead-in to the asking about more 'sensitive' issues. This general questionnaire was administered to 571 women and 429 men.

One of the aims of this stage of the study was to generate data on the attitudes of men to domestic violence, so a section of the questionnaire was directed at male respondents only. Vignettes were used detailing where in a 'conflict' situation, men could see themselves as using violence. Dobash and Dobash have suggested that, 'the four main sources of conflict leading to violent attacks are men's possessiveness and jealousy, men's expectations concerning women's domestic work, men's sense of the right to punish 'their' women for perceived wrongdoing, and the importance to men of maintaining or exercising their position of authority' (1992, p. 4) and it was this that we tried to reflect in designing the 'conflict' situations. The 'conflict' situations, therefore, included quarrels over domestic arrangements, child care, infidelity and so on. This was supplemented by male self-report questions on actual violence: men were asked if they had ever hit their partner in any of the 'conflict' situations. Obviously if you ask men directly if they had hit their partner, they will reply 'no', but if you present them with a 'conflict' situation it was conjectured that this might elicit a different response[3]. Whilst it is true that even using such an approach, some men will see their violence as not 'severe' enough to mention or feel it is not relevant having occurred outside the scope of the 'conflict' situation or will simply lie, such data gives us a baseline. It enables us to say that *at least* this proportion of men would be liable to use violence against their partners. This section was included in order to move away from the conventional research emphasis on women alone; it is, after all, *men* not women who largely perpetrate violence on women and as such we should provide some focus on their behaviour.

The vignettes were also presented to 100 women respondents, they were asked if they could predict their partners likely response in any of these 'conflict' situations. This was to provide comparative data for the male responses and to discover whether women, in·relationships where violence has not occurred, are still controlled by its possibility. That the violence has not occurred may well be due to avoidance of the 'conflict' situations. Every woman interviewed was, in addition, asked about her experiences of domestic violence, mainly to act as a control to test the method used in Stage 2 of the project.

Stage 2

This stage involved women respondents only, the method used has been termed the 'piggy-back' method. Every woman interviewed for the first stage of the project was handed a supplementary self-complete questionnaire on domestic violence, together with a stamped addressed envelope. The interviewer was instructed to emphasise that the information recorded would be treated with confidence and that the respondent's identity would not be revealed to anyone. The personal contact made in the formal interview situation (Stage 1 of this project) had previously been found to motivate the respondent to complete and return the questionnaire, thus boosting the response rate. Pilot work had shown that this method generates a better and more accurate response than that of the traditional victimisation survey. This is likely to be because the method assures the respondent of her anonymity. Given the intrinsically private nature of domestic violence, it is easier for the respondent to record her experiences on paper than relate them verbally to a stranger, no matter how good an interviewer, standing on the door-step. Postal surveys also allow time for the respondent to reflect on questions which results in more considered, precise answers. This stage included questions on: definitions of domestic violence, the different forms of domestic violence perpetrated by husbands and boyfriends, including ex-husbands and ex-boyfriends; their incidence and prevalence; the use of various agencies by women and their assessment of the various agencies effectiveness. Questions were also included on physical violence and sexual assaults from other family members and sexual assault and rape from men women have dated/ gone out with on not more than five occasions. Despite such a wide scope, the questionnaire was kept as short and concise as possible to ensure that it would be filled-in and returned. So as not to have to ask the same questions twice, particularly those designed to collect demographic data, each supplementary questionnaire was given a number allowing it to be matched with the main questionnaire. In addition, to completing the questionnaire, many respondents wrote detailed accounts of their experiences thus generating qualitative data around a quantitative survey.

A key aspect of the self-complete questionnaires was that they were only given out to women whose partners were not at home at the time of the interview. They, therefore, not only gave the respondent time to reflect in answering questions when compared to the interview situation, they also had the vital element of secrecy. Questionnaires were handed out to 535 women. They, therefore, *represent a second survey selected on this criterion* and the response rate is calculated in terms of the numbers handed out. It is important to stress that the sample was not selected in terms of the willingness of women to answer a supplementary questionnaire. This would have perhaps biased it towards those who had experienced domestic violence. We had 430 questionnaires returned which represented a response rate of 80 per cent.

Stage 3

This final stage of the project consisted of in-depth interviews with women who had experienced domestic violence. Women who had spoken to the interviewer about their experiences in Stage 1 of the project were asked if they would mind doing a further interview. Fifteen were interviewed. In-depth interviews were included in response to the widespread recognition of the importance of a 'triangulation' of method (Denzin, 1970; Jupp, 1989). That is, the collection of both qualitative and quantitative data are essential if the experience of domestic violence is to be accurately portrayed. Qualitative data, such as that generated by in depth interviewing, are necessary to fully interpret survey data and, likewise, quantitative data are necessary to fully interpret the typicality of case studies. The intention of this stage was to provide information on the individual impact of domestic violence, the context of the violence and contribute to the understanding of the longitudinal development of domestic violence. Qualitative interviews further tackle the problem of 'incessant' violence, that is when violence occurs with a regularity it is simply not quantifiable in terms of the discrete, 'event orientation' implicit in victimisation surveys (Genn, 1988; Walklate, 1989).

A SELECTION OF THE FINDINGS[4]

Violence from Husbands and Boyfriends

Stages 2 and 3 of the project covered definitions of 'violence', women's experiences of different forms of violence from husbands and boyfriends, including ex-husbands and ex-boyfriends; the impact that these experiences have had and the levels of reporting to the various agencies.

How do women define domestic violence?
As previously indicated there is a wide variation with respect to what might be defined as 'domestic violence'. Women were, therefore, asked what actions they would designate as 'violence' in a relationship between a husband and wife or boyfriend and girlfriend. The results are presented in Table 11.1.

Thus, as would be expected, 92 per cent of women consider physical violence that results in actual bodily harm to be domestic violence

Table 11.1   *Women's definitions of domestic violence*

Behaviours	Agreed with statement (%)
A Domestic violence includes mental cruelty. Mental cruelty includes verbal abuse (e.g. calling of names, being ridiculed especially in front of other people), being deprived of money, clothes, sleep, prevented from going out, etc.	80
B Domestic violence includes being threatened with physical force or violence, even though no actual physical violence occurs	68
C Domestic violence includes physical violence (e.g. grabbing, pushing, shaking) that does not result in actual bodily harm	76
D Domestic violence includes physical violence that results in actual bodily harm (e.g. bruising, black eyes, broken bones)	92
E Domestic violence includes being made to have sex without giving consent.	76

$n = 430$.

but mental cruelty is also seen by the vast majority of women as domestic violence (80 per cent). Indeed, more women would define this as domestic violence than threats of physical violence (68 per cent). Important also to note is that rape, defined on the questionnaire as 'made to have sex without giving consent', (whether or not actual physical violence is used or threatened) is seen as part of domestic violence. This indicates that most women do not support the myth that rape is only an offence if the woman is beaten (that is, if there is bruising, black eyes and so on) and the man is a stranger. Indeed the survey showed a clear majority of *all* women would define all of these five aspects (mental cruelty, threats, physical violence without actual bodily harm, physical violence with actual bodily harm and made to have sex without consent) as constituents of what makes up domestic violence.[5]

This broad definition of domestic violence reflects women's attitudes to what amounts to intolerable coercion in their lives. Each aspect, of course, may occur together and compound the problem which women face. Furthermore, it would be wrong to view such violence as a simple continuum of seriousness ranging from mental cruelty through to threats and actual bodily violence. For example, prolonged mental cruelty may have greater impact than the sporadic, isolated incident of actual bodily violence. Clearly, however, women's prioritisation of this range of events under the rubric of 'domestic violence', would suggest a demand for a wide range of agency intervention. For example, not only the police and General Practitioners but also counsellors, social services and informal support groups. To argue that such a multi-agency approach is necessary is not, of course, to suggest that any one agency has a magic wand which will simply 'solve' the problem. All agencies are important and the particular configuration of agencies involved, together with the decision about which are to take a leading role, will be dependent on the problems of specific groups of women and the stage at which a violent relationship is being confronted.

Incidence, Prevalence and Time Span

Our questionnaire allowed us to separate out the incidence and prevalence of domestic violence. Incidence refers to the number of incidents of violence occurring; prevalence to the number of individuals affected. Obviously incidence rates will be higher than prevalence rates as the same individual may have several incidents within a given time span. In terms of time, we asked both 'have ever' questions and whether the violence occurred in the last 12 months. 'Have ever' questions are important in that they estimate the percentage of individuals who have been affected at some time in their lives and it should be stressed that women's fear and concern about domestic violence will relate to such lifetime experiences. As one woman who had been sexually assaulted over two decades ago said, 'I should be over it, but you never forget, just little things said or done can make you remember.' The events in the last 12 months are vital in order to know what individuals are affected in a year (prevalence per year) and what number of incidents occur per year (incidence per year). The *latter* figures represent the yearly potential demand on the agencies concerned. This being said it should be stressed that the figures throughout represent the number of women who have revealed their experiences to us. However high they may seem, and however well the research method has facilitated response, the percentages presented here represent bottom line figures. For many women will undoubtedly still have been too fearful, embarrassed or unwilling to reveal their hidden experiences to strangers.

The Prevalence of Domestic Violence in a Woman's Lifetime

Women were presented with a range of different types of violence and questioned as to whether they had experienced any of these at some time in their lives. The results are recorded in Table 11.2.

Table 11.2 *The prevalence of domestic violence in a woman's lifetime, by type of violence*

Violent behaviours	Percentage
Mental cruelty Including verbal abuse (e.g. the calling of names, being ridiculed in front of other people), being deprived of money, clothes, sleep, prevented from going out, etc.	37
Threats of violence or force	27
Actual physical violence	
Grabbed or pushed or shaken	32
Punched or slapped	25
Kicked	14
Head butted	6
Attempted strangulation	9
Hit with a weapon/object	8
Injuries	
Injured	27
Bruising or black eye	26
Scratches	12
Cuts	11
Bones broken	6
Rape[6] (defined as being made to have sex without consent)	23
Rape with threats of violence[7]	13
Rape with physical violence	9
Composite violence	30

n = 430.

Note that all of these behaviours have been defined by the majority of women as domestic violence. As can be seen from Table 11.2, violence from a partner is scarcely a rare phenomenon. Whether it is defined as mental cruelty, threats, actual violence with injury or rape, it has occurred to at least one quarter to a third of all women in their lifetime. There is, of course, a continuum in terms of frequency: mental cruelty is more common than actual physical violence, actual physical violence more common than violence which results in an injury. But *all* are common occurrences. Indeed even if we were to take one of the more extreme definitions of domestic violence, where bones have actually been broken, one in sixteen have been so inflicted. Furthermore, as has been stressed, all of these forms of domestic violence may occur together, and may have equal and compounding impact whether mental cruelty or broken bones. Indeed mental cruelty was seen by many women to be particularly damaging, thus confirming the finding by Walker (1979). One woman wrote, 'in my opinion mental cruelty is equally as bad as physical violence except the scars do not show and never heal', another reported, 'it is not the physical bashing so much as what you are told constantly – the belittling really wears you down – it is the mental abuse that really does the damage'.

In terms of the mode of physical violence, as would be expected there is a continuum from being pushed or shaken to being hit by a weapon. But even attempted strangulation, which might be considered the more serious end of this continuum, has occurred to just under one in ten women and assault with an object or a weapon to over one in twelve.

In order to achieve a general rate of violence to facilitate the cross-tabulation of the data, the categories: punched or slapped, kicked, head-butted, attempted strangulation and hit with a weapon/object were combined (that is, excluding mental cruelty, rape, threats of violence and 'grabbed, pushed and shaken'). Despite excluding some aspects of violence, 30 per cent of women had had acts perpetrated against them by partners or ex-partners at sometime in their lives which fell into this category. We termed this general rate 'composite domestic violence'.[8]

In this section, it is important, also, to comment on how widespread rape is from men against their partners. Just under a quarter of women had been raped. Furthermore, this had occurred with threats of violence to over one in seven women and with actual physical violence to just under one in ten women in the population surveyed.[9]

Women, in addition, on the supplementary questionnaires and in the in depth interviews spoke of being bitten, burned with cigarettes, scalded, knocked unconscious and of having experienced miscarriages as a result of an assault. Indeed it was not unusual for violence to begin or escalate in pregnancy, a time when women reported feeling especially physically and emotionally vulnerable.

The Prevalence of Domestic Violence in the Last 12 Months

Women were asked whether the various forms of domestic violence – mental cruelty, threats, physical violence, violence with injury and rape – had occurred within the last 12 months and the number of times that such violence had been inflicted (see Table 11.3).

Thus 12 per cent of women had experienced actual physical violence (including being grabbed or pushed or shaken, punched or slapped, kicked, head butted, attempted strangulation, hit with a weapon/ object) from their partners in the last 12 months, 8 per cent of all women had been injured and 6 per cent raped by their partner. These figures, alone, over such a short period illustrate the enormity of the problem.

From the above figures we are also able to ascertain the extent to which domestic violence is an infrequent occurrence or a repeated event. Thus if we distinguish those events which have occurred five or less times in the

Table 11.3 *The prevalence of domestic violence in the last 12 months, by type of violence*

Type	All (%)	No. of times (%)			
		1–5	*6–10*	*11–20*	*20+*
Mental cruelty	12	5	2	1	4
Threats of violence	8	5	2	0.2	1
Physical violence	12	8	2	0.5	1
Injuries	8	6	1	0.5	0.5
Rape	6	4	1	0	0.5
Composite domestic violence	10	–	–	–	–

$n = 430$.

Table 11.4 *Frequency of domestic violence incidents in last 12 months, by type*

| Type | Percentage of incidents | | |
	Less than 5	6–10	Over 11
Mental cruelty	42	17	42
Threats of violence	61	24	15
Physical violence	70	17	13
Injuries	75	13	13
Rape	73	18	9

n = 430.

year, six to ten times and over eleven times, we can make a breakdown of the figures as shown in Table 11.4.

As can be seen from Table 11.4 domestic violence is often repeated in all categories even over a relatively short period of time such as 12 months. More than a quarter of all injuries, for example, have occurred more than five times a year.

In terms of estimating the amount of potential demand on agencies with regards to domestic violence it is important to distinguish the number of incidents which have occurred per year (incidence rate) in contrast to the number of individuals involved (prevalence rate, see Table 11.5).

Incidence rates are the usual way of expressing crime rates, for example, the number of burglaries per 100 of the population. If we consider domestic violence where injury has occurred and where legal action would certainly be possible, we have an astonishingly high assault rate of 17 per cent (that is, allowing for rate per *total* population of men and women) due to domestic violence.

Average victimisation rates are the average number of times a person has been victimised: that is incidence divided by prevalence. As we can see the average rate of domestic violence committed against each woman is high for every type of victimisation. Domestic violence is far from a one-off occurrence. Thus the average number of times a woman who has been physically injured in the last 12 months has been injured overall is four. Domestic violence is thus not only widespread but frequently

Table 11.5   *Prevalence rate, incidence rate and rate of multiple victimisation over a 12 month period, by type of domestic violence*

Type	Prevalence rate by 100 women	Incidence rate by 100 women	Average victimisation rate
Mental cruelty	12	123	10.3
Threats	8	73	9.1
Physical violence	12	85	7.1
Injuries	8	34	4.3
Rape	6	25	4.2

$n = 430$.

repeated over a relatively short period of time. These figures illustrate the degree to which the national British Crime Surveys have underestimated the scale of the problem.

The Nature of the Relationship

In this section more specific details of the nature of the relationship were sought, in particular whether they were living together when the last incident of violence occurred or did not live together and whether it occurred before or after the relationship had broken up (see Table 11.6). From this point onwards all the figures presented, unless otherwise stated, refer to 'composite domestic violence'.

What is of interest here is that a significant proportion of incidents occurred with men who the woman was not living with or indeed had never lived with – 12 per cent of life-time incidents and 22 per cent of those in the last 12 months. The absence of domestic circumstances clearly does not seem to guarantee non-violence nor does not being in a relationship: a quarter of violent incidents occurring in the last 12 months involved former partners. Overall, 37 per cent of women experiencing domestic violence in this time period were not living with their partner or were not in a relationship with him. If the man was a former husband or boyfriend

Table 11.6   *The nature of the relationship in which domestic violence occurred*

	Violence	
Relationship	*At any time (%)*	*Last 12 months (%)*
Husband or live-in boyfriend	62	63
Current boyfriend (not living with)	4	11
Former husband or former live-in boyfriend	26	14
Former boyfriend they had never lived with	8	11
	$n = 129$	$n = 43$

women were, in addition, asked if violence had occurred whilst they were together. In 6 per cent of the life-time cases and 2 per cent of those in the last 12 months it occurred only *after* the break-up of their relationship. It is clearly necessary for agencies to be aware that domestic violence does not always come from within the home[10].

Impact of the Violence

The serious nature of domestic violence is illustrated by the finding that 8 per cent of women, experiencing violence at some time in their lives, had stayed overnight in hospital as a result, 20 per cent had taken time off work, 46 per cent reported 'feeling depressed or losing self-confidence' and 51 per cent felt 'worried, anxious or nervous'. The qualitative data further supported the degree to which the experience of domestic violence affected women emotionally and psychologically, as the following comment shows:

> Your own self-worth diminishes, even to the point of blaming yourself for the situation. You really begin to believe that you can't make a life on your own – after all you're not in control of your own life situation are you? You've had your 'stuffing' – your sparkle, spirit and joy of life – knocked out of you.

Several women, in addition, reported having had nervous breakdowns, suicidal thoughts and a few even attempted suicide. In addition, fear of reprisals was a commonly expressed worry and, as the relationship data reveals, these fears are based in reality given the number of women who are subjected to violence from ex-partners.

Reporting of the Violence

With regards to the reporting of violence, the predominant persons informed of domestic violence are friends and relatives rather than formal agencies. Friends are, however, considerably more likely to be informed than relatives: 46 per cent in comparison to 31 per cent. However, the response women received from friends and relatives varied: some were 'wonderful', 'very supportive', whereas, others expressed disbelief, blamed the woman and even pressurised her into staying in the relationship. Pahl (1985) has pointed out that it is only when these informal sources of support prove inadequate that women report to official agencies.

Of the agencies: General Practitioners and the police are the two front line agencies: 22 per cent reported to General Practitioners, 22 per cent to the police. The reporting to General Practitioners is in line with the findings of the percentage of women who need medical attention and with the emphasis on keeping domestic violence private. For, given the restrictions placed on doctors with regards to confidentiality, what is revealed is seen as going no further than the consulting room. The finding that around one quarter of all life-time experiences are reported to the police is high compared to previous estimates. The Women's National Commission Report (1985), for example, suggests two per cent and Walker (1979) 10 per cent but such differences may merely reflect different definitions of what constitutes domestic violence. The figures quoted in this section refer to a composite of domestic violence incidents all of which are incontestably actual physical assaults; if a wider definition of domestic violence were used (including mental cruelty, threats and 'grabbed or pushed or shaken') the figure for reporting to the police would fall to 11 per cent.

Although the finding that 22 per cent of those experiencing domestic violence (in accordance with our composite definition) report their assault to the police is high in terms of comparative estimates it still, of course, reveals a hidden figure of violence which is a cause of concern. The Domestic Violence Units set up by the police across London since 1987, with the intention of providing women with support and practical advice, are a major step forward. But it is vital not only that women should have confidence in these new initiatives but also that they should *know* about them. As it is, only 41 per cent of women who had experienced domestic violence in the last 12 months had heard of the Units and only 37 per cent of women in general.

The proportion of women consulting a solicitor was also found to be high (21 per cent) and, once again, emphasises the severity of the problem whilst creating worries with regard to the present cutbacks in Legal Aid in Great Britain. Only a small proportion contacted a women's refuge (5 per cent) which is likely to reflect their restricted finances and the regrettably limited services they can provide. Those women who had gone to a women's refuge were almost without exception very impressed with the response they received. They were described as 'offering valuable support', 'a safe atmosphere'. One woman stated, 'it was so good to be among women who were on my side'.

The Findings from the Vignettes

Male attitudes to domestic violence
As previously stated, in Stage 1 of the project men were presented with vignettes detailing a number of stereotypical 'conflict' situations and asked whether they could see themselves as hitting their partner in any of the situations and if they had actually hit her. Thirty-seven per cent of our total sample of men claimed that they would never act violently, about half said they could see themselves as doing so in up to two of the vignettes and 17 per cent said they would act violently on every example. The most frequently cited situation was sexual infidelity where just under a third of all men said they would be liable to hit their partners. Nineteen per cent of men actually admitted to using violence against their partners at least once within the range of incidents presented to them. Seven per cent had acted violently in two or more of the situations. These results – even though they are base-line figures – support the other findings presented in this paper in that they show that domestic violence is a common occurrence.[11]

Women's responses
One hundred women were asked if they could envisage their partner hitting them in any of the 'conflict' situations. The results were similar to those generated by the male questions: 35 per cent said their partners would not act violently in any of the situations, 18 per cent said they would on every example, 61 per cent in two or more of the vignettes. Of those women who responded to this section who had *not* reported on the supplementary questionnaires that they had been threatened with violence

or experienced actual physical violence, slightly over half said they would expect their partner to hit them if one or more of the situations occurred. That there has been no violence of this nature may well be due to avoidance of such 'conflict' situations which indicates that the behaviour of some women in domestic relationships is controlled by the *possibility* of male violence.

FURTHER COMMENTS

From these results, it is evident that the survey has uncovered high levels of domestic violence. On a methodological level, we must, therefore, ask two main questions of this work. Firstly, is the area in which it took place an exceptional one? The answer to this is 'no', the study was conducted in an urban area and it is important to emphasise that most people in Great Britain live in urban areas; further, it is an area that is mixed both in terms of class and ethnicity. The results can, therefore, be regarded as representative of the experiences of a wide range of urban women. Secondly, why did the study generate such large figures? Clearly this is to do with the method employed: the project used well-trained, sensitive interviewers; carefully worded questionnaires (which, for example, would repeat questions as to whether violence had occurred); a supplementary self-complete questionnaire and vignettes. We found that some women who had said to the interviewer in the first stage of the project that they had not experienced domestic violence, went on to report that they had on the supplementary questionnaires.

In terms of policy, on the basis of these results, we would argue for support to be built up for women experiencing domestic violence, on both an informal and formal basis. Given the number of women who told friends and family and the mixed response they received we must ensure through public education campaigns that *everyone* is aware of the extent of domestic violence and the problems women face. And it is an urgent priority that all relevant agencies are resourced and adequately funded and that women are informed of the help that is available. It is apparent that such a large problem has to be dealt with on a multi-agency basis because of both the size and the range of problems which women experience. For it is important for all concerned to recognise, as McGibbon *et al.* (1989) have pointed out, that women see themselves, the perpetrator and the violence, differently at different stages in the relationship and, therefore, their needs and concerns will change in accordance with this.

The results of the North London Domestic Violence Survey will be presented to the various agencies to assist them with policy development, particularly with respect to the patterning of potential demand.

Notes

1. The work of the Family Research Laboratory – often described as the 'family violence' approach – has been subject to detailed criticisms by feminists (see, for example, Kelly, 1988; Walklate 1992a, b; Dobash and Dobash, 1992; Brush, 1993; Kurz, 1993).
2. These researchers are associated with the 'family violence' approach.
3. This method is distinct from the Conflict Tactic Scales used by the 'family violence' researchers which does not suggest specific scenarios (Straus, 1979; Straus *et al.*, 1981).
4. Further findings are discussed in *The Hidden Figure: Domestic Violence in North London* (Mooney, 1993) and *Violence, Space and Gender: the Social and Spatial Parameters of Violence Against Women and Men* (Mooney, 1994).
5. When the data was analysed by age, class and ethnicity some differences between women in defining domestic violence did emerge (see Mooney, 1993). For example, women who were fifty-five years and over were less likely than other age groups to define the behaviours listed as domestic violence: a variation which indicates that there may well have been a change in attitude over the years with respect to what constitutes domestic violence and in levels of tolerance over what is 'acceptable' behaviour within a relationship.
6. As many commentators have pointed out (Clark and Lewis, 1977; Hall, 1985; Estrich, 1987) many rapes are accompanied by non-physical forms of coercion (i.e not by overt threats of violence or actual physical force or violence e.g. bruising, broken bones, etc.). Social and economic forms of coercion, for example, are likely to occur, particularly when rape takes place in the context of a relationship. It must also be stressed that rape is a violent act in itself whether or not achieved by threats of or actual physical violence. Unfortunately, whilst being made to have sex without giving consent is defined in law as 'rape', it is often only when physical forms of coercion are involved that society and particularly the criminal justice system – and then not always (see Lees and Gregory, 1993) – is prepared to accept that a rape has taken place.
7. It should be noted that threats of violence and actual physical violence are not mutually exclusive as some women will be threatened and/or have physical violence used against them in different incidents.
8. This is not, of course, to suggest that violence does not occur outside the composite or is less serious for, as it has been shown, this is manifestly untrue. Indeed this study starts from the premise that mental cruelty, threats, sexual violence, physical violence and any other form of controlling behaviour used against a woman are all to be seen as violence.

However, we found in both our quantitative and qualitative work that the composite is a definition of violence which virtually all women agree about whilst with other forms of violence there is a greater divergence of opinion. The use of a consensus definition enables us to counter the argument that violence rates are simply a reflection of definitional variations between different parts of the population (see Hough, 1986; Young, 1986). Composite domestic violence is incontestably domestic violence whoever's definition one utilises.

9. Rape and sexual assault on dates were likewise found to be not uncommon experiences: for example, 9 per cent of women reported being raped on a date at sometime in their lives.

10. Information was also collected in the survey on threatening and obscene telephone calls from ex-partners (see Mooney, 1993).

11. These data will be further analysed to determine the social characteristics of the least violent and the most violent men. Data has also been obtained on men's experiences of physical violence as children, when cross-tabulated by the vignette data this should enable us to explore the inter-generational transmission of violence hypothesis.

References

Bains, S. (1987), *Manchester's Crime Survey of Women for Women* (Manchester Council: Police Monitoring Unit).

Bograd, M. (1988), 'Feminist Perspectives in Wife Abuse: An Introduction', in K. Yllo and M. Bograd (eds), *Feminist Perspectives on Wife Abuse* (Beverly Hills, CA: Sage).

Brush, L. (1993), 'Violent Acts and Injurious Outcomes in Married Couples: Methodological Issues in the National Survey of Families and Households', in Bart, P. and Moran, E. (eds), *Violence Against Women* (Beverly Hills, CA: Sage).

Clark, L. and Lewis, D. (1977), *Rape: The Price of Coercive Sexuality* (Ontario: The Women's Press).

DeKeseredy, W. and Hinch, R. (1991), *Woman Abuse: Sociological Perspectives* (Ontario: Thompson).

Denzin, N. (1970), *The Research Act* (Chicago, IL: Aldine).

Dobash, R and Dobash, R. (1992), *Women, Violence and Social Change* (London: Routledge).

Edwards, S. (1989), *Policing 'Domestic' Violence* (London: Sage).

Estrich, S. (1987), *Real Rape* (London: Harvard University Press).

Gelles, R. and Cornell, C. (1985), *Intimate Violence in Families* (Beverley Hills: Sage).

Genn, H. (1988), 'Multiple Victimisation', in Maguire, M. and Pointing, J. (eds), *Victims of Crime: A New Deal* (Milton Keynes: Open University Press).

Hall, R. (1985), *Ask Any Woman*, Report of the Women's Safety Survey conducted by Women Against Rape (Bristol: Falling Wall Press).

Hanmer, J. and Saunders, S. (1984), *Well-Founded Fear* (London: Macmillan).

Hough, M. (1986), 'Victims of Violent Crime: Findings from the First British Crime Survey', in Fattah, E. (ed.), *From Crime Policy to Victim Policy* (London: Macmillan).

Jones, T., Maclean, B. and Young, J. (1986), *The First Islington Crime Survey*, Middlesex Polytechnic: Centre for Criminology.

Jupp, V. (1989), *Methods of Criminological Research* (London: Unwin Hyman).

Kinsey, R. (1985), *First Report of the Merseyside Crime Survey* (Liverpool: Merseyside County Council)

Kish, L. (1965), *Survey Sampling* (New York: Wiley).

Kelly, L. (1988), *Surviving Sexual Violence* (Cambridge: Polity Press).

Kurz, D. (1993), 'Social Science Perspectives on Wife Abuse: Current Debates and Future Directions', in Bart, P. and Moran, E. (eds), *Violence Against Women* (London: Sage).

Lees, S. and Gregory, J. (1993), *Rape and Sexual Assault: A Study of Attrition* (Islington Council: Police and Crime Prevention Unit).

Mayhew, P., Elliot, D. and Dowds, L.(1989), *1988 British Crime Survey* (London: HMSO).

McGibbon, A., Cooper, L. and Kelly, L. (1989), *What Support?* (London: PNL & Hammersmith and Fulham Council Community Committee Domestic Violence Project).

Mooney, J. (1993), *The Hidden Figure: Domestic Violence in North London* (Islington Council: Police and Crime Prevention Unit).

Mooney, J. (1994), *Violence, Space and Gender: The Social and Spatial Parameters of Violence Against Women and Men* (Middlesex University: Centre for Criminology)

Pahl, J. (1985), *Private Violence and Public Policy* (London: Routledge & Kegan Paul).

Radford, J. (1987), 'Policing Male Violence – Policing Women', in Hanmer, J. and Maynard, M. (eds), *Women, Violence and Social Control* (London: Macmillan).

Smith, L. (1989), *Domestic Violence* (London: HMSO).

Straus, M. and Gelles, R. (1988), 'How Violent are American Families? Estimates from the National Family Abuse Violence Resurvey and Other Studies', in Hotling, G., Finkelhor, D., Kirkpatrick, J. and Straus, M. (eds), *Family Abuse and its Consequences* (Newbury Park: Sage).

Straus, M. and Gelles, R. (1986), 'Societal Change in Family Violence from 1975 to 1985', *Journal of Marriage and the Family*, vol. 48, pp. 465–79.

Straus, M., Gelles, R. and Steinmetz, S. (1981), *Behind Closed Doors: Violence in the American Family* (New York: Anchor Books).

Straus, M. (1979), 'Measuring Intrafamily Conflict and Violence', *Journal of Marriage and the Family*, vol. 41, pp. 75–88.

Todd, S. and Butcher, B. (1982), *Electoral Registration in 1981*, OPCS (London: HMSO).

Walklate, S. (1989), *Victimology* (London: Unwin Hyman).

Walklate, S. (1992a), *The Kirkby Inter-Agency Response to Domestic Violence* (University of Salford: Department of Sociology).

Walklate, S. (1992b), *Responding to Domestic Violence* (University of Salford: Department of Sociology).

Walker, L. (1979) *The Battered Woman* (New York: Harper & Row).

Women's National Commission (1985), *Violence Against Women* (London: Cabinet Office)

Young, J. (1986), 'Risk of Crime and Fear of Crime: A Realist Critique of Survey-Based Assumptions', in Maguire, M. and Pointing, J. (eds), *Victims of Crime: A New Deal* (Milton Keynes: Open University Press).

12. Masculinity, Emotion and Sexual Violence*

PAULINE FULLER

Over the past three decades feminist writers and theoreticians have been elaborating ideas which make connections between gender and sexual violence. This approach has been applied to the analysis of child sexual abuse and it has been argued that since the vast majority of known abusers are male,[1] the social construction of masculinity within a patriarchal culture may be an important contributory factor.[2] It is important to note what this does not mean; a physiological state of maleness does not itself produce sexual violence. Rather, there exists a social construction of masculinity, which is dominant in Western culture, and which contains elements enabling sexual and other violence against women, children and men.

In this research the possible links between the structurally dominant construction of masculinity and child sexual abuse have been investigated. David Finkelhor (1984) has noted that little empirical research directed toward the identification of such links has been conducted. The research outlined here is based on interviews with thirteen men who had experienced a sexual relationship with a child. Most of the respondents were contacted through a Probation Service Sex Offender's Group and all had been convicted for sexual offences against children or adolescents. The sample is, therefore, in no way representative of the majority of such abusers, who have neither been reported or arrested.

Each respondent was asked to give an account and explanation of his 'offence'.[3] Additionally, a 'mini' life-history was elicited, in which the respondent was encouraged to draw attention to events and experiences he thought may have been relevant to his sexual behaviour. In this way the respondent's 'world view' and understanding of his own behaviour became apparent, being implicit in his life 'stories'. The stories were analysed for evidence of whether the respondent was strongly influenced in his attitudes and behaviour by the structurally dominant form of masculinity. Feminist theories suggest a variety of connections between

*This paper is based on research funded by the Economic and Social Research Council and the Fuller Bequest, Department of Sociology Research Fund, University of Essex.

masculinity and child sexual abuse, at several levels of social life. In view of this I identified five areas for analysis where such connections might be found. These might be summed up as Women, Sex, Men, Emotion and Childhood.

In this chapter I will briefly outline the theoretical perspectives employed in this research, followed by an account of some of the research findings. These are divided into five parts that correspond to the five areas identified above.

THEORETICAL PERSPECTIVES: INTERACTIONISM, MASCULINITY AND EMOTION

The five areas of analysis were derived from a feminist Interactionist perspective much influenced by the 'Scripting Theory' of John Gagnon and William Simon (1987) and the 'Emotion Management Perspective' of Arlie Hochschild (1979). These writers share a concern with socially derived scripting, either of sexual activities and conduct, or emotional conduct. Both imply an individual self actively engaged in this process, whereby emotional and sexual life is managed or staged; sometimes according to cultural prescription, sometimes against it.

Each area represents a collection of social constructions, be they ideologies, images or social rules regarding behaviour, dress and conduct. Additionally, each includes the meanings individuals attach to these and their own physical and emotional feelings about them. Clearly these constructions and meanings vary across time, culture, class, ethnicity and gender.

At the structural level of society ideals, cultural prescriptions and social rules may all be understood as 'scripts' or 'cultural scenarios' (Simon and Gagnon, 1987, p. 365), which are available as patterns for the production of individual or group styles. Some of these hold a strong position as a cultural norm in our society and may thus be deemed to have gained structural dominance. At the social level such norms are negotiated, maintained or challenged in the interactions between people. Interactions may be face-to-face or involve an individual interacting with cultural representations of various kinds. For example in the media, art, music or law. Individual perceptions of the five areas, of 'femininity', 'sexuality', 'masculinity', 'emotion' and 'childhood', are built up through such processes; as are the social rules and meanings which become attached to these constructions. Interactions between people may be described as 'interpersonal scripts' (Simon and Gagnon, 1987, p. 365), drawing on cultural scenarios for shared meanings and the rules of conduct which apply to that situation. Individuals draw upon both these sources in their development of their own 'intrapsychic scripts' (Simon and Gagnon, 1987, p. 366). Individuals and groups may also produce new scripts, enhancing or contravening those already in existence. In this way social action and social structure may be seen to articulate, at the structural, social and individual levels of analysis.

Thus socially constructed definitions of masculinity vary across time, place, class, race and religion. [4] For this reason it is possible to say that there is not one 'masculinity' but that there are 'masculinities'; typical forms associated with for example class or race. It is, therefore, possible for several constructions of masculinity to co-exist in one time and place (Ehrenreich, 1983). Contemporary examples can be readily cited: Sporting Man, Macho Man, Business Man, Working Class Man, Middle Class Man, Homosexual Man, and these constructions can be seen to overlap to a great extent (often in the same individuals). Alongside these, other constructions have recently become available. Gay Man and New Man appear to contradict much of the content of the more conventional constructions. The point is, conventional constructions of masculinity all share aspects of a single idealised form of 'masculinity' and it is the unequal power relationship between women and men which connects them. There are various terms for this central form in the literature, but the best for several reasons is 'hegemonic masculinity' (Connell, 1987). This concept allows that a particular form of masculinity can be the dominant available model. However, by attaching Antonio Gramsci's concept of 'hegemony' to this notion of a dominant ideal of masculinity, the active agreement, co-operation and collaboration of individuals is implied. Additionally, we gain the insight that this ideal form is embedded in social practice. This has the advantage of highlighting the articulation between the structural, social and individual levels of society, in the creation of a 'gender order' (Connell, 1987, p. 119). Hegemonic masculinity fashions structures of power while being continually formed by them. It also offers what might, borrowing from Simon and Gagnon, be called a 'script' for the individual performance of masculinity.

The ideals, cultural prescriptions, social rules and norms attached to hegemonic masculinity may all be understood in terms of Scripting Theory. Cultural scenarios relating to hegemonic masculinity are available as patterns for the individual production of corresponding interpersonal and intrapsychic scripts. The most easily identified examples of cultural scenarios regarding the performance of hegemonic masculinity can be gleaned from the popular newspapers:

Men think about sex every five minutes.   (*Daily Star*, 10 May 1990)

Romeo Craig tells of his wild romps, *Home and Away* Hey – My 140 girls, by TV hunk who had three in a bed sex session
(*The News of the World*, 17 June 1990)

Brain, Body and Emotions – Make the difference between Men and Women.
  Will you pass your sex test?:
Question 6: Out of men & women, who needs to have good love more than good sex?
Correct answer: Women are more sensitive and so love is more important.
Question 20: Of men & women – who needs sexual satisfaction far more than they need romance and emotional love?
Correct answer: Men – to them the physical act is much more important.
(*News of the World Sunday Magazine*, 1 July 1990)

The above quotes make it clear that the sexes are different and illuminate some important emotional and sexual aspects of the cultural scenarios for hegemonic masculinity. The implications are that men are sexually insatiable, while women take the emotional and sexual responsibility for them.

I have outlined a model in which individual men are presented with an idealised form of masculinity which they *may* adopt *in full, or part, or reject*. Many men adhere to the ideologies inherent in the cultural scenarios associated with hegemonic masculinity. Similarly, many women adhere to such scenarios in their expectations of individual men. A central aspect of the heterosexual relationship and hegemonic masculinity is emotion.

Recently there has been an explosion of men talking about their emotional lives, or more accurately, their lack of connection with their emotional lives. For example the 'Men's Recovery' movement is encouraging men to rediscover their emotions. What this illuminates is that men are increasingly dissatisfied with their emotional development. Men's 'emotional illiteracy' (Glaser and Frosh, 1988) and the strong social constraints against male expression of most emotions, have been highlighted by a number of theorists of masculinity. [5] My interpretation of this is that hegemonic masculinity involves a distancing of the individual from his emotional life.

The approach of feminist Object Relations Theory in this area is of considerable relevance (Chodorow, 1978). Building on this work, Luise Eichenbaum and Susie Orbach point to patriarchal forms of masculinity and femininity as the means by which men learn not to express emotions or how to deal with them in others. Since this is women's work, men's dependency. . . . remains the best kept secret, the terrifying taboo, of masculinity . . . . boys experience and expect nurturing simply as 'part of the fabric of life'.   (Eichenbaum and Orbach, 1983, p. 75)

Thus the most fully theorised explanation of why masculine sexuality should enable sexual violence, comes from the application of feminist Object Relations Theory (Metcalf and Humphries, 1985; Glaser and Frosh, 1988; MacLeod and Saraga, 1988). Sex becomes one of the few avenues to emotional expression, but since masculine identity is centred on the denial of emotions, sex becomes dangerous or a means of expressing all emotions. Thus it is argued child sexual abuse is 'inherent in a mode of personality organisation that rejects intimacy' (Frosh in MacLeod and Saraga, 1988, p. 42). The cultural scenarios of hegemonic masculinity may therefore contribute to the development of the sexually abusive male.

A major criticism of feminist Object Relations Theory is that the individual becomes a passive receptor of social imperatives. Personal and social change become impossible and 'masculinity' and 'femininity' can never be broken down or challenged. However, Hochschild's Emotion Management Perspective resolves this problem. Hochschild assumes independent human action by arguing that adults actively manage their emotions. Hochschild applies the term 'feeling rules' to those social rules which refer to emotional conduct, arguing these are culturally and socially variable. Emotion management is a kind of work where we change an emotion in 'degree or quality' (Hochschild, 1979, p. 561). Emotion work is performed by self on self and others, and by others on self. It has two forms: the evocation and shaping of feelings, or their suppression and control. This requires

> one to induce or suppress feeling in order to sustain the outward countenance that produces the proper state of mind in others.
>   (Hochschild, 1983, p. 7)

Hochschild argues that we usually perform such work when we become conscious of a dissonance between what we feel and feeling rules. This can have damaging psychological effects if prolonged, for example, in those who sell their emotional labour. In Western culture, Hochschild argues, emotion management capabilities are promoted in women and inhibited in men through socialisation processes. Feeling rules are gender differentiated. This is born out in the media quote above, where male and female approaches to emotion are taken to be entirely opposite. Hochschild argues that both women and men do emotion work, but this is more important to women as a resource to exchange for men's material property. The subordinate position of women means they must become better emotion managers than men. Women are not more emotional than men, but do more emotion work; they may express emotionality more, but be more in control of their feelings. Hochschild explains this in terms of feminist Object Relations Theory, which suggests that boys reject feminine aspects of self in order to attain manhood. This results in men's 'repression of feeling generally' (Hochschild, 1983, p. 164) and has been noted by many as forming a structural constraint upon men. The cultural scenarios of hegemonic masculinity can be interpreted as offering feeling rules for the performance of masculine emotion in our society. As the foregoing suggests, the major feeling rule would be the non-expression of most emotions. At the level of the intrapsychic script, this rule would dictate the non-feeling of these emotions. Unlike Hochschild, I would argue this is as an extreme act of emotion management, involving as much suppression of emotion as possible. This implies the potential for psychic damage noted by Hochschild and explains the increasing dissatisfaction of some men with their emotional lives. I will now move on to a brief description of the research findings.

HEGEMONIC MASCULINITY AND CHILD SEXUAL ABUSE

The findings of this research fall into five categories which approximate to the five areas outlined earlier. These are illustrated with extended quotations from the interviews in my thesis, but clearly they cannot be reproduced here.

(1)　Sexual Ideologies Regarding Women

The term 'sexual ideologies' relates to all five areas in some way, however in this research it is used specifically in relation to the respondents' ideas about, and actions towards, women. Eight of the respondents were or had been husbands. All eight were found to have been abusing the power associated with this 'role'. This was chiefly through the abuse of their economic and physical power over wives. Each wife could be defined, from a feminist viewpoint, as a victim of domestic violence.[6] This use of power ranged from physical assault and verbal abuse, to husbands absenting themselves from family life. Thus one respondent abused his power by leaving all decision making to his partner and by absenting himself physically from the home for most of the week – despite her objections. This was compounded by his emotional absence from partner and children when he was present, as well as his sexual abuse of a daughter.

For these respondents their 'right' to engage in abusive behaviour was founded upon their status as 'breadwinner'. All eight had greater earning power than their wives and they demonstrated their 'rights' through their definitions of wives' responsibilities. Wives were expected to 'stand by their men'. For example, wives were praised when they did not demand divorce as a result of the respondents' offences. However, wives who did demand a divorce were seen as uncaring. They were frequently blamed for their lack of support, which it was implied had some input into the respondents' offending. A related belief was that wives should be sexually faithful. This was found even where a respondent was himself sexually unfaithful and in two accounts, was seen as good reason for the use of violence. [7] Wives were expected to fulfil husbands' sexual and emotional needs. This came out very clearly in respondent's explanations of their offences in which various strategies for blame shifting were identified.[8] One strategy, found in four cases, was to blame the wife for not sexually satisfying the husband: thus leading him to seek sexual satisfaction from a child. This strategy was also identified by Judith Herman and Lisa Hirschman (1981) in their study of incest survivors.

Another common strategy was to blame the wife for not giving enough emotional support and comfort, for not talking to her husband enough. A final wifely duty was to take total responsibility for housework and childcare.

These kinds of ideas were repeated by the unmarried heterosexuals among the respondents. The non-heterosexual respondents (two identified themselves as gay and one as a paedophile) gave no instances of sexist views regarding women. I speculate that they did not need to indulge in this tactic in order to legitimate their behaviour toward women, since they did not have intense relationships with them. However, *all* the respondents were found to have an expectation of emotional care from the women around them. It is noteworthy that it was generally females who cared for the respondents after their offences had been disclosed.

The above outlines of the respondents' ideas regarding women are examples of cultural scenarios for heterosexual relations, as they appear in individual action. The cultural scenario is re-enacted, supported and maintained through practice. Each part sustains another. Thus men's power, while resting on economic and physical advantage, is none the less sustained by women's sexual and emotional responsibilities.

(2) Sexual Scripts

The respondents' sexual scripts were deduced from their accounts of their sexual acts with adults and children. A variety of heterosexual cultural scenarios were in evidence in the respondents' scripts. A hierarchy of sexual acts was identified in these accounts, such that kissing or fondling was the lowest form of sexual activity, while penetrative sex was at the apex of the hierarchy. This hierarchy clearly reflects male power, since the centre of attention in this view of sex is the penis, the emphasis is upon male sexual pleasure. The best sex was penetrative sex. However, this hierarchy was also present in the respondents' views on child sexual abuse. In this context the hierarchy took the same form but the meaning placed upon the acts was reversed. Thus penetrative sex became the worst sexual act and several respondents were keen to tell me that they would never have gone *that* far. This interpretation is not born out in studies of the effects of sexual abuse upon survivors.

Four other heterosexual cultural scenarios were identified in the respondents' accounts. Two of these have already been noted in the media example used earlier. The first is 'men want sex, women want love'. This was demonstrated in the last section in relation to women's responsibilities for the sexual and emotional care of men. The other side of this arrangement was found in the respondents' general lack of emotional skills (see below) and their expectation that their sexual needs ought to be satisfied. A clear example of this was the use of justifications that rested upon the cultural scenario of male lack of sexual control.[9] This rests on the cultural scenario that males have an innate need for sex owing to biological imperatives. A related Western cultural scenario is that of man as active and woman as passive. This was seen in the respondent's accounts of how they initiated their sexual activities with children and adolescents: they all actively planned these contacts. A fifth related cultural scenario is that of the seductive woman. Since this contradicts the cultural scenario of the passive female, such actions are usually defined as 'bad'. Thus one frequent justification for sexual contact with a child was the child's seductive behaviour.[10] Whilst this may undermine the scenario of the active male who initiates sex, it can be seen that both scenarios arise from ideas round female passivity. Taken together they enabled the respondents to 'have it both ways' − not uncommon for a ruling class. The cultural scenarios identified here are mutually supportive and provide males with justifications and excuses for their sexually abusive acts in all circumstances; they are also constitutive of the cultural scenarios for heterosexual relations.

(3)   Hegemonic Masculinity

The respondents were all from a working class background, although three
had run their own businesses. I have noted that a specifically 'working
class' variety of masculinity has been identified and have argued that hegemonic masculinity provides the thread of continuity between several conventional constructions of masculinity. The respondents' accounts revealed
five 'core attributes' of hegemonic masculinity that I would argue illuminate the continuities between conventional constructions of masculinity.

The first core attribute was the possession of work and money. These
were of huge importance in the respondents' conceptions of self and identity. For example several had experienced financial or work problems and
like most people they found this stressful. However, if they were 'bread-
winners' they also felt extremely guilty, because being a 'breadwinner'
was deemed by these respondents to be their main function and duty as
husbands and fathers. The power of the 'breadwinner' is based to a large
extent on his economic power. Problems in work struck at the heart of this
power and each man's sense of self.

The second core attribute is that of heterosexuality. The non-heterosex-
uals and one bisexual among the respondents, defined their sexual identity
in relation to the heterosexual cultural scenario. All had felt that their
sexual identity was not ideal and accepted societal stigmatisation of their
sexual activities. While two gay respondents had struggled to accept their
sexual identities, one of these had not managed this until after his offence
had been disclosed. Among the heterosexual respondents there was no
question as to the 'rightness' of their sexual identity. Those who could
demonstrate sexual experience were quick to do so, while those who had
sexual problems found these highly stressful. There are a number of aeti-
ologies of paedophilia which cite 'stress' as a causal factor (Howells,
1981) and a majority of respondents cited stress as a condition of their
lives at the time of their offences. (Several men used this as an excuse or
justification.) What is interesting is that these stresses all concerned work,
money and sex. A combination of all three was experienced as particularly
disastrous. Earlier academic work identifying 'stress' as a causal factor
might, therefore, be re-interpreted. It is these particular types of stress
which threaten a male sense of 'manhood'; which is why they were experienced as so devastating.

The third core attribute of hegemonic masculinity is 'to not be feminine'.
Only two respondents defined themselves as having any 'feminine' qualities
at all. However, six of the eight husbands did carry out some kinds of housework and childcare. On closer examination it became clear that, as shown

earlier, women were seen as responsible for these tasks. The respondents saw themselves as 'helping' Several respondents saw this as evidence of how well they treated their wives, while others used this to show what 'bad' mothers their wives had been. Three rules applied to men taking part in this work: Men who were in full time work had the right not to do any of these tasks, regardless of the wife's paid work commitments. Men should not be required to carry out 'polluting' activities, such as hand washing or changing nappies. Men did not have responsibility for these tasks.[11]

The fourth core attribute was the demonstration of 'manliness'. This had several aspects, but displays of strength were crucial to it. Strength could be demonstrated in several ways and physical strength was clearly quite important, as might be expected of a working class construction of hegemonic masculinity. One respondent gave many accounts of his physical strength, even demanding my admiration of his biceps. However, in common with middle class constructions of masculinity, the respondents gave accounts of their mental strength. Examples of this concerned 'standing your ground' and perseverance. One man felt that giving himself up to the police had demonstrated 'bottle', another refused to move house after his offences became public knowledge and several felt they could always get what they wanted. These kinds of example were connected with an overall ability to be in control of situations. The man being in control is entirely consistent with the unequal power arrangement inherent in the cultural scenarios for heterosexual relations.

Four respondents, looking back on their actions and armed with new definitions of their behaviour towards women and children, described themselves as selfish. My interpretation is that many instances of exerting control are defined as displays of 'manliness', but can also be defined as selfishness. Men who act on the cultural scenarios for hegemonic masculinity become accustomed to being selfish without defining it as such. Thus 'manliness' underpins much abusive behaviour.

(4) Emotion

The final core attribute of hegemonic masculinity relates to emotion. Two major 'feeling rules' were identified in the respondents accounts:

(1) That men may feel and express aggression;
(2) That men may not feel or express emotions of vulnerability.

Thus anger could be expressed but only in violent, usually physical, ways. Three respondents even limited the definition of 'emotion' to 'anger'.

Additionally, the respondents described themselves as unable to talk to anyone about their emotional lives. They 'bottled up' their vulnerable emotions and were performing a considerable degree of emotion work. These two feeling rules are consistent with the requirements of the interpersonal and intrapsychic scripts for hegemonic masculinity. Displays of defencelessness, of 'soft' or vulnerable emotions can only be interpreted as weakness in the context of hegemonic masculinity. Such behaviour would conflict with the necessity of being in control and maintaining power. The violent display of aggression is also a useful aid in the maintenance of power.

The 'feeling rules' identified here correspond to those for femininity, whereby emotion management becomes a sphere of female activity. The consequences for the respondents were that they had never learned how to manage emotion in themselves or others. Thus several respondents were able to ignore the signs of emotional upset in their victims. The respondents had problems empathising because they had difficulty in interpreting others' emotions. They lacked emotion management skills and frequently displayed an unfamiliarity with emotion talk. Several respondents confused one emotion with another or replaced emotional displays with other actions, such as defining affection as the giving of presents. The emotional trap of hegemonic masculinity is that it denies the existence of emotional vulnerability in men. The consequent individual lack of emotion management skills enables such men to abuse without understanding the full implications of what they are doing. These emotional characteristics support demonstrations of 'manliness' and the unequal power arrangement in heterosexual relations.

The exploration of the respondents ideas and behaviour toward women has revealed inequalities inherent in the conventional cultural scenario for heterosexual relations. The power and rights men accrue by this arrangement enables the abuse of that power. These same cultural scenarios provide the sexual scripts employed in the sexual abuse of children, as well as excuses and justifications for this. The attributes of hegemonic masculinity have also been shown to be linked to child sexual abuse. The stress often cited as a cause is clearly linked to problems of 'manhood'. Demonstrations of manliness and the feeling rules associated with hegemonic masculinity, have been shown to underpin each other in the expression of selfishness, sexual abuse and violence. These rules also act as a block to emotional awareness of the victim. The links thus identified make it possible to argue that the construction of hegemonic masculinity is implicated as one *enabling* condition of child sexual abuse.

(5)   Childhood

A further 'enabling' condition for child sexual abuse was identified in all the respondents' lives. This was the experience of 'abuse' as a child or adolescent. This is 'abuse' as defined by me, not always by the respondents themselves.[12] Twelve respondents can be defined as experiencing various kinds of abuse within the nuclear family and five as experiencing sexual abuse from sources outside it. Thus all thirteen were defined as having been the victim of abusive experiences.

Within the nuclear family the sources of abuse were mothers and fathers. However, mothers were experienced as much less abusive than fathers. Of the twelve mothers present during these respondents' childhoods, five were experienced as abusive. All five were described as emotionally distant for at least some of the time. Additionally, one mother was physically abusive on occasions and one was physically neglectful. However, three of these respondents also described close, supportive relationships with their mothers as well. Thus of twelve respondents with mothers, two had only negative feelings for them while seven had only positive feelings for them. All the respondents had a father present during some part of their childhood. Of these only one had no negative feelings toward his father. Twelve respondents experienced their fathers as emotionally distant, of whom one was severely emotionally abusive. Three men experienced their lone fathers as physically neglectful. Five respondents' fathers were physically abusive and two were sexually abusive. When the respondents accounts of their fathers were analysed it became clear that the fathers could all be demonstrated to display an adherence to the interpersonal scripts for hegemonic masculinity. Thus the abuse perpetrated by the fathers was greater in occurrence and severity than that by the mothers. Interestingly, a recent study of undetected rapists has similar findings regarding mothers and fathers (Lisak, 1991).

Additionally, the respondents' fathers followed an authoritarian model of fathering. This in itself may be related to the requirements of hegemonic masculinity, since many of these are derived from ancient Western ideas regarding the power of fathers. The respondents accounts of their relationships with their children revealed they had replicated their fathers' authoritarian approach. Consistent with the cultural scenarios for hegemonic masculinity and heterosexual relations, these respondents treated their sons and daughters in different ways. The respondents often seemed to expect emotional care from their daughters while three expressed a fear that they were too emotionally distant from their sons.

Thus individual adherence to hegemonic masculinity as well as abusive behaviour was being passed down the generations. Additionally, the cultural scenario that children deserve less respect than adults, was identified. This was seen in some respondent's descriptions of children as 'less human' than adults and in a willingness to mete out physical punishments to their own children. Nine respondents appeared to have developed a severe lack of self-esteem and confidence as a result of their childhood experiences. These kinds of emotional effect were in my view compounded by the feeling rules of hegemonic masculinity. Because emotion must be suppressed and denied, emotional problems cannot be admitted or dealt with. Exclusion from emotional talk denied these respondents the skills to communicate their problems and to manage them on an emotional level. Similarly, the experience of sexual attraction to a child may be defined by many potential abusers as 'wrong', but if they are also hemmed in by this particular set of emotional rules how are they to deal with this attraction? The experience of abuse must be regarded as an important 'enabling' condition for child sexual abuse to occur. Of this sample, seven men had experienced sexual abuse as children or adolescents (six of these 'abusers' were male). Two of these respondents described the incidents as very pleasurable, but these acts were not equal ones; in both cases the other was significantly older than the respondent. It is probable that these specifically sexual incidents of abuse provided the respondents with an inherently unequal sexual script. This replicates the inequality inherent in dominant cultural scenarios and sexual scripts for heterosexual relations. In the presence of other 'enabling' conditions, the respondents went on to enact these scripts. Six of those who had been sexually abused also experienced other kinds of abuse as children, as did the rest of the sample. Thus *any* experience of serious abuse may be an 'enabling' condition for child sexual abuse. However, so many children experience instances of serious abuse that this statement must be taken in conjunction with the other 'enabling' conditions already identified – and probably others. The experiences of these respondents are highly influenced by hegemonic masculinity in several ways. Hegemonic masculinity shaped much of the abuse they experienced and was expressed in the interpersonal scripts of their fathers. The respondents themselves adhere, relatively uncritically, to these scripts in their sexual, personal and family relationships. The scripts enabled these men to carry out and justify their sexually abusive acts towards children. Finally, the respondents' adherence to the emotional feeling rules for hegemonic masculinity, prevented them from dealing with their own emotional problems and also enabled them to abuse.

CONCLUSION

The research outlined in this paper addressed the question of whether there are links between masculinity and child sexual abuse. Thirteen men who had been arrested for sexual offences against children were interviewed in depth. The respondents' accounts and explanations have been analysed through five themes relating to their perceptions of women, men, childhood, sex and emotion, and connections between the five themes and a variety of theoretical perspectives has been demonstrated. These perspectives included feminist analyses of child sexual abuse, social constructionist approaches to gender, a socialist feminist model of hegemonic masculinity, feminist Object Relations Theory and the Interactionist influenced Scripting Theory and Emotion Management Perspective. A major concern in this research has been to give consideration to structural, social and individual levels of society. This particular combination of theoretical approaches avoids the problems of purely structural approaches to human behaviour, by retaining the concept of an active subject throughout.

A discussion of these theoretical approaches indicated that a particular construction of masculinity was implicated in the development of sexually abusive behaviour toward children. It was suggested that this construction might be 'hegemonic masculinity'. This was defined as the structurally dominant form of masculinity, evidence of which is found in 'cultural scenarios'. These are available for adoption by males in the construction of conventional 'masculinities'. The cultural scenarios offered interpersonal and intrapsychic 'scripts' for the individual performance of hegemonic masculinity. This was achieved through individual and group interaction with the cultural scenarios. The sets of cultural scenarios attached to hegemonic masculinity and its associated arrangement of heterosexual relations, were revealed as mutually supportive. Many instances of these cultural scenarios were identified in the respondents accounts in the form of interpersonal and intrapsychic scripts. Cultural scenarios provide the scripts; personal enactment of the scripts informs and maintains the cultural scenarios. Hegemonic masculinity was also seen to be constructed round the denial of emotion. This was shown to be essential to male expressions of power and male dependence upon female emotion management skills.

The respondents accounts revealed particular aspects of hegemonic masculinity that were interpreted as 'enabling' child sexual abuse. Generalised abusive behaviour was seen to exist in the sexual and family lives of the respondents. Being accustomed to exerting power, having control and getting what you want, was interpreted as conducive to abusive behaviour of all kinds. These behaviours occurred in the context of hegemonic masculinity, which enabled such acts to be defined as biological imperatives, 'manly' and excusable in most circumstances. The feeling rules attached to hegemonic masculinity were revealed as a barrier to understanding victims' feelings. These rules also allowed for displays of power whilst excluding displays of caring, nurturance and empathy.

A further enabling condition was identified in the respondents' experiences of abuse as children and adolescents. Those who experienced sexual abuse had an inherently unequal sexual script made available to them. This was seen to replicate the inequality inherent in dominant cultural scenarios and sexual scripts for heterosexual relations. In the presence of other 'enabling' conditions, these respondents went on to enact these scripts. A majority of the respondents also experienced other kinds of abuse. Thus any experience of serious abuse could be seen as an 'enabling' condition for child sexual abuse. It was therefore argued that the experience of abuse was significant in the development of sexually abusive behaviour when it occurred *in conjunction with* other enabling conditions. These enabling conditions include the influence of hegemonic masculinity.

The experiences of these respondents were highly influenced by hegemonic masculinity in several ways. Hegemonic masculinity shaped much of the abuse they experienced and it was expressed in the interpersonal scripts of their fathers. Thus patterns of abusive behaviour passed from father to son. The respondents tended to accept the cultural scenarios for hegemonic masculinity and heterosexual relations uncritically. The corresponding interpersonal and intrapsychic scripts were evident in their sexual, personal and family relationships. These scripts enabled the respondents to carry out and justify their sexually abusive acts towards children. Finally, the respondents' adherence to the emotional feeling rules for hegemonic masculinity, prevented them from dealing with their own emotional problems and also enabled them to abuse.

An adherence to the cultural scenarios for hegemonic masculinity was important in the lives of this small sample of men who had a sexual relationship with a child or adolescent. It was therefore argued that this particular construction of masculinity was implicated as one *enabling* condition of child sexual abuse. This argument does not exclude other 'enabling' conditions, or imply that all persons who adhere to constructions of hegemonic masculinity would inevitably sexually abuse a child. Such men might for example adhere to the 'protective' cultural scenarios associated with hegemonic masculinity and never act abusively toward those defined as weaker than themselves. Additionally, this argument implies that constructions of masculinity not informed by hegemonic masculinity may not provide enabling conditions for child sexual abuse. These findings indicate that feminist-influenced interpretations of child sexual abuse are correct in their insistence upon the links between masculinity and child sexual abuse. A unitary explanation of child sexual abuse is not possible and a multiplicity of individual, social and structural factors must be taken into account in explaining each occurrence. These findings support 'cycle of abuse' theories, but the relevance of conventional masculinities has been identified at several points in such a cycle. The research also supports analyses of child sexual abuse which take account of many factors. The multi-factor analysis provided by Finkelhor (1984) is one such approach. My argument is that the most significant of these factors is the patriarchal cultural context in which child sexual abuse is validated, encouraged and concealed. The abuser is a 'normal' man.

Notes

1. Studies of the sexual experiences of adults when they were children suggest that between 80 and 97 per cent of 'abusers' are male. For a review of this work in the USA and UK see David Finkelhor *et al.* (1986).
2. See Herman and Hirschman (1981), Rush (1980), Russell (1984), Finkelhor (1984, 1986), Glaser and Frosh (1988), Kelly (1988), MacLeod and Saraga (1988), Hearn (1990) and Scully (1990).
3. For a discussion of 'accounts', 'explanations' and 'justifications' see Stanford Lyman and Marvin Scott (1989) and Diana Scully (1990).
4. See Tolson (1977), Ehrenreich (1983), Metcalf and Humphries (1985), Connell (1987), Hearn and Morgan (1990) and Segal (1990).
5. See particularly: Tolson (1977), Siedler in Metcalf and Humphries (1985), Seidler (1989), Brittan (1989) and Jackson (1990).
6. Liz Kelly found in her study that domestic violence frequently involved the sexual abuse of wives and children in conjunction with other forms of physical or emotional violence.
7. Diana Scully identifies a belief in the sexual double standard as characteristic of the convicted rapists she studied. Scully terms a whole set of beliefs surrounding the sexual double standard 'pedestal values' which 'are characterised by an intensely rigid double standard of moral and sexual conduct – a standard that both denies a woman the rights accorded to men and requires her to have the protection of a man' (Scully, 1990, p. 165).
8. See note 3.
9. Scully notes the use of this kind of justification by those rapists she classes as 'admitters' – an appeal 'to forces beyond their control' (Scully, 1990, p. 163).
10. Scully refers to this kind of justification as denial, whereby 'injury is denied by portraying the victim as willing' (Scully, 1990, p. 164).

11. These findings concur with many feminist studies of housework and child-care. Lynne Segal (1990, pp. 33–7) addresses these matters specifically with respect to masculinity.

12. For example, nine respondents described experiencing extreme physical punishments. Often the respondents did not define these incidents as abusive and justified them by telling me they had deserved it.

References

Brittan, A. (1989), *Masculinity and Power* (Oxford: Basil Blackwell).

Chodorow, N. (1978), *The Reproduction of Mothering* (London: University of California Press).

Connell, R. W. (1987), *Gender and Power* (Oxford: Polity Press).

Ehrenreich, B. (1983), *The Hearts of Men* (London: Pluto Press).

Eichenbaum, L. and Orbach, S. (1983), *Understanding Women* (Harmondsworth, Middx: Penguin).

Finkelhor, D. (1984), *Child Sexual Abuse: New Theory and Research* (New York: Free Press).

Finkelhor, D. *et al.* (1986), *A Sourcebook on Child Sexual Abuse* (Beverly Hills, CA: Sage, 1986).

Glaser, D. and Frosh, S. (1988), *Child Sexual Abuse* (Basingstoke and London: Macmillan).

Hearn, J. (1990), '"Child Abuse" and Men's Violence', The Violence Against Children Study Group, *Taking Child Abuse Seriously: Contemporary Issues in Child Protection Theory and Practice* (London: Unwin Hyman).

Hearn, J. and Morgan, D. (1990), *Men, Masculinities and Social Theory* (London: Unwyn Hyman).

Herman, J. and Hirschman, L. (1981) *Father–Daughter Incest* (Cambridge, Mass.: Harvard University Press).

Hochschild, A. R. (1979), 'Emotion Work, Feeling Rules and Social Structure', *American Journal of Sociology*, vol. 85, no. 3: pp. 551–75.

Hochschild, A. R. (1983), *The Managed Heart: Commercialization of Human Feelings* (Berkeley, CA: University of California Press).

Howells, K. (1981), 'Adult Sexual Interest in Children: Considerations Relevant to Theories of Aetiology', in Cook, M. and Howells, K. (eds), *Adult Sexual Interest in Children* (New York: Academic Press).

Jackson, D. (1990), *Unmasking Masculinity: A Critical Autobiography* (London: Unwin Hyman).

Kelly, L. (1988), *Surviving Sexual Violence* (Cambridge: Polity Press).

Lisak, D. (1991), 'Sexual Aggression, Masculinity and Fathers', *Signs*, vol. 16, no. 2, pp. 238–62.

Lyman. S. M. and Scott, M. B. (1989), *The Sociology of the Absurd* (New York: General Hall.

MacLeod, M. and Saraga, E. (1988), 'Challenging the Orthodoxy', *Feminist Review*, vol. 28, pp. 16–55.

Metcalf, A. and Humphries, M. (eds) (1985), *The Sexuality of Men* (London: Pluto Press).

Plummer, K. (1982), 'Symbolic Interationism and Sexual Conduct; An Emergent Perspective', in Brake, M. (ed.), *Human Sexual Relations: A Reader* (Harmondsworth: Penguin).

Rush, F. (1980), *The Best Kept Secret: Sexual Abuse of Children* (Englewood Ciffs, NJ: Prentice hall).

Russell, D. (1984), *Sexual Exploitation: Rape, Child Sexual Abuse and Workplace Harassment* (Beverly Hills, CA: Sage).

Scully, D. (1990), *Understanding Sexual Violence: A Study of Convicted Rapists* (Boston, Mass.: Unwin Hyman).

Segal, L. (1990), *Slow Motion: Changing Masculinities, Changing Men* (London: Virago Press).

Seidler, V. J. (1989), *Rediscovering Masculinity: Reason, Language, and Sexuality* (London: Routledge).

Simon, W. and Gagnon, J. H. (1987), 'The Sexual Scripts Approach', in Greer, J. and O'Donoghue, W. (eds), *Theories of Human Sexuality* (New York: Plenum Press).

Tolson, A. (1977), *The Limits of Masculinity* (London: Tavistock).

13 The Impact of Political Conflict on Domestic Violence in Northern Ireland*

JOAN McKIERNAN and MONICA McWILLIAMS

There is a well-developed body of literature on the subject of domestic violence and the societal constraints facing abused women. There has, however, been less examination of the interrelationship between violence against women in the home and the political violence occurring in the wider society. This was one of the issues studied in a recent research set in Northern Ireland before the ceasefire. Here we will discuss the implications for abused women and children living in a society, such as Northern Ireland, which has been dominated by a high level of political conflict. It will also examine the state response to such abuse occurring in the midst of that conflict. Raising the issue of domestic violence is problematic when it is considered to be a distraction from the policing of other forms of violence in what has been one of Europe's longest running political conflicts. When violence occurs in the more private domestic arena of the family home and when the society also happens to be a more traditional, religious oriented one then further constraints can exist in recognising domestic violence as a serious problem.

Studying any form of violence in the context of a political conflict can have a particular significance for those being studied and is often reflected in the way the violence itself is portrayed and defined. We found that there are various types of acceptable and unacceptable forms of violence. Often these can exist alongside and overlap each other. For example, there is enormous condemnation when hospitals, school playing grounds, community centres, churches and universities are affected by the political conflict. A woman's own home has not, however, received public recognition as a neutral area or safe place in the same way and there is little public condemnation when women are abused or killed by their partners.

---

*Please note that although the research reported here was completed before the ceasefire, findings are sometimes recorded in the present tense.

When a woman becomes the target of a sectarian killing or bombing, there is invariably a much greater sense of outrage than when the victim is a man. Approximately two hundred women and young girls have died since 1969 – killed by bomb explosions, gun attacks and plastic bullets. These deaths have raised the question about the morality of killing women, and the unacceptable level of the current violence. The sense of public outrage, however, stands in sharp contrast to the limited attention paid to the deaths of women as a result of domestic violence and makes public once again the contradictory messages about women's lives in Northern Ireland society.

This contradictory message is also witnessed in areas of public policy. Decisions relating to social, economic and political policies have been dominated by the political conflict. McLaughlin (1991) argues that the focus of the media, research and government bodies on what is seen to be the main problem – sectarianism and political conflict – has obscured the reality of other areas of inequality, with gender inequality very low on the list of priorities. For example, current reports on public expenditure show that government funding directed at reducing the divisions between Catholics and Protestants is over five times the amount spent addressing the inequality of women in society.[2]

TRADITIONAL SOCIETY

There is also support for the view that Northern Ireland is a more traditional society than Great Britain. One of the most important influences on women's lives in Northern Ireland society is the conservative part played by Church and State which combine to ensure that women remain in the primary role of wife and mother. The survey of social attitudes in Northern Ireland showed the predominance of conservative attitudes on issues such as sexuality, abortion and divorce (Montgomery and Davies, 1991). There was a ten-year delay in extending divorce reform legislation to Northern Ireland because of the objection of both Catholic and Protestant churches. Abortion is only available in the most restricted circumstances. Legislation on homosexual rights was only introduced after coercion from the European Commission of Human Rights. Most recently, Catholic and Protestant activists publicly combined to try to prevent the opening of the Brook Advisory Clinic which provides information on contraception to teenagers in Belfast.

Legislation providing for protection and exclusion orders for victims of domestic violence applied only to married women when it was first introduced in Northern Ireland in 1980 (Domestic Proceedings (NI) Order). There were major objections by elements of the judiciary who thought family life was being threatened by the introduction of exclusion orders. One local magistrate found it hard to believe that 'a man could be put out of his own home' (McWilliams, 1991). As a result of these attitudes it took another four years before cohabiting women could obtain court orders against violent partners (Family Law (Miscellaneous Provisions) (NI) Order, 1984).

Mitchison (1988), describing the role of women's groups in Northern Ireland, has argued that it is more difficult for women to assert their independence as a result of the entrenched conservatism of the society in which they live and the extent to which the political situation has reinforced traditional family networks. Both of these, she claims, have disallowed a radical reappraisal of politics within the home and kept women's liberation very far down the political agenda. Mitchison also notes that in addition to these features of the society, the militarisation of Northern Ireland has meant that domestic violence can go relatively unchecked. The extent to which this is the case currently (1993) was one of the main features of this research.

THE RESEARCH

The research referred to in this chapter was a one-year project resulting from an initiative of the Ministerial Committee on Women's Issues which recommended that health and social service professionals should examine ways of dealing more effectively with those experiencing domestic violence. The research was intended to provide baseline information for a demonstration project on domestic violence in Northern Ireland, so the focus of the research was to indicate experiences particular to women living in Northern Ireland and to assess the extent to which the help-seeking process differed from elsewhere. There were two stages of data collection. The first involved in-depth interviews with women who had recent experience of domestic violence; the second involved interviews with 120 help-providers and focused on professional practice in relation to domestic violence. The second phase was designed to build on the first so that the various agencies would have the opportunity to respond to the specific problems reported by the women.

The research focused on two localities, one urban and one rural. Interviews were carried out in a predominantly Catholic area and a predominantly Protestant area in both localities in order to assess whether there were any differences among the help-seekers and the help-providers in relation to the religious/political divide in Northern Ireland. In-depth interviews were carried out with 56 women who had experienced domestic violence. One group of women (22) were interviewed in Women's Aid refuges. Another group (28) had already ended their relationships and were resettled in the community. A smaller number of women (6) were still living with their partners. The sample included women from the two largest communities in Northern Ireland, Protestant (23) and Catholic (30), and a smaller group from the Traveller community (3). The sample of women was predominantly working class, but women from middle class or professional households and farming families were also represented. Most of the women came from large towns, but we were able to interview a small number of women living in more rural areas.

METHODOLOGY

In planning the interviews with the women we felt there was little point in approaching those who had experienced domestic violence with a predetermined schema and a range of deductively derived concepts. Our research started with women's articulation of their experience and general concepts were derived in negotiation with the women themselves. As far as possible, the women were allowed to be the authors of their experiences and in the case of Traveller women their storey as it was told directed the method rather than the other way round. This is a process which Liz Kelly (1988) calls building 'a cooperative framework' while Dobash and Dobash (1979) describe it as 'learning about the problem in its concrete form'. Although this proved to be a time consuming exercise, it was, none the less, a productive part of the study.

From the outset of the project the authors were fully involved in every aspect of the research work. Group discussions with women in refuges were used to develop a suitably robust instrument to gather the information as well as to identify issues that were not developed in the literature but which were felt to be important to explore in the specific context of Northern Ireland. These group discussions also enabled the researchers to find ways to talk to women about their horrific encounters as well as to discuss sources of help and suggestions for change.

RESULTS

The interviews provided a vivid picture of the nature of domestic violence, with women describing violent acts which would not be tolerated in any context other than the home. The interviews confirmed the findings in the literature that domestic violence has serious consequences for the well-being of both women and children. The women's experiences demonstrated the complexity of their reactions to the violence and their decision making process. They also illustrated the particular constraints placed on their actions because of the long history of political strife in Northern Ireland. Traditional attitudes toward marriage and family confirmed the extent to which women were prepared to keep the violence hidden which in itself constituted a major obstacle to the help-seeking process.

The Violence

The women described a number of horrific injuries which they sustained while living with their partners. Over half said they needed medical treatment for their injuries, while almost a quarter of the sample required hospital treatment at least once. Over a third were hit while they were pregnant and two women suffered miscarriages. A number of women told us they were raped. Several women told us that they had sex when they did not want to and others had given in just to please their partner. Marital rape was one of the problems that women were most reluctant to disclose and they commented on the rapes almost as an afterthought. Often the women saw no escape from the brutality except by inflicting harm on themselves or even by attempting to end their own lives. Eight women in this survey had taken overdoses as a result of the violence; one had done this four times.

Weapons

The men used a variety of weapons to assault their partners. Research by Montgomery and Bell (1986) has shown that the increased availability of guns in Northern Ireland means that more dangerous forms of torture can be used against the abused women. Several of the women were threatened with guns whilst another woman whose husband did not have a gun told her several times he knew where he could get one to use on her. Women told us of their experiences when a gun was put to their heads but they never knew whether or not there was a bullet in the gun. This 'game' which the men enjoyed playing is known as Russian Roulette and has been widely used on prisoners captured during war. Such psychological torture can have long-term psychological consequences with an additional problem for the women in that it leaves no physical marks. The women consequently have difficulty making those in positions to help them believe their stories.

Traditional Attitudes

The interviews conducted for this research clearly illustrated the barriers imposed on women by social and religious attitudes in Northern Ireland and supported the findings of conservative attitudes toward marriage and divorce, even among the younger women in the group. The most common religious belief which affected women's decisions was the idea that marriage is forever. Both Catholic and Protestant women had problems because of their families' fundamentalist views. Specific religious objections to divorce were mentioned by several women, but religion was not the basis of the objection to divorce for all women. For many women marriage was serious and 'you worked at it'.

During the interviews the very high value and expectations that women placed on their marriages was evident. The importance of this for women within local communities and the attitude toward lone parenthood made leaving violent partners more difficult. Because they wanted to make their marriages work, the women would try again and again and hope for change. Publicly admitting their marriage had failed was particularly difficult since the women felt they would be blamed. They also feared exposure because of the stigma against lone parents which women felt still operated in Northern Ireland. They thought there was an additional stigma against women who had been separated or divorced, had been victims of domestic violence or had lost custody of their children.

Impact of the Political Conflict

Much emphasis in the literature and in professional practice is placed on an examination of the reasons why women do not act to stop the violence and leave the relationship. The women in this study showed that they had an amazing ability to cope and were not in any sense the passive victims portrayed in much of the professional literature. These women did resist but they had to make their decisions about resistance within a framework of knowledge about what was realistically possible for them. Their resistance was frequently constrained by men's insistence on coming back to their partners. This was a major problem for many of the women, some of whom had to leave Northern Ireland despite the fact that they would have had more support remaining near their marital home. As one woman explained, 'I just can't be in the same country as him. I just have to stay out of the way completely.' Recently research has shown that when a woman threatens to leave or has left a relationship, the incidence of murder/suicide increases (Marzmuk *et al.*, 1992). In a recent case in Northern Ireland a man who could not accept that his wife had left him made arrangements to meet her, used a shotgun to kill her and then turned the gun on himself. This case was similar to many others which so often go unreported in Northern Ireland and which indicate that even when women escape they are still not safe.

There were also women who remained in Northern Ireland, but had to break all connections with communities and families and go 'underground' by disappearing into another area where they hoped to remain anonymous. This option presented enormous difficulties for women who had previously had a family and social network for support. It proved to be particularly problematic for women from the Traveller and Asian communities. The feelings of separation from their distinct cultural groups and the loss of friends and social networks were exacerbated by the experience of moving into an alien settled or English speaking environment. The isolating effects of such experiences influenced some women to return to their abusive partners.

Other women took advantage of the violence in Northern Ireland to escape their partners. They deliberately chose to move to Northern Ireland from the Republic of Ireland and Great Britain in the expectation that the political turmoil might deter their partners from following them. Some women chose particular communities within Northern Ireland to resettle where it would be dangerous for their husbands to follow. It is ironic that the much publicised violence of Northern Ireland should become a refuge in itself for women who were trying to find some kind of sanctuary.

Police in Northern Ireland

Researchers such as Weitzer (1985) and Farrell (1983) argue that the Northern Ireland police force, the Royal Ulster Constabulary (RUC), has been seen as a highly partisan force organised in defence of the state and opposed to the interests of the Catholic minority. Moreover, according to Weitzer (1985) in spite of British government efforts to transform the RUC into a 'normal' modernised police force, police attitudes, time and resources have been concentrated on the political conflict. It is not surprising then that the Chief Constable of the RUC disclosed that 80 per cent of police time is involved in security duties (cited in Weitzer, 1985). The result has been a lack of interest in and limited resources available for the victims of the violence that occurs in the home.

The RUC does not have any domestic violence units which are now well established by many of the police forces in Great Britain. Domestic violence work is subsumed within units responsible for rape and child abuse although police in these units are already overburdened with the increasing workload on these cases Police officers have publicly stated that they do not have the resources to set up a specialist unit on domestic violence since they have to concentrate on catching 'terrorists'. But who defines the concept of terrorism in this situation? For the women in our study, the terrorism they spoke of was from the men they lived with. However, in Northern Ireland this domestic terrorism is not as important as what is perceived to be political 'terrorism'. For the acceptable work of defeating political 'terrorism' the police in Northern Ireland are well equipped. The RUC has the largest proportion of police officers per head of population in the United Kingdom with one police officer for every 193 people compared to one for every 531 in East Anglia. (HMSO, 1993) Despite its size, it has the lowest percentage of women officers in the force even though experience in other areas has shown that women police officers are essential for dealing with crimes such as rape, child abuse and domestic violence.

Counting Domestic Violence

In contrast to the sophisticated computerised data collection system available to the RUC to combat political 'terrorism', basic information on the occurrence of domestic violence in Northern Ireland is lacking. For example, the Chief Constable's Annual Report still does not list domestic violence as a separate notifiable offence. The latest report lists a total of 3338 offences against the person in Northern Ireland, but of that number, 2263 are grouped in a catch all category of 'other offences against the person'. Domestic violence offences are lost, unlisted in that category. Neither are there official data collected on the number of women murdered by their partners every year. Most homicides in Northern Ireland are directly related to the political situation. There are about 25 domestic (non-political) homicides each year. A study showed that 10 (40 per cent) of the non-political homicides in 1991 were the result of domestic violence (McWilliams and McKiernan, 1993).

Although sophisticated computer technology is available for anti-terrorist work, it has taken over two years to sort out the recording of domestic violence disputes reported to the police. Since the publication of the new guidelines on domestic violence (Force Order No. 7/91) all calls to the police relating to domestic disputes must be recorded and a quarterly statistical return must be submitted. To date, the only information that is available from this procedure is the number of incidents of domestic disputes that are reported to the police, which totalled over 2800 in 1991. Caution must be taken with the figures produced because uniform procedures and definitions of domestic violence have not yet been established.

The data provided does not indicate whether these are new cases or repeats, nor do they indicate the gender of the victim or the relationship of the victim to the abuser. As well, the accuracy of those statistics is problematic because of differential reporting levels in nationalist (Catholic) and unionist (Protestant) communities and because of police attitudes which may not consider such work the best use of their time. In the course of the research, it was found that one-third of the police stations in Northern Ireland were regularly months late in turning in their reports.

Women's Attitudes to the Police

Women were asked if there were particular difficulties as a result of the political conflict, known locally as the 'Troubles'. The problem most reported was women's reluctance or perceived inability to make contact with the police about domestic violence. This was the perception mainly of women living in nationalist sections in both urban and rural areas.

There was very little indication that there would be community disapproval if women did contact the police, though one woman reported that she was warned by others not to bring the police in. There was, however, a greater sense that the police are 'not there to help you'. Nationalist communities, particularly in urban areas, are regularly patrolled by large joint army/police patrols, either on foot or in armed convoys. But when the women were asked if they would contact the armed patrols as they came down the street, the response was 'they are not there to help. In this area police are not the people that you normally go to'. One woman explained that they do not go to the police because 'We look after ourselves. When we look for help, the police are never included. They are always seen to be the harasser, you know. I feel even when I went to the police station, they didn't really care, like I mean: '"You'se lot out there look after yourselves, you know. You're forever shooting us and abusing us when we're on the street and we're not going to help you".'

Women's Experience with Police

In spite of the contradictions about using the police, 62 per cent of the respondents in our survey did contact the police. This is a similar level of contact found by Montgomery and Bell (1986) but higher than previous research (Evason, 1982; Bowker, 1983) has found in Northern Ireland and elsewhere. Women from both Catholic and Protestant areas contacted the police either directly about the violence or because of breach of protection and exclusion orders. There was actually a higher level of contact made by women living in Catholic areas with 72 per cent (24) making contact compared to 50 per cent (11) of women from Protestant communities.

Although the women often phoned the police, and waited until the situation was particularly critical to do so, only 26 per cent of women who were in contact with the police found them to be helpful. Similar proportions of Protestant and Catholic women found the police helpful. Those few who had a positive response thought the police were helpful because they removed the abuser from the house or talked to or cautioned the partner. But most women in the survey group did not have a positive experience, even though the police introduced new guidelines for a proactive policy on domestic violence in 1991.

Many of the reasons given by women who thought the police were not helpful are similar to responses found in British research which found low rates of arrest, non-intervention responses and attempts to defuse the situation (Smith, 1989). Montgomery's Northern Ireland study (1991) found that the most frequent police action taken was confined to the removal of the man from the home with no further action being taken. Women reported police claims that there was 'nothing we can do, it's domestic'. The interviews with women supported research in Britain which showed that the police did not treat the issue of domestic violence as a serious matter (Faragher, 1985; Bourlet, 1990). In Brewer's ethnographic study of the RUC, family disputes were grouped in the category of problem solving calls for the police such as helping owners with injured dogs. Such calls were thought to be helpful in breaking up a boring night and getting away from paperwork. 'Police work involves so much bloody paperwork these days and a lot of boring stuff that a family row can quite spice up a night' (Brewer, 1990, p. 46).

The onus was placed on the women to do something such as charge the husbands or leave the home themselves. The police supported husbands or minimised the violence. Women found that the police did not believe them and let their partner stay in the house. The attitude to domestic violence was clear in one case when the police refused to arrest the man because he had hit his partner, but arrested him for hitting the police.

As indicated above, the possession and use of guns was a particularly threatening aspect of domestic violence cases. However, when the police were called in, a few women found that the police would not remove their husbands' guns. In one incident when the police did remove the gun from a husband who was a policeman, he was able to retrieve it from the police station the next day.

The most common response reported by women was police refusal to answer calls. This is in contrast to police statements reported by Brewer

(1990) that domestic violence calls were routinely attended for the purpose of preventing crime, rather than law enforcement. Most of the women who reported 'no action' came from west Belfast and other nationalist areas. Women, professionals and the police agreed that there is a slow response time, up to six hours, in these areas because of the police need to organise security for themselves. Since so many of the professional helping agencies recommend that women call the police either in the first instance or to enforce protection and exclusion orders, the lack of police response in these areas has serious implications for the policy of these agencies. Often telling women to call the police has no meaning if the police will not or cannot come out. Several women reported that when they phoned, the police replied, 'We are not going out there because it could be a set up, anybody could phone us up and tell us that.'

Given research findings (Bowker, 1983) that women only phone the police when the violence has become more severe, this lack of police response has serious implications for the safety of women who do call the police and get no response. Several women reported, 'I waited outside the house all night.' These women also reported that they were not even informed by the police that they could not come out so that the women would try to make some alternative arrangements to escape. They also pointed out that there was no follow up; no one checked up the next day to see if they were still alive. Lack of police response also undermines the value of any court orders women may get which depend on police action for their enforcement.

As a result of the potential for paramilitary attacks, police have long argued that they cannot answer calls from nationalist areas without taking precautions. In order to avoid the possibility of 'being set up', they phone back to check on the call and organise protection for themselves. However, while there have been instances of traps being set for police in these areas, there is no known evidence of domestic violence ever being used as an excuse to set a trap for police.

The police are considered as 'legitimate' targets by the IRA and have suffered one of the highest death and injury rates of any police force in the world. During the period of 'Troubles' 288 police officers have been killed with 7031 injured.[3] However Weitzer (1985) argues that the decline in police deaths and attacks on police stations since the early years of the 'Troubles' has not been matched by a change in the nature of policing. Contradictions have been raised by local women who argue, 'the police and army are in here all the time. They come in whenever they want to raid houses looking for people or weapons. Why can't they come out for domestic violence?'

Evidence of police counter-insurgency tactics taking precedence over the needs of abused women is seen in the well-developed system of informers used by the police. During the years of the 'Troubles' many men who have been arrested by the police for non-political offences have agreed to act as informers in return for having charges dropped. In our interviews some women were afraid that if they reported men to the police because of domestic violence, the Special Branch might try to recruit them as informers. In a society where exposed informers are shot, this practice placed further pressure on women not to report their violent partners to the police.

As a result of the security precautions the police take in nationalist areas, there is a very long response time if they answer a call. If the police do come, they are escorted by the British Army. This arrangement usually entails a convoy of heavily armoured vehicles full of soldiers and police causing further embarrassment for the women involved. The experience of having to climb into the back of an armoured landrover accompanied by policemen wearing flak jackets and carrying submachine guns is regarded by women as one more humiliation which further reduces their dignity.

Problems for women living in some rural nationalist areas are compounded by the fact that police and army do not consider it safe to travel by road. One woman was both relieved that the police had responded but was also worried about neighbours' reaction when the police arrived by helicopter in answer to her call.

It is not only domestic violence calls that police are accused of refusing to answer. The police are coming under increased community pressure to take action on other areas of non-political crime such as joyriding, drugs and sexual violence. However, in the case of domestic violence, the police argument about their own personal security must be assessed within the context of their traditional attitudes toward domestic violence and their understanding of what they consider to be proper police work.

Paramilitaries

There is evidence to suggest that residents living in nationalist areas look to the IRA to control the level of crime in local areas (Fairweather *et al.,* 1989). Community policing has been carried out by paramilitaries in both Protestant and Catholic areas who mete out strict punishments, such as kneecapping, for crimes such as joyriding and burglary. This development began early in the 'Troubles' when 'no go areas' were set up and has continued because of local reluctance to depend on the police and the perception of police neglect of criminal activity in the nationalist communities. Each side has its interest to defend. While the aim of the security forces is the defeat of the paramilitary organisations, the aim of the paramilitaries is to keep the police and army out of local areas. The police have long been accused of allowing criminal activity to continue unhindered in nationalist areas such as West Belfast in an attempt to alienate the community from the IRA. And it is the interest of the paramilitaries to keep police out of their areas both to heighten their own control of the area and to protect their military organisation and equipment.

Interviews with women activists in nationalist areas support the view that paramilitaries are looked to and do take action against men who are violent toward their wives. 'Some women come to us and we put him out so she can come back to her home. In some cases men have been put out of the country'. However, very few women in our study stated that paramilitary groups got involved in the domestic violence issue and there was only one case in which such action was taken. Several women knew they could go to them for help but one woman thought the IRA in her area would take the attitude, 'We don't like getting involved.'

In the interviews we found the initiative to consult paramilitaries came primarily from families', neighbours and from paramilitary groups themselves. A woman living in a Protestant area went to the Ulster Defence Association (UDA), a loyalist paramilitary organisation, and they came and got her partner out of the house, 'quicker than the police'. But afterwards she was afraid that they might expect something in return. The decision to involve paramilitaries can be fraught with danger as this woman experienced. Women said they would not call the paramilitary groups because they thought they would be exploited later by being asked for favours, such as hiding weapons in their houses. Other women told us that when their husbands were reported to the police or to a paramilitary group then action would be taken if the partner was wanted for some criminal offence. These women felt that the various policing forces, both official and unofficial, would only condemn or punish the offender for his violent behaviour in the home if he was wanted for some other offence. The women said this was no solution for them because it left them vulnerable to retaliation by their partners, or by his friends, who would interpret it as 'informing' on him.

Most of the women who considered involving paramilitaries decided against it for many of these reasons. But, as well, they did not want their partners to be physically harmed. One violent partner had already been threatened by the IRA for petty crime and his wife 'knew they are looking for an excuse to do him, but I wouldn't have that on my conscience. But if I thought they could advise him – I would have gone and said he won't leave me alone. But they go too far.' In a Protestant area, when a woman found no support from the police, the UDA offered to do something about her husband. 'They would have give him the same as he gives me.' She said no 'so that he can't claim I did him any harm.'

There is additional difficulty for women living with violent men who are members of paramilitary organisations. There are many complicated pressures on these women not to report violent incidents. Exposing a 'war hero' to the police is not acceptable, and the policing by paramilitary organisations of their own members is not always effective. One woman who was abused by a republican ex-prisoner pointed up the hypocrisy involved when paramilitaries are willing to police others, but not members of their own organisations. 'I know a lot it's happened to, there is a lot of favouritism and in some cases they don't take action. When I told my husband I was getting the boys, he laughed. He said who are you gonna get, there's nobody going to take me outta here.'

Women political activitists in nationalist areas face a complex dilemma. They cannot go to the police for assistance, nor can they count on their own organisation for support against violent partners. One woman reported that the police told her husband 'he should have danced on me, he done me right. That is because I am a republican and they don't like me. They were more worried about charging me with assault.' Since she was assaulted by her husband, the police have used the incident to taunt her when they patrol through the area. Women like these have been active in raising women's issues in their own organisations and opening women's centres in local areas to provide women-centred assistance for abused women.

Women are not safe from abuse even when their husbands are imprisoned for political offences. Prison warders did not stop one man who was beating his wife while on a prison visit. The husband was upset because she was wearing too much makeup. The violent was stopped by fellow prisoners who later warned him because he was letting down the 'macho line of the organisation'.

Security Force Families

The political violence also has an impact on the lives of women whose partners are in the prison service, police and the British Army serving in Northern Ireland. Because of the emphasis on the 'real troubles', domestic violence is minimised or rationalised. Wives of prison officers and police found their husbands' supervisors unwilling to believe their stories of domestic violence and reluctant to censure the husbands. One welfare officer in the army was not surprised to learn from Women's Aid that the police and soldiers used particularly horrific forms of violence against their partners. He claimed that since his soldiers were trained as 'lean, mean killing machines' then it was to be expected that they would occasionally explode and end up fighting with their female partners.

In our research we interviewed a number of police and army wives who had limited options in responding to domestic violence. Army wives often do not have the support of their families readily available. Reporting domestic violence might result in the family being ignominiously shipped back to England or a reduction in rank and wages for the man so there was pres sure on women not to tell. When policemen abuse their wives there is general acknowledgement of the stressful nature of their work in Northern Ireland. They are often given counselling and support to deal with the stress. However, women in the study received no such consideration. Several women lost custody of children because they were under stress from the violence of their police husbands. The ready availability of weapons, especially for policemen who carry a personal protection weapon, was a particular hazard. As a result of the political situation, police weapons have been returned to violent husbands in spite of their use against wives. These women have few alternatives in dealing with the violence. They are reluctant to bring charges which might result in jail sentences because of the potential danger a prison sentence might bring for these men.

CONCLUSION

The impact of societal conflict has been researched extensively in Northern Ireland but to date very little is known about how women's lives are affected by this conflict. Our research has shown that twenty-five years of political conflict and the traditional attitudes toward marriage and the family have intermeshed to impose considerable constraints on women affected by violence in the private sphere. As in other areas of political conflict throughout the world, women's needs and demands for equality have not received the public focus given to conflict in the public arena. The terror that women experience due to domestic violence is minimised; it does not feature in public attention or in the allocation of state resources. As a result, women are left vulnerable in their homes with few options open to them in the public sphere of life.

Important contradictions and difficulties were uncovered in studying police involvement in domestic violence. It is contradictory to respect women to phone police for support in areas where the dominant community perception of the police is one of repression rather than a source of

ovpport, On the other hand, the attitudes and responses of the police themselves combine tradilluiial attitudes towards domestic violence with a
heightened perception of their role as an anti-terrorist force which does
more than normal policing.

As a result of the 'Troubles', the normal remedies that might be available to women cannot always be assumed to be options in Northern
Ireland. Police support is not always available and police involvement
may actually increase the difficulties. Women in some areas do have
access to and use alternative support from paramilitary organisations.
Professional agencies must recognise that different patterns of help provision are used by women who are increasingly looking for greater control
over this process. During our study, women suggested that what is needed
is the establishment of centres for abused women in local communities.
Such centres would be run by the women themselves, totally separate from
the police and social services, thereby avoiding the stigma of using these
agencies. Women, often overcoming political and religious differences,
have recently been struggling to find a space in the public arena to have
their voices heard and their needs recognised. In doing so they have
created alternative and innovative networks that have helped to combat
the violence that has destroyed so many lives. Their efforts should be
recognised, resourced and taken more seriously in the future.

Notes

1. The Northern Ireland Estimates indicates that in 1992 £5.1 million was
    spent on the Fair Employment Commission and cross community projects
    aimed at combatting religious and political sectarianism compared to
    £1 million given to the work of the Equal Opportunities Commission which
    addresses gender inequality in Northern Ireland.
2. Reported by RUC Inspector Peters at the Lisburn Conference on Domestic
    Violence, June 1992.
3. Reported by RUC Press Office, Belfast, February 1993,

References

Bourlet, A. (1990), *Police Intervention in Marital Violence* (Milton Keynes: Open
    University Press).
Bowker, L. (1983), *Beating Wife-Beating* (Lexington, Mass.: Lexington Books).
Brewer, J. (1990), *Inside the RUC* (Oxford: Clarendon Press).
Dobash, R. E. and Dobash, R. (1979), *Violence against Wives* (New York: Free
    Press).

Evason, E. (1982), *Hidden Violence: A Study of Battered Women in Northern Ireland* (Belfast: Farset Press).

Faragher, T. (1985), 'The Police Response to Violence against Women in the Home', in Pahl, J. (ed.), *Private Violence and Public Policy* (London: Routledge & Kegan Paul).

Fairweather, E., McDonough, R. and MacFadyean, M. (1984), *Only the Rivers Run Free* (London: Pluto Press).

Farrell, M. (1983), *Arming the Protestants: The Formation of the Ulster Special Constabulary and the Royal Ulster Constabulary* (London: Pluto).

HMSO (1993), *Regional Trends* (London: HMSO).

Kelly, L. (1988), *Surviving Sexual Violence* (Cambridge: Polity Press).

Marzmuk, P. *et al.* (1992), 'The Epidemiology of Murder–Suicide', *Journal of American Medical Association*, vol. 267, pp. 3179–83.

McLaughlin, E. (1991), 'Introduction: A Problem Postponed', in Davies, C. and McLaughlin, E. (eds), *Women, Employment and Social Policy in Northern Ireland: A Problem Postponed* (Belfast: Policy Research Institute).

McWilliams, M. (1991), 'Women in Northern Ireland: an Overview', in Hughes, E. (ed.), *Culture and Politics in Northern Ireland 1960–1990* (Milton Keynes: Open University Press).

McWilliams, M. and McKiernan, J. (1993), *Bringing It Out in the Open: Domestic Violence in Northern Ireland* (Belfast: HMSO).

Mitchison, A. (1988), 'Ulster's Family Feminists', *New Society*, 19 February.

Montgomery, P. (1991), 'Police Response to Wife Assault in Northern Ireland', *Violence and Victims*, vol. 6, pp. 43–55.

Montgomery, P. and Bell, V. (1986), *Police Response to Wife Assault: A Northern Ireland Study* (Belfast: Women's Aid Federation).

Montgomery, P. and Davies, C. (1991), 'A Woman's Place in Northern Ireland', in P. Stringer and G. Robinson (eds), *Social Attitudes in Northern Ireland* (Belfast: Blackstaff Press).

Smith, L. (1989), *Domestic Violence: Home Office Research Study 107* (London: HMSO).

Weitzer, R. (1985), 'Policing a Divided Society: Obstacles to Normalization in Northern Ireland', *Social Problems*, vol. 33, pp. 41–55.

Index